The Prehistoric Settlement at Winnall Down, Winchester:

Hampshire Field Club and Archaeological Society: Monograph 2
General Editor: Kenneth E Qualmann

M3 Archaeological Rescue Committee Report No. 8

The Prehistoric Settlement at Winnall Down, Winchester:
Excavations of MARC3 Site R17 in 1976 and 1977

by P J Fasham
with a Preface by Prof B W Cunliffe

and contributions by

P J Bates, J Bayley, C Catling, T C Champion, B M Dickinson, J W Hawkes, H M Jecock,
V A Jones, C Keepax, D F Mackreth, J M Maltby, W H Manning, C Mason, M A Monk,
E L Morris, D P S Peacock, F V H Powell, S J Shennan, R F Tylecote and R P Winham

Published by the Hampshire Field Club
in co-operation with the Trust for Wessex Archaeology
1985

HAMPSHIRE FIELD CLUB MONOGRAPH 2
Published by the Hampshire Field Club and Archaeological Society in co-operation
with the Trust for Wessex Archaeology

This monograph is published with the aid of a grant from the Historic Buildings and
Monuments Commission (England). Crown copyright is reserved in respect of
material in it resulting from central government expenditure.

ISBN 0-907473-01-6

Produced for the Society by
Alan Sutton Publishing, Gloucester
Printed in Great Britain by
Redwood Burn Limited, Trowbridge, Wiltshire

CONTENTS

PREFACE by Prof B W Cunliffe xiii

AUTHOR'S NOTE AND ACKNOWLEDGMENTS by P J Fasham . . . . xiv–xv

ABSTRACT xvi

Chapter 1   INTRODUCTION 1–8
            The Background 1
            The Site 3
            Excavation and Post-Excavation Methods 5

Chapter 2   THE DEVELOPMENT OF THE SITE 9–45
            Phasing
            Phase 2. Bronze Age 9
                Phase 2a. Middle Bronze Age 9
                Phase 2b. Late Bronze Age 9
            Phase 3. Early Iron Age 11
                The Enclosure Ditch 11
                The Gate Structure 11
                Circular Structures 12
                Two, Four and Six Post Structures 13
                Pits 13
                Other Structures 13
                Fences 13
                Features Outside the Enclosure 17
                Human Remains 17
                Dating Evidence 18
                The Radiocarbon Dates by S J Shennan 18
            Phase 4. Middle Iron Age 18
                Circular Buildings 18
                Rectangular Structure D 22
                Four Post Structures 22
                Pits 22
                Pit 5548 by R P Winham 22
                Pit 6595 by J M Maltby 25
                Pit 7399 25
                Other Structures 25
                Human Remains 25
                Dating Evidence 26
                Comments on the Radiocarbon Dates by S J Shennan . . . 30
            Phase 5. Late Iron Age – Romano-British 31
            Phase 6. Romano-British 31
                The Ditches 31
                Pits 31
                Rectangular Post-built Structures 31
                Four-Post Structures 33
                Fence 33
                Human Remains 39
            Phase 7. Medieval 39
            Unphased Features 41
                Probable Quarry Scoops 41
                Possible Structures 44

vi

Chapter 3   THE FINDS   46–96
            Finds of Metal by R P Winham   46
                Bronze
                    Coin by C Catling   46
                    Brooches by D F Mackreth   46
                    Other Bronze Objects by R P Winham   47
                Speculum   47
                Lead   47
                Iron   48
                    Brooches by D F Mackreth   48
                    Other Iron Objects   48
            The Pottery by J W Hawkes   57
                Introduction   57
                Method   57
                Phasing   57
                Reliability   57
                The Prehistoric Pottery   60
                    Fabrics   60
                    Phase 2. Bronze Age: Deverel-Rimbury   61
                    Phase 2. Late Bronze Age   61
                    Phase 3. Early Iron Age   61
                    Phase 4. Middle Iron Age   62
                    Discussion   67
                The Roman Pottery   69
                    Fabrics   69
                    Phase 5. Pre-Conquest   69
                    Phase 6. Early Roman   72
                    Amphorae   73
                    The Samian by V A Jones   73
                    The Stamps by B M Dickinson   75
                    Discussion   76
                Medieval   76
            The Briquetage by E L Morris   76
                Macroscopic Identification   76
                Vessel Forms   76
                Microscopic Analysis   76
                Discussion   76
            Stone Objects   76
                Introduction by D P S Peacock   76
                The Querns – Some Observations by H M Jecock   .   .   .   77
                Other Objects of Stone   80
                Chalk by J Bayley   80
                Miscellaneous Stone Objects by T Champion   81
                Flint by R P Winham   84
            Daub and Burnt or Baked Clay by P J Bates and R P Winham   .   .   .   86
                Fabric Description   86
                Considered by Phase   88
                Brick and Tile by R P Winham   90
            Loomweights by P J Bates and R P Winham   90
                Chalk   90
                Clay   90
            Metal Working Debris based on reports from J Bayley   .   .   .   92
                Crucibles   92
                Over-fired Clay   92
                Slag   93
            Bloomery Iron by R F Tylecote   93
            Marcasite and natural Ironstone Formations   93
            Glass   93
            Antler and Bone Objects by R P Winham   93
                Red Deer Antler   93
                Bone   96

Chapter 4   THE ENVIRONMENTAL EVIDENCE 97–125

    The Animal Bones by J M Maltby 97
      Phase 2. Bronze Age 97
      Phase 3. Early Iron Age 97
        The Enclosure Ditch 5 97
        The Pits 97
        The Quarry Areas 99
        Postholes and Scoops 99
        Intra-Site Variability 99
        Cattle 101
        Horse 101
        Sheep/Goat 101
        Pig 102
      Phase 4. Middle Iron Age 102
        The Pits 102
        The Ditch 104
        The Hut Gullies 104
        The Scoops, Quarries and Postholes 104
        Intra-Site Variability 104
        Cattle 105
        Horse 106
        Sheep/Goat 106
        Pig 107
        Dog 107
      Phase 5. Late Iron Age – Romano-British 107
      Phase 6. Romano-British 108
        Ditches and Gullies 108
        The Pits 108
        The Scoops and Hollows 108
        The Postholes and Other Features 108
        Intra-Site Variability 108
        Cattle 110
        Horse 111
        Sheep/Goat 111
        Pig 112
        Dog 112
        Domestic Fowl 112
      Shell 112
    The Plant Economy by M A Monk 112
      Phase 2. Late Bronze Age and Phase 3. Early Iron Age . . . 112
      Phase 4. Middle Iron Age 112
        The Building Gullies 112
        The Pits 113
        The Function of the Pits 113
        A General Appreciation of the Plant Economy of Winnall Down in the
          Middle Iron Age 115
          Distribution of the Main Cereal Taxa across the Site . . . 115
          Weed Seed Contaminants and the Ecological Implication . . 115
      Phases 5 and 6. The Late Iron Age – Early Romano-British Period 116
      Unphased Contexts 116
      Summary 116
      Pit 5548 116
    Wood Charcoal by C Keepax 117
    Human Skeletal Remains by J Bayley, P J Fasham and F V H Powell . 119
      Infants 119
      Children 119
      Adolescent 119
      Adults 119
      Cremation 121
      Discussion 122
    Land Molluscs by C Mason 122
      Interpretation 122

Chapter 5   DISCUSSION AND GENERAL OBSERVATIONS 126–143

    Phase 2. The Bronze Age 126
    Phase 3. The Early Iron Age 126
      The Enclosure Ditch 127
      Structures 127
      Activities outside the Enclosure 127
    Spatial Relations and Activity Areas in the Early Iron Age 127
    Phase 4. The Middle Iron Age 130
      The Structures 130
      The Pits 130
      Environmental 131
      Pottery 131
    Spatial Relations in the Middle Iron Age 131
    Phases 5 and 6. Late Iron Age – Early Romano-British 134
    Spatial Relations in the Late Iron Age – Early Romano-British Period 134
    General Considerations 134
      Animal Husbandry by J M Maltby 137
        Density Data 137
        Analysis of Bone Preservation 137
        Butchery and Carcase Division 137
        The Exploitation of the Domestic Stock 138
      Pits, Houses and People by P J Fasham and J W Hawkes . . . 138
      Social and Economic 142
    In Conclusion 142

Chapter 6   THE ARCHIVE 144–145
    Structure Concordance 144
    Index to the Archive 145

REFERENCES 146–149

LIST OF ILLUSTRATIONS

Fig 1.   Map showing location of site.   2
Fig 2.   Aerial view showing the Winnall Down Early Iron Age enclosure, 'Celtic' field traces and a second enclosure to the northeast. (Photo: National Monuments Record, reproduced by permission of the Royal Commission on Historical Monuments England. Crown copyright reserved.]   3
Fig 3.   General plan of the site showing all excavated features.   4
Fig 4.   Aerial view of the site during the 1976 excavations. (Photo: National Monuments Record, reproduced by permission of the Royal Commission on Historical Monuments England. Crown copyright reserved.)   5
Fig 5.   Aerial view of the site during the 1977 excavations. (Photo: Army Air Corps.)   6
Fig 6.   Summary phase plan.   8
Fig 7.   Plan of all features of Phase 2: Late Bronze Age.   10
Fig 8.   Detailed plan of Late Bronze Age Features.   11
Fig 9.   Plan of all features of Phase 3: Early Iron Age.   12
Fig 10.   The development of the gate to the Early Iron Age enclosure.   13
Fig 11.   Detailed plans of Early Iron Age houses E, F, G and L.   14
Fig 12.   Detailed plans of Early Iron Age houses H, I, J and K.   15
Fig 13.   Plans of selected 2, 4 and 6-post structures, and of structures B and C.   16
Fig 14.   Sections of selected Early Iron Age pits, with key to conventions for all sections.   17
Fig 15.   Plan of all features of Phase 4: Middle Iron Age.   19
Fig 16.   Detailed plans of Middle Iron Age houses B, M, N, P and V.   20
Fig 17.   Detailed plans of Middle Iron Age houses S, T and W, and structures E and F.   21
Fig 18.   Detailed plans of structure D and house R.   23
Fig 19.   Sections of selected Middle Iron Age pits (for key see Fig 14).   24
Fig 20.   View of the Middle Iron Age burial area in the quarries at the northwest of the site. (Photo: J Lockett).   26
Fig 21.   Middle Iron Age inhumations from the burial area in the quarries at the northwest of the site.   27
Fig 22.   Middle Iron Age inhumations 156, 174, 487, 488, 500, 531, 567 and 574.   28
Fig 23.   Middle Iron Age inhumations 35, 143, 159, 161, 420 and 629.   29
Fig 24.   Plan of all features of Phase 5: Late Iron Age/Early Romano-British.   30
Fig 25.   Sections of Late Iron Age/Early Romano-British pits and ditches (for key see Fig 14).   32
Fig 26.   Plan of all features of Phase 6: Romano-British.   33
Fig 27.   Schematic plan of Roman enclosures in probable chronological sequence.   34
Fig 28.   Sections of Roman ditches (for key see Fig 14).   35
Fig 29.   Sections of Roman ditches (for key see Fig 14).   36
Fig 30.   Sections of Roman pits (for key see Fig 14).   37
Fig 31.   Detailed plans of Roman structures G, H, J, K, and L, and 4-post structure ss.   38
Fig 32.   Detailed plans of Roman burials.   39
Fig 33.   Plan of all Phase 7 (Medieval) and unphased features.   40
Fig 34.   View of the quarry area in the southeast of the site. (Photo: J Lockett).   40
Fig 35.   View of the quarries in the northwest of the site, showing house N and the Early Iron Age enclosure ditch. (Photo: J Lockett).   41
Fig 36.   Plan of part of the quarries at the northwest of the site.   42
Fig 37.   Sections of quarries at the northwest of the site (for key see Fig 14).   43
Fig 38.   Sections across part of the northwest quarry area and house N (for key see Fig 14).   44
Fig 39.   Plan and sections of quarries in the southeast of the site (for key see Fig 14).   45
Fig 40.   Plan of unphased features 4641, 4715 and 4739.   44
Fig 41.   Bronze objects.   48
Fig 42.   Objects of bronze, speculum and lead.   49
Fig 43.   Iron objects.   50
Fig 44.   Iron objects.   51
Fig 45.   Iron objects.   53
Fig 46.   Iron objects.   54
Fig 47.   Iron objects.   55
Fig 48.   Iron nails.   56

Fig 49.   Pottery – form/fabric correlation.   58
Fig 50.   Pottery fabrics by phase.   59
Fig 51.   Bronze Age pottery.   61
Fig 52.   Early Iron Age pottery.   62
Fig 53.   Early Iron Age pottery.   64
Fig 54.   Middle Iron Age pottery.   66
Fig 55.   Rim diameters of incurving and straight-sided saucepan pots.   67
Fig 56.   Middle Iron Age pottery.   68
Fig 57.   Late Iron Age and Early Roman pottery.   71
Fig 58.   Early Roman pottery.   72
Fig 59.   Rim diameters of bead rim jars.   74
Fig 60.   Rim diameters of 'southern Atrebatic' chamfered rim jars.   74
Fig 61.   Decorated samian.   75
Fig 62.   Diameters of rotary querns.   77
Fig 63.   Querns.   79
Fig 64.   Chalk objects.   82
Fig 65.   Chalk objects.   83
Fig 66.   Stone objects.   84
Fig 67.   Metrical analysis of flint flakes.   85
Fig 68.   Worked flint.   87
Fig 69.   Daub and burnt/baked clay.   89
Fig 70.   Loomweights.   91
Fig 71.   Loomweight types by phase.   92
Fig 72.   Crucible.   92
Fig 73.   Antler.   94
Fig 74.   Antler and worked bone.   95
Fig 75.   Distribution of cattle and sheep/goat elements in a range of Early and Middle Iron Age
            contexts.   100
Fig 76.   Numbers of cattle and sheep/goat fragments in Middle Iron Age pits.   103
Fig 77.   Ageing analysis of cattle and sheep/goat mandibles from Middle Iron Age contexts.   106
Fig 78.   Percentages of bone elements of cattle and sheep/goat in Romano-British deposits.   110
Fig 79.   Measurements of cattle astragali from Phases 3, 4 and 6.   110
Fig 80.   Ageing analysis of sheep/goat mandibles from Romano-British deposits.   111
Fig 81.   Charcoal taxa from samples from Phases 3, 4 and 6.   117
Fig 82.   Number of charcoal fragments for each taxa identified per sample.   118
Fig 83.   Summary histogram of snails from selected features.   124
Fig 84.   Distributions of selected elements in the Early Iron Age.   128
Fig 85.   Distributions of animal and human bones in the Middle Iron Age.   132
Fig 86.   Distributions of selected elements in the Middle Iron Age.   133
Fig 87.   Distributions of selected artifact types in the Roman period.   135
Fig 88.   Densities in fragments per m³ of animal bones in the Roman period.   136
Fig 89.   Measurements of pits.   139
Fig 90.   Volumes and types of pits.   140
Fig 91.   Late Bronze Age – Middle Iron Age houses in order of rank size by floor area.   141
Fig 92.   Possible population sizes based on Winnall Down grain production and floor areas.   142

LIST OF TABLES

Table 1.   All features ordered by feature type and contents.   6
Table 2.   Phased features ordered by feature type.   7
Table 3.   Unphased features ordered by feature type.   37
Table 4.   The distribution of metal objects by phase.   46
Table 5.   Pottery: later Bronze Age – Iron Age fabrics.   60
Table 6.   Pottery: forms/fabrics in Phase 3 (Early Iron Age).   63
Table 7.   Pottery: Phase 3 (Early Iron Age) vessel association table.   65
Table 8.   Pottery: forms/fabrics in Phase 4 (Middle Iron Age).   65
Table 9.   Pottery: Phase 4 (Middle Iron Age) vessel association table.   67
Table 10. Pottery: Late Iron Age/Roman fabrics.   70
Table 11. Pottery: forms/fabrics in Phase 6 (Roman).   73
Table 12. Stone fragments not identified as artefacts.   77
Table 13. Querns by form and phase.   78
Table 14. Stone artifacts, excluding querns.   81
Table 15. Distribution of flint artifacts by phase.   85
Table 16. Daub and burnt/baked clay.   89
Table 17. Metal-working debris and occurrences of iron-bearing stone.   93
Table 18. Objects of worked antler and bone by phase.   96
Table 19. The distribution of animal bone fragments from Early Iron Age features.   98
Table 20. The variation of principal stock animal fragments against selected features in the Early Iron Age.   99
Table 21. The distribution of animal bone fragments from Middle Iron Age features.   102
Table 22. The variation of principal stock animal fragments against types of features in the Middle Iron Age.   105
Table 23. The distribution of animal bone fragments from features in Phase 5 (Late Iron Age/Romano-British).   107
Table 24. The distribution of animal bone fragments from Early Romano-British features.   109
Table 25. The variation of principal stock animal fragments against types of features in the Romano/British period.   109
Table 26. Plant remains from Phase 4 (Middle Iron Age).   113
Table 27. Plant remains from Phases 5 and 6 (Late Iron Age and Roman).   114
Table 28. Distribution of complete human skeletons and 'loose' human bones by phase.   120
Table 29. Human remains: skull measurements.   121
Table 30. Human remains: measurements of adult bones.   122

Preface

The Hampshire Field Club has had a long and distinguished involvement in active archaeological field-work within the county beginning with the brilliant programme of research excavations undertaken at the Iron Age hillfort St Catherine's Hill (and published so thoroughly as Vol XI of the *Proceedings*), and culminating with the carefully designed series of Iron Age excavations, energetically pursued by Christopher Hawkes, Dorothy Liddell and others, which made the decade of the 1930s a time of remarkable achievement and advance. In those heady pre-war days a Society such as ours could instigate and largely finance excavations of national and international importance. Since the war, and more particularly in the last 15 years, escalating costs and the greatly increased scale of excavation, has tended to diminish the innovative role which local societies can hope to have: to cope with large-scale threats of destruction professional Rescue excavation units have had to be called into existence.

In Hampshire we have been particularly fortunate. In the 1970s, in the face of specific threats, committees like the M3 Archaeological Rescue Committee were set up with professional staffs, to undertake what archaeological work they could in the face of massive earth-moving machines. This present volume, dealing with a major late prehistoric and Roman site on Winnall Down, is one of the fruits of their endeavours. The scale of the work and the sheer professionalism with which it was undertaken under Peter Fasham's direction, are self-evident. That the report was completed under the auspices of the Trust for Wessex Archaeology is a reflection of a reorganisation of Wessex archaeology within the last few years which has seen Rescue archaeologists pooling their efforts and coming together in larger and more powerful regional bodies.

Greater professionalism in archaeology of this kind is inevitable but this does not mean that county societies no longer have a function – far from it. Their members are a vital component of the county archaeological fabric and contribute in a variety of ways: they serve on the management committees of our units, take part in the excavations themselves, and provide the substructure of informed interest within the county, so necessary if archaeology is to thrive. Moreover our Society has always performed a major function as the publisher of archaeological research. Now, it has taken a major step forward by instigating a monograph series of which this is the first excavation report (the first, we hope, of many). It is a historic moment, reflecting, as it does, the Society's continuing involvement in archaeology and its willingness to respond readily to the present day needs of the discipline.

This monograph, on the Winnall Down excavation, sets high standards for the future: its preparation and presentation are a credit to the professional team involved, its appearance as a Field Club monograph is a credit to the Society.

Professor B W Cunliffe
Oxford

Author's Note

This report was substantially completed in the spring of 1980, awaiting only a couple of outstanding specialist reports. It was submitted to the Hampshire Field Club and Archaeological Society a year later but the Field Club was unable, for sound reasons of its own, to proceed with the publication. The financial structure of the Field Club has been reorganised and I am pleased that this latest report on the archaeology of the M3 Motorway through central Hampshire should, like all the other reports, be published by the Field Club.

In 1982 and during the construction of the motorway in 1983 a substantial area west of the Winnall Down site was investigated and revealed a sequence of funerary and settlement remains starting in the later Neolithic. The results of that work will form a separate monograph in the future. The 1980 account of the 1976/7 excavations has not been revised as I feel that attempts to reconsider Winnall Down in light of the more recent excavations would be premature until post excavation analyses are more advanced. Indeed Professor Cunliffe's report on the first ten years of excavation at Danebury, which has been published while this comment was being written, will have a bearing on the ceramics and chronology of Winnall Down. Nevertheless any reconsideration of the data base at the moment would disturb the balance of this report and further delay its appearance. I therefore present these thoughts as an indication of the contents of the archive which students have already started to reconsider.

P J Fasham
April 1984
Salisbury

Acknowledgements

The excavation of a complex site such as Winnall Down, the preparation of an archive and of the report are essentially a team effort. Mr R Clarke gave permission for the excavation to take place. The excavation supervising team included Peter and Judith Bates, Abigail Borrow, Eric Elias, Sally Fasham, Martin Herdman, Graham Kelsey, Jerry Lockett, David Maynard, Peter Mills, Joyce Nunn, Jane Ross, Christine Rowley and Caroline Sturdy. The post-excavation team included Peter and Judith Bates, Ingrid Clifford, John Hawkes, Charlotte Matthews, Jane Ross, Peter Winham and the computer of the Hampshire County Council and our contact there, David Lloyd. The drawings are the work of Sheila Cresswell, Peter Cox, Sue Davies, Kevin Feeney, Jo Gingell, Lorna Jones, Fiona Leah, Carol Mason and David Ormerod. Pat Coulson produced the typescript. To all these and to the specialists named in the report I am deeply grateful. The staff of the Ancient Monuments Laboratory greatly facilitated the production of many of the specialist reports.

The M3 Archaeological Rescue Committee, especially the successive chairmen, Professor Martin Biddle and Collin Bowen (then of the Royal Commission on Historic Monuments) and the Department of the Environment's representatives Dr G J Wainwright, Dr C J Young and Mr S Dunmore provided constructive advice and comments during and after the excavation.

The entire project has been financed by the Department of the Environment.

Mr Maltby wishes to thank Roger Jones, Ancient Monuments Laboratory, for his time, advice and guidance in the production of the computer archive for the animal bone and Jennie Coy for her valuable comments and encouragement.

Collin Bowen, Dr Tim Champion, Dr Geoffrey Wainwright, Professor Barry Cunliffe and Dr Ann Ellison have kindly commented on the text, but the author remains responsible for errors and omissions.

Finally I should like to thank my colleagues at the Trust for Wessex Archaeology for their work during the later stages of this project. I recognise a special debt to John Hawkes whose contributions ensured that this report and its supporting archive were completed.

P J Fasham

Abstract

The excavation in 1976 and 1977 of an enclosure on Winnall Down, discovered by aerial photographs, revealed a complex sequence of occupation and activity from the later Bronze Age to the second century AD. A small later Bronze Age settlement was succeeded by an Early Iron Age settlement enclosed by a ditch. The ditched enclosure was in turn followed by an open settlement of the Middle Iron Age. In the early Roman period a series of enclosures linked by a track was constructed.

This report contains, in summary form, details of all these phases with major contributions on animal and crop husbandry. The archive is housed at the Hampshire County Museum Service.

Chapter 1

Introduction

The Background

Less than two kilometres north-east of Winchester Cathedral an enclosure complex was discovered and photographed from the air by Collin Bowen in 1974. The photographs had been taken as part of the survey of archaeological sites along the proposed route of the M3 extension (Biddle and Emery 1973).

The proposals for the M3 motorway and its interchanges meant that the whole of the site was to be destroyed. There have been few total excavations of Iron Age sites on the chalkland of central southern England. In 1938 and 1939 Dr Gerhardt Bersu commenced excavation of the Little Woodbury site for the Prehistoric Society but the project was curtailed by the Second World War (Bersu 1940). In the early 1970's Dr S Champion undertook the total excavation of a large Iron Age site on the Portway Industrial Estate at Andover but unfortunately the results of that excavation have not yet been published. At about the same time Mr M Bell excavated an Iron Age enclosure at Bishopstone in Sussex (Bell 1977). In 1972 Dr Wainwright totally excavated an Iron Age settlement at Gussage All Saints, Dorset, as a consequence of a research project aimed at reviewing Dr Bersu's excavations at Little Woodbury. In the introduction to his report of the Gussage All Saints excavation Dr Wainwright (1979 *xi*) wrote 'A great deal has been deduced in economic, social and cultural contexts from the site (Little Woodbury) but only one third of the interior was investigated and arguments have constantly been inhibited on account of this fundamental defect. For many years it has been apparent that the total excavation of a Little Woodbury type enclosure was a prime necessity for the advancement of socioeconomic theory in Iron Age studies . . .'

Winnall Down was neither a Little Woodbury nor a Gussage All Saints. The aerial photographs revealed that, prior to its excavation, Winnall Down was smaller and lacked the antennae ditches at the entrance. As this report shows, the site was more complex and had a longer history than either of the other two.

It is against this background of re-evaluation of the social and economic basis of Iron Age sites in central southern England that the excavation and, more particularly, the post-excavation work at Winnall

Down must be seen. It was intended that the excavation should provide a context for the non-settlement sites that had been examined previously by the M3 Archaeological Rescue Committee. There is considerable emphasis in this report on Mr Maltby's very important assessment of the animal bones and Mr Monk's observations on the carbonised plant remains. Aspects of Mr Monk's work have already been published (Monk and Fasham 1980).

There are attempts to analyse spatial patterning and the relationship between possible grain storage capacity and population. Many of these exercises are capable of different interpretations and the archive is so ordered that other scholars should be able to reassess this site as further models are developed.

The M3 Archaeological Rescue Committee hoped to excavate the site over a period of six months during the winter of 1976–7. However, agricultural needs dictated that the site would be available intially for just seven weeks and excavation occurred from August 1st to September 20th 1976. As the topsoil was stripped it was obvious that there was a more complex series of archaeological features than indicated by the aerial photographs, which could not be completely excavated within the available time. The immediate aims of the excavation therefore became to provide a minimal data-base by determining the stratigraphic relationship of all inter-cutting features and to obtain, normally by half-section, chronological, cultural and morphological data for all features. Even these modest aims could not be achieved within the time limit, so following discussions with Mr Clarke, the farmer, the site was made available until September 1977. The aims of the second season's work, from February 28th to July 1st 1977, were to complete the unfinished 1976 programme and to examine the area around the enclosure, underneath the spoil heaps, paying particular attention to the westward extent of the Middle Iron Age unenclosed settlement, the track that appeared to approach from the east, the irregular mark ('splodge') on the aerial photographs at the north and part of a second enclosure at the south. This led to the discovery of the later Bronze Age settlement. The cereal crop of 1977 had been sown up to the edge of the 1976 spoil heaps which accounts for the irregular outline of the final excavation, when the

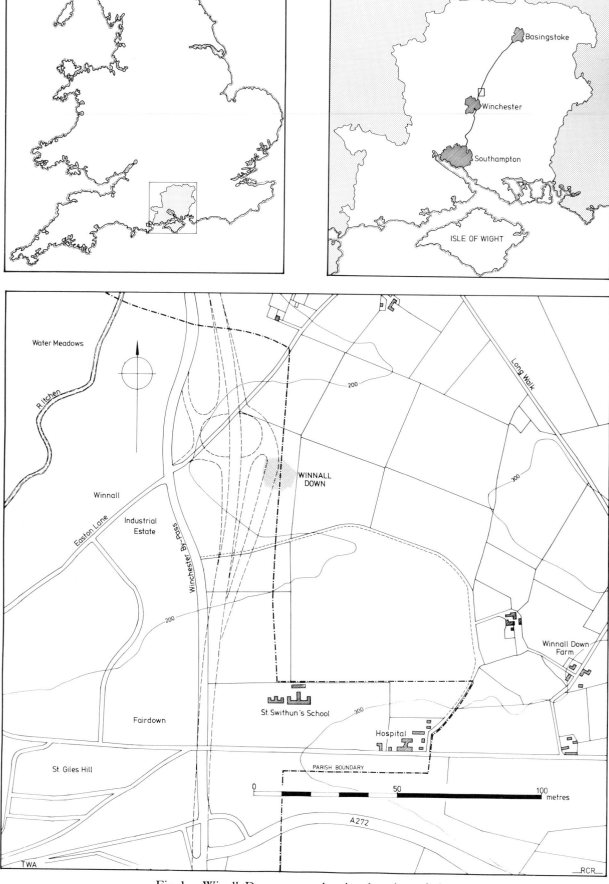

Fig 1.   Winall Down: map showing location of site.

spoil heaps were pushed into the interior of the enclosure.

The report of this excavation aims to be a 'synthesis and archive' report in the manner indicated by Frere (DoE 1975). Consequently only relevant data are published here. The full archive is deposited with the finds in the Hampshire County Museum Service and a microfiche copy is deposited with the National Monuments Record.

The Site

The site is 800m east of the River Itchen at SU 498303. It lies on the Upper Chalk and, at 67m AOD, is 30m above the valley bottom, over which it looks (Fig 1). The land also falls away slightly to the north and south, in the latter direction towards a dry valley. The boundary between the parishes of Winchester and Chilcomb bisects the site.

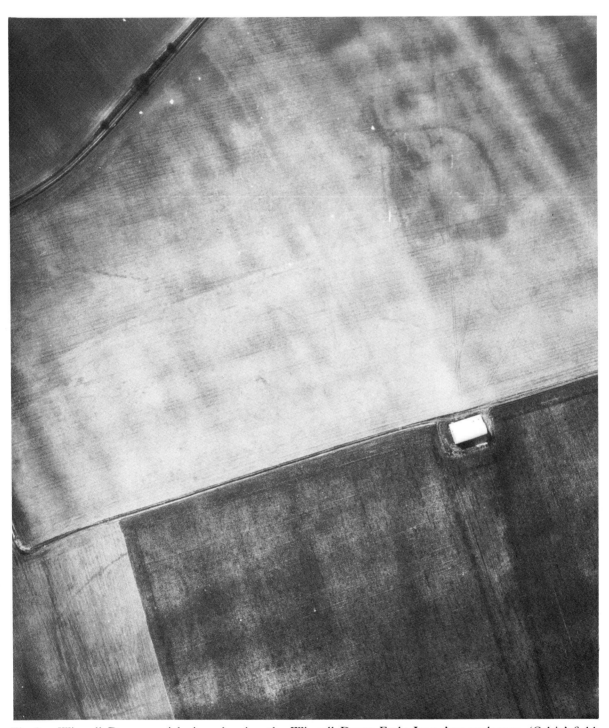

Fig 2. Winnall Down: aerial view showing the Winnall Down Early Iron Age enclosure, 'Celtic' field traces and the second enclosure to the north-east. North is at the bottom. (Photo: National Monuments Record).

The site was not discovered until 1974 when it was recorded in aerial photographs taken by H C Bowen, M F Hughes, and G E Peake and in April 1975 by the National Monuments Record. Aerial photographs of the site were taken under a range of different soil and crop conditions and at various times before the excavation. No single photograph revealed all the features and the following description of the air photographic data is based on the study of all the available photographs. Even so, not every major element of the site was detected by aerial reconnaissance. There were two enclosures, approximately the same size, about 300m apart in a matrix of vestigial 'Celtic' fields (Fig 2). A ditch, 60m long, linked the north-east corner of the eastern enclosure with a pentagonal soil mark within which was a rectangular mark. The linking ditch continued east of the pentagonal shape and, with a second parallel ditch, formed a track. The linking ditch/track ran along the edge of a 'Celtic' field. A second double-ditched track, or possibly originally a double-

lynchet, started 100m south of the eastern enclosure and ran west to the north-east corner of the western enclosure complex. The western complex consisted of a D-shaped enclosure with the second double-ditched trackway running down the straight eastern side, a small rectangular enclosure at the north-east, at least one, if not two, small sub-rectangular enclosures to the south and a series of dark areas or 'splodges'. A third, small, sub-rectangular enclosure had been observed some 30m south of the whole complex. Examination of Figures 2 and 3 shows that only the principal, D-shaped enclosure and the surrounding 10–20m were excavated.

The field was walked as part of the preliminary survey of the line of the M3 (Biddle and Emery 1973) when a few post-medieval sherds were recovered. Further casual finds made in the autumn of 1974 included thirteen medieval or later sherds, a Georgian halfpenny, two copper objects, two Roman and one prehistoric sherds. The lack of prehistoric or

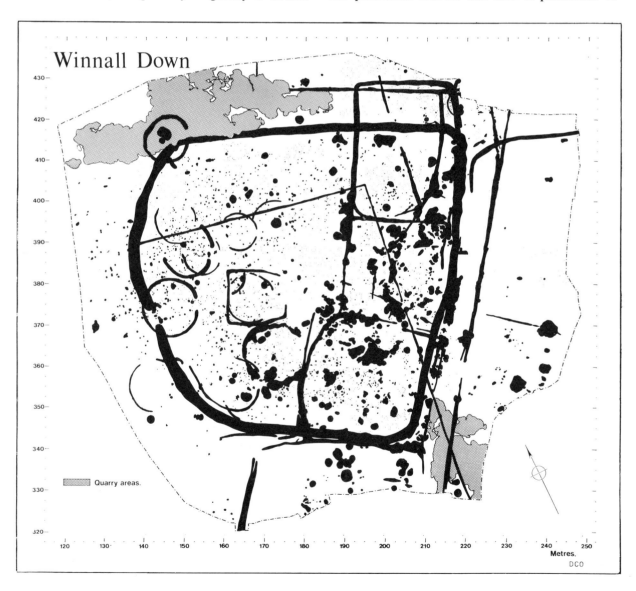

Fig 3.   Winnall Down: general plan of site showing all excavated features.

Fig 4.   Winnall Down: aerial view of the site during the 1976 excavations. (Photo: National Monuments Record).

Roman finds from the ploughsoil was probably due to the depth of the soil, 17–27cm, and the shallowness of recent cultivations. There had been earlier and deeper ploughing which had disturbed the upper part of the archaeological deposits, as was revealed when trial trenches were excavated by machine. The only other pre-excavation exercise performed was the collection and analysis of ten soil samples for available phosphorus. Five samples were taken from the topsoil within the enclosure and five from outside. The former samples all produced higher readings than the latter indicating that the archaeological phosphorus had not been masked by the relatively recent phosphorus-based fertilizers (Fisher 1978).

Excavation and post-excavation methods

Four trial trenches were mechanically excavated with a Cat DC9 to locate the sides of the D-shaped enclosure and to assess plough-damage. As ploughmarks were clearly visible in the surface of the chalk, and because time was restricted, it was decided to remove the topsoil mechanically to the surface of the chalk over all of the D-shaped enclosure (Fig 4).

In 1977 the spoil heaps from 1976 were pushed onto the completed part of the site and the area beneath the spoil heaps was similarly stripped (Fig 5). A total of 1.26 hectares (3¼ acres) was examined. Features exposed in the top of the chalk were then excavated by hand and sections and profiles recorded. The dark 'splodges' created a challenge and two approaches were tried: either the splodge was exca-

vated on a 1m alternate box system as in the south-east corner; or with longer, but alternate, 1m wide lateral trenches off an axial base line, as at the north-west of the site.

Each deposit or feature was given a unique number (Jefferies 1977) and a total of 11,465 contexts were recorded; post-built structures were numbered within that system but, as many were indicated during post-excavation analysis, the total number of stratigraphic units for the site is 11,278. Plans were drawn at 1:50 and sections at 1:10 or 1:20, as necessary. Unique numbers were also allocated to recorded finds, ie objects of metal, stone, bone, identifiable pieces of baked clay etc, and to samples. Flotation samples were taken for carbonised seeds and cereals. The majority of the samples were from Middle Iron Age or Romano-British contexts and it is therefore not possible to do a statistical analysis of the carbonised waste material from and between each phase.

Table 1 summarizes the totals of features and layers excavated, the numbers of samples collected, the numbers of recorded finds and the numbers of occurrences of general finds of different types in different contexts.

A large number of analyses were done in the post-excavation stage; some are considered in detail, others referred to and yet others not mentioned. Most of the data was manipulated by computer; the full details are in the archive. The purpose of the post-excavation analysis was to understand and provide a 'best-guess' interpretation of the recorded data. Instead of having, for example, 2138 meaning-

Fig 5. Winnall Down: aerial view of the site from the west during the 1977 excavations. In the foreground are the post-holes of the Bronze Age occupation. The quarries are clearly visible to the north and south. (Photo: Army Air Corps).

Table 1. Numbers of features by feature type; layers within those features; samples (soil, snails *etc*) taken from those features; recorded finds (individual finds of note – querns, metal objects, diagnostic pottery sherds *etc*) and numbers of unrecorded find records (*ie* bone, shell, pottery of one fabric, which will include recorded finds *etc*, and may refer to many individual artifacts). Other features included at least 320 segments of linear ditches and gullies which were recorded as separate feature records.

	Gully	House Gully	Linear Ditch	Pit	Posthole	Quarry Pit	Scoop	Stakehole	Shallow Scoop	Other Features	Row Totals
Features	25	14	22	270	2027	92	493	111	18	538	3610
Layers	29	34	23	1644	2445	1165	944	71	30	1470	7855
Samples	3	1	5	1411	32	81	87	–	–	426	2046
Recorded Finds	16	3	34	1039	104	199	354	–	1	1252	3002
Unrecorded Finds	66	34	74	2499	389	479	972	1	12	2388	6914
Column Total	139	86	158	6863	4997	2016	2850	183	61	6074	23427

less stake- and post-holes, the repeated analyses have allocated 933 post- and stake-holes (46%) to structures. Artifacts from post-holes forming structures and specialised analysis of the structures themselves have allowed many structures to be tentatively allocated to a phase. Certain structures can be more confidently proposed than others; the former are shown on the phase plans with the post-holes joined by solid lines, the latter joined by dotted lines. It must be stressed that the linking of post-holes is, in this case, a statement of confidence about the plan of the structure and has no other architectural significance whatsoever. Post-holes with datable artifacts are referred to in the text or in the archive. This approach provides the reader with an opportunity to assess the data base and re-interpret the suggestions put forward in this report.

The animal bones were examined at the Faunal Remains Project, Department of Archaeology, University of Southampton. Each fragment was examined and computer recorded using an expanded version of the system devised by Jones (1977). This enabled a detailed record of metrical data, fragment size, butchery, ageing, pathology, sexing, bone-working and preservation evidence to be stored in an archive. The discussion of the animal bones in this report is a synopsis of that information.

A site that has been occupied for 1,000 years from the later Bronze Age to the Roman period presents problems of residuality and of intrusiveness. Artifactual material is always likely to be moved around and re-deposited, and its final deposition need not reflect either its functional or chronological origin. Pit 7399 is a clear example of the process of redeposition. The upper fills of features can often contain material considerably younger than the feature. As each feature, rather than each layer within that feature (except for enclosure ditch 5), has been phased, the tables, patently the pottery ones, will often contain residual or intrusive traces. Where the artifactual material is too mixed or too infrequent, features have not been phased. There are therefore many features within the enclosure which have not been phased and it must be remembered that each phase probably contains more features than are portrayed on the plans.

The dark 'splodges', probably quarry areas, presented great problems for analysis, despite careful excavation and the observation of more than one kilometre of sections. Some can be tentatively phased on stratigraphic grounds but, as they have been recut on numerous occasions, they cannot be securely phased on the rather minimal artefactual remains they contained. For the ceramic analyses, the quarry pits have generally been regarded as unphased, although an attempt to show their extent for each phase has been made and is portrayed in the individual phase plans.

1,631 (46%) of the features were not phased. As Table 3 demonstrates, 1,078 were post-holes and stake-holes and 362 were scoops, mainly in the areas of quarrying. Thus 92.5% of the unphased features were of a type which are not expected to be readily allocated to phase on an open area site with no stratigraphic depth. Scoops have been defined as irregularly shaped, usually shallow, holes and pits as having a more definable plan, profile and base.

Table 2. Phased features ordered in feature type.

Table summarising the numbers of the main feature types and expressing them as percentages of the total of the phased feature type recorded.

	2	3	4	5	6
Post-holes and stake-holes	12%	25%	46%	1%	16%
Scoops and shallow scoops	1%	35%	14%	6%	44%
Pits and quarry pits	4%	40%	32%	5%	19%

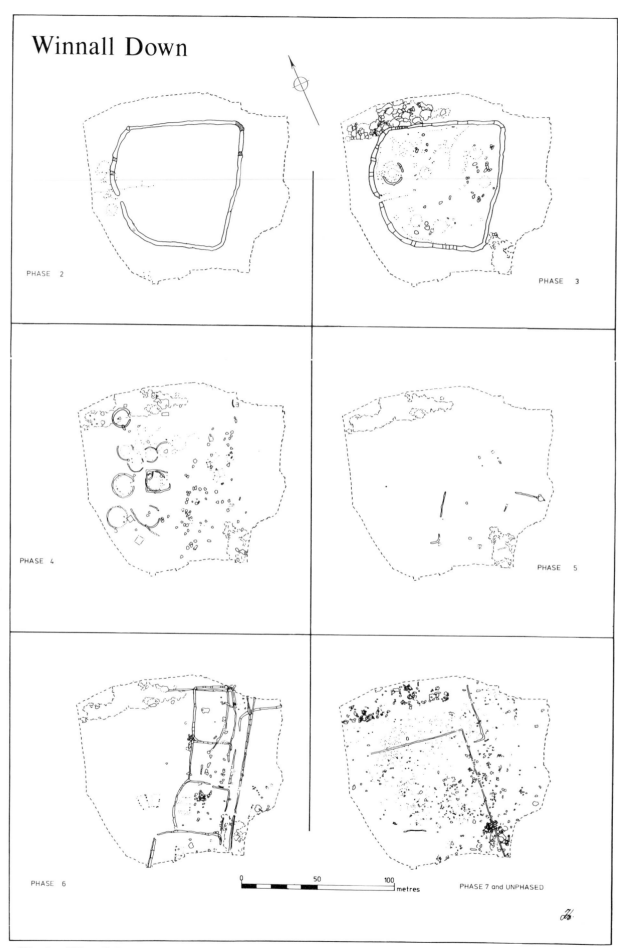

Winnall Down

PHASE 2

PHASE 3

PHASE 4

PHASE 5

PHASE 6

50   100
metres

PHASE 7 and UNPHASED

Fig 6. Winnall Down: summary phase plan.

Chapter 2

The Development of the Site

Phasing Summary

The general limitations of the data for phasing have been described in Chapter 1. Nevertheless, there are seven distinctive periods of activity represented by features on the site, Fig 6. In referring to the Iron Age the terms Early, Middle and Late are used. These compare broadly with Collis's general classification (Collis 1977a).

Phase 1. Neolithic. The interrupted ring-ditch, feature 1972, is the subject of a separate report and will not be discussed here (Fasham 1982).

Phase 2. Bronze Age. This can be subdivided on ceramic grounds to a residual element containing Deverel-Rimbury type material mainly from the Phase 3 enclosure ditch (Phase 2a), and a later Bronze Age phase (Phase 2b).

Phase 3. Early Iron Age.

Phase 4. Middle Iron Age.

Phase 5. Late Iron Age/Early Roman.

Phase 6. Early Roman.

Phase 7. Medieval.

Phase 2. Bronze Age (Fig 7)

Phase 2a. Middle Bronze Age

One feature can be assigned to this period. The small pit 4786 on the east side of the site contained the lower portions of a bucket urn which, in turn, contained some unidentifiable fragments of bone. The pit was amongst a group of pits and scoops whose observed relationships suggest that pit 4786 was later than Phase 3 enclosure ditch 5. The urn however seemed to be in its original place of deposition with its upper part damaged by later activity and it seems likely that some of the stratigraphy was incorrectly observed in a complex area.

Other Middle Bronze Age material was recovered in residual contexts in the Phase 3 enclosure ditch. Most of the pottery was from a bucket urn of a coarse and decaying fabric, fabric 12, found in ditch segment 5C on the west of the site. Human bones were also discovered in the same segment. A few small sherds of comparable fabric were found in ditch 5 at the north-east corner and on the east side just south of pit 4786.

Phase 2b. Late Bronze Age (Fig 8)

This phase was represented by four possible post-built round houses and a fence, all located on the west side of the site. As the fence line and one of the houses intersected, they could only be broadly contemporary. There were no direct stratigraphic relationships. Three houses are partly conjectural and only two of the houses, the fence and the pits can be dated by their associated finds. The entrances of Houses A, B and C can be identified with reasonable confidence.

House A was the sole discrete, post-built round house from the entire excavation that was not damaged by subsequent activities. This slightly oval structure, 8m by 7.5m, had a simple entrance porch facing south-west. Pottery found in three post-holes included parts of a wide-mouthed bowl (Fig 51.2), an indented base in post-hole 6370 and a jar (Fig 51.3) in post-hole 6404. This house was adjacent to segment C of enclosure ditch 5 which produced Deverel-Rimbury pottery.

House B, adjacent to and south of house A, was cut by the Early Iron Age enclosure ditch 5 and, because of the method of excavation, was not observed *in toto* in the field. It was oval, 8m by 7.5m, with a west-facing porch longer and more elaborate than that of House A with a probable double door, as indicated by the replaced or double post-holes in the middle. There were no associated finds.

House C, south of house B, was oval and measured 7.75m by 7m. It had a splayed west-facing entrance porch. The eastern part of the structure is conjectural as it was cut by enclosure ditch 5 and the associated Early Iron Age gate structure. The isolated internal post-hole, 6482, contained rims of two wide-mouthed jars (not illustrated), a retouched flake, burnt animal bone, five fragments of white quartzite sandstone, with traces of burning similar to the burnt sarsens from Burntwood Farm (Fasham 1980), and probably from a quern. Two body sherds, two fragments of a greensand quern of unidentifiable form and fragments of a triangular loomweight were found in post-hole 6490. It could be argued that the entrance porch was an isolated 5-post structure, that there is no house at this point and that fence 1 can therefore be regarded as contemporary with the other structures. The south-west arc of the structure from post-hole 10404 to post-hole 1536 does, however, strongly indicate the presence of a circular structure.

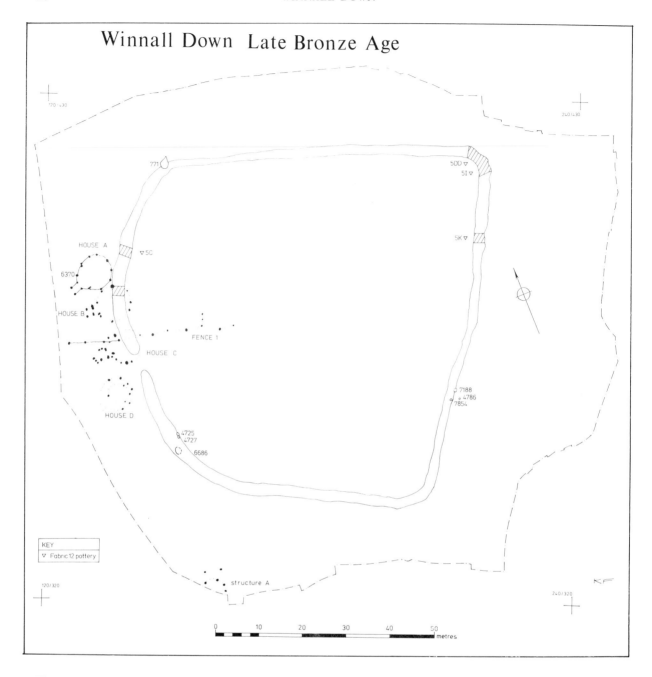

Winnall Down Late Bronze Age

KEY

▽ Fabric 12 pottery

Fig 7.   Winnall Down: Bronze Age. Plan of all features belonging to Phase 2.

House D, the southernmost house, comprised eleven post-holes in two concentric arcs which probably represent the eastern half of a structure with a diameter of about 7.5m. All the post-holes were shallow, only two being deeper than 0.1m. This lack of depth may account for the partial survival of the structure. The diameter of the inner ring was 5m and this would tend to be too small for an individual structure; the best interpretation must be that the two rings were contemporary and part of a single structure. There were no associated finds.

Structure 11189, a short line of three posts just in front of the south side of the porch of house C, may have formed a windbreak to that porch; alternatively it could be associated with fence 1.

Fence 1 comprised ten posts and extended for a distance of 38m (Fig 7). The westernmost post-holes were undoubtedly part of this fence; the remaining post-holes, including two forming a right-angled extension to the north, were added at the post-excavation stage and form a conjectural extension. A perforated sandy sherd was found in post-hole 6468 and burnt bone, a cylindrical loomweight (Fig 70.2), fragments of a second cylindrical loomweight and rims from at least six wide-mouthed jars (Fig 51.4–9) were found in post-hole 6466.

Structure A in the south-west corner of the site was a group of six post-holes for which three possible interpretations can be proposed: the post-holes formed a north-facing porch with part of the

Winnall Down
Late Bronze Age Houses

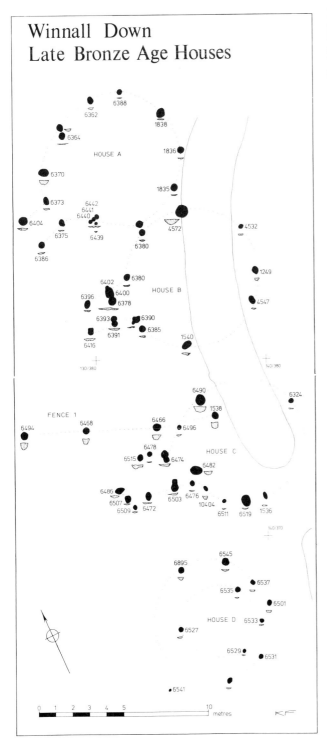

Fig 8. Winnall Down:

detailed plan of Late Bronze Age features.

circle of another round house; or the southern four were part of an arc; or the northern four were a four–post structure. There were no associated finds and thus they cannot be dated, neither can they be phased on spatial grounds because of their isolated location.

Apart from 21 fragments of animal bone, the environmental data from this phase is limited to the recovery of a single grain of barley from scoop 4786.

The distribution of all artifacts has been outlined above in terms of related structures. Several other features were cut by the Phase 3 enclosure ditch and must pre-date it. They contained no diagnostic artifacts and it is impossible to suggest a date for them. They are features 771, 1662, 4725, 4727, 6686, 7188 and 7854 (Fig 7).

Phase 3. Early Iron Age (Fig 9)

An area of just over 0.4 hectares (1 acre) was enclosed by a ditch of V-profile. The enclosure was D-shaped with a single, formal, entrance on the curving west side. The associated features will be described in the following order: the ditch, the gate structure, circular structures, four- and six-post structures, pits, other structures and features outside the enclosure.

The enclosure ditch 5

A total of 31 trenches was excavated across the ditch to obtain a minimum 25% sample from all sides of the ditch. Eventually 78.5m of the total length of 267m (29.4%) were excavated. The ditch was of V-profile with a flat bottom (profiles on Fig 9). The top width varied from 1.3 to 3.35m, mean 2.16m, standard deviation 0.51m; depth ranged from 0.7m to 1.48m, mean 1.12, standard deviation 0.20m; and the cross-sectional area was from $0.5m^3$ to $2.2m^3$, mean $1.22m^3$ and standard deviation of $0.45m^3$. Consideration of these measurements shows that the ditch was larger and more impressive by the entrance than elsewhere except at the north-east corner. The east side particularly was small, the cross-sectional area being as little as one quarter of that on the west. The segments with cross-sectional areas one standard deviation less than the mean area were 5D, E, EE, HH, II and MM. Those with cross-sectional areas greater than the mean plus one standard deviation were 5B, J and FF (Fig 9). The ditch silted up mainly by natural processes although occasionally there were rubbish deposits such as the discarded hearth in segment A and a large spread of burnt flints in the top of the ditch between segments A and AA and in segment B. In places on the western side the ditch must have been deliberately back-filled.

The volume of the ditch was in the order of $330m^3$, which represents about 660 tonnes weight of chalk excavated. The vertical distribution of pottery attributable to Phase 3 suggests that 85% of the ditch was filled during Phase 3. The greatest density of pottery per m^3, both in numbers and weight, occurred on the east side, followed by the west, north and south. The examination of the mean and standard deviation of occurrence by numbers, weight and numbers and weight per m^3 shows that segments C, L, AA, FF and GG had consistently high quantities while segments B, P, EE, MM and JJ suggested high densities.

There was no clear indication from the stratigraphy for the position of the bank, if indeed there had been one. However, there was an irregular series of large, but shallow, post-holes which were traceable on the north and south sides of the site, and may have been related to structural timberwork in the bank, Fences 2 and 3.

The gate structure (Fig 10)

The entrance was formed by a causeway about 3.8m wide in the middle of the west side. The gate structure had been rebuilt at least twice (archive number 11199).

Period 1. The original rectangular gate of four posts measured 0.6–1.2m by 2–2.5m between post-pits. The north-west post was replaced.

Winnall Down Early Iron Age

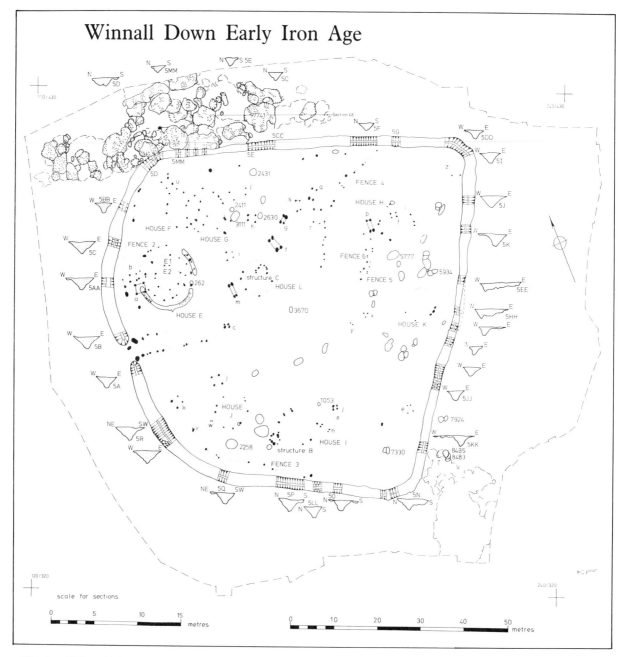

Fig 9.   Winnall Down: Early Iron Age. Plan of all features belonging to Phase 3.

Period 2. The gateway was rebuilt to a length of 5.8m and reduced to an entrance width of 2.1m splaying to 3.4m in the interior where there was a central post. Structures 11200 and 11201 may have extended the entrance-way into the interior.

Period 3. The final modification produced a trapezoidal structure which may have included two central posts giving three narrow entrances of 0.6–0.7m width. It is unlikely that the central posts were contemporary with one another. The northern posts were replaced and the north-west corner was strengthened by a post erected in the partially silted ditch and which rose along the slope of the ditch terminal.

Circular structures (Figs 11 and 12)

Five complete and two partially complete post-built circular structures were recognised during both the excavation and the post-excavation analysis. Additionally, one circular gully with internal post settings has been assigned to this phase.

House E, with internal post settings E1 and E2, was circular with an external diameter of about 14m. It was represented by a penannular gully up to 0.75m wide and 0.30m deep. The entrance faced south of east and was clearly defined by the sloping terminals of the gully. The north-west quadrant of the gully was not present but an arc of seven post-holes completed the gap (Fig 11). The gully had straight sloping sides and a flat bottom. There were not many finds, but the majority occurred in the south-west segment. No traces of post-holes were discernible cutting through the lower chalky silt to reach natural, but post- and stake-holes were seen in the upper part of that fill. The implications are not clear and, although the possibility of posts resting in the bottom of the trench, particularly in the south-west sector, cannot be ruled out, it does look as if the gully was partially filled before the posts were set in it. The gully does not appear to be a drainage feature.

Internally there was a double circle of posts: the larger, E1, comprised 15 posts and had a diameter of 10.5m; the smaller, E2, consisted of eight posts and had a diameter of 6.5m. Assuming the gully and the two post-circles were contemporary and not succes-

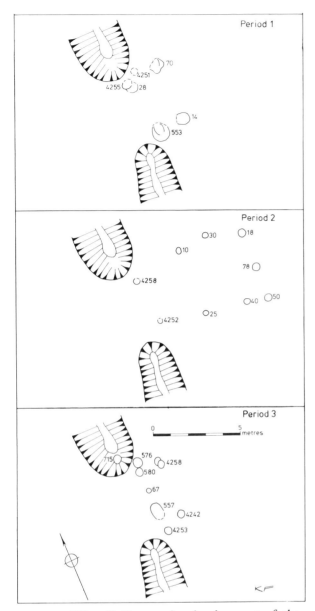

Fig 10. Winnall Down: the development of the gate to the Early Iron Age enclosure.

sive, the structure was fairly elaborate. It is assigned to the Early Iron Age, as it was cut by a post of four-post structure *a*, which, on the evidence of a shouldered jar in another of the post-holes, must date to the Early Iron Age.

House F, 8m in diameter, consisted of eleven fairly small and shallow post-holes. The simple porch faced south-east.

House G, 8m in diameter with nineteen post-holes, was a replacement for or was replaced by House F. Pottery in post-hole 2673 was of Early Iron Age type.

Two areas of closely-spaced post-holes formed House H, diameter 8.5m. A rim sherd of a haematite-coated bowl was in post-hole 4313.

House I, diameter 8m, consisted of ten posts with a small, porched entrance which faced north into the centre of the enclosure.

House J contained ten posts spaced 2–4m apart, forming a circle of 7.5m diameter.

The incomplete House K was represented by five posts which would have formed a circular building of 7–8m diameter. The distribution of pits around House K suggests there had been a structure there.

The other incomplete building was House L with six shallow posts forming slightly more than a semi-circle, with a conjectural diameter of 7m.

Two, four and six post structures

Two pairs of post-holes may represent two-post structures, *v* and *z*. There were nineteen four-post structures within the enclosure. The spacing of the posts enables their division into four groups (Fig 13), which were applicable to all phases on the site.

Group A. Small squarish structures, 0.8–1.6m long and with a length : width ratio less than 2:1. Eight Early Iron Age examples: *b, c, d, e, f, g, h, i.*

Group B. Large squarish structures, 2.0–3.2m long. Four in this phase: *a, j, k, l.*

Group C. Elongated rectangular structures, 2.0–3.3m long and with a length : width ratio greater than 2:1. The seven Early Iron Age ones are *m, n, p, q, r, s* and *t.*

Group D. Any structure with length greater than 4m; none in this phase.

The six-post structure, *u*, measured 3.2 by 2.0m.

Pits

Twenty-seven pits are attributable to this phase, sixteen of recognisable forms. There were five sub-rectangular pits with flat bottoms, four beehive-shaped, and seven cylindrical pits. The remainder were ovoid with flat bottoms or shallow with circular or oval plans (Fig 14).

Thirteen pits had volumes of less than 0.5m^3, four of between 0.5 and 0.99m^3, six of 1–2m^3 and four greater than 2m^3. The number of sherds and the mean number of sherds per m^3 were calculated, to investigate possible spatial patterning of pottery within the pits. The number of sherds per m^3 in the pits was usually less than 74 except for pits 2630 (79), 7330 (129), 3670 (321) and 1053 (1,754). The mean pot density/m^3 was calculated and only pit 1053 lay outside one standard deviation for both weight and number of sherds, pit 5934 was outside in terms of weight.

Other structures

Structure *B* was a small circle, 2.0–2.5m diameter, of nine closely-spaced post-holes (Fig 13). A sherd of Early Iron Age pottery was found in post-hole 4371.

A similar but less regular structure than *B* was represented by the eight posts of structure *C* (Fig 13).

Fences

Fence 4 was 30m long and composed of 13 irregularly spaced post-holes. Post excavation work, including measuring of modern fences, related to the Roman fences on Burntwood Farm (Fasham 1980), revealed that even an apparently regular fence has some disparity in the spacing of its posts.

Fence 5 was 10m long and the eight post-holes were set in a curve. Fence 6, of nine post-holes, lay immediately west of 5.

Structures *v* and *w*, south-west of House J, were a pair of two-post structures which may have formed a gate to an enclosed area between the hut and Fence 3.

Structures *x* and *y* were arrangements of three and two posts, respectively.

Winnall Down Early Iron Age Houses

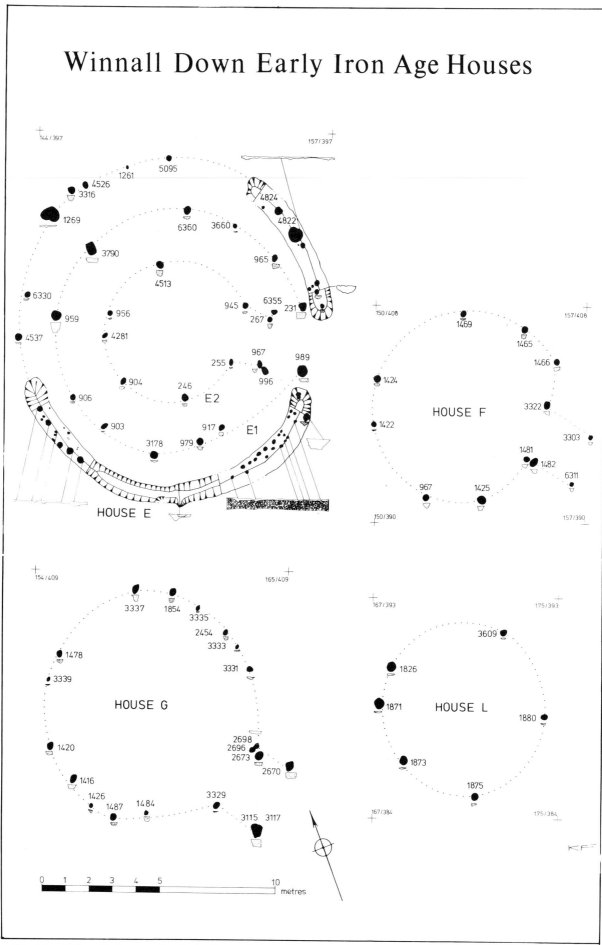

Fig 11. Winnall Down: detailed plans of Early Iron Age houses E, F, G and L.

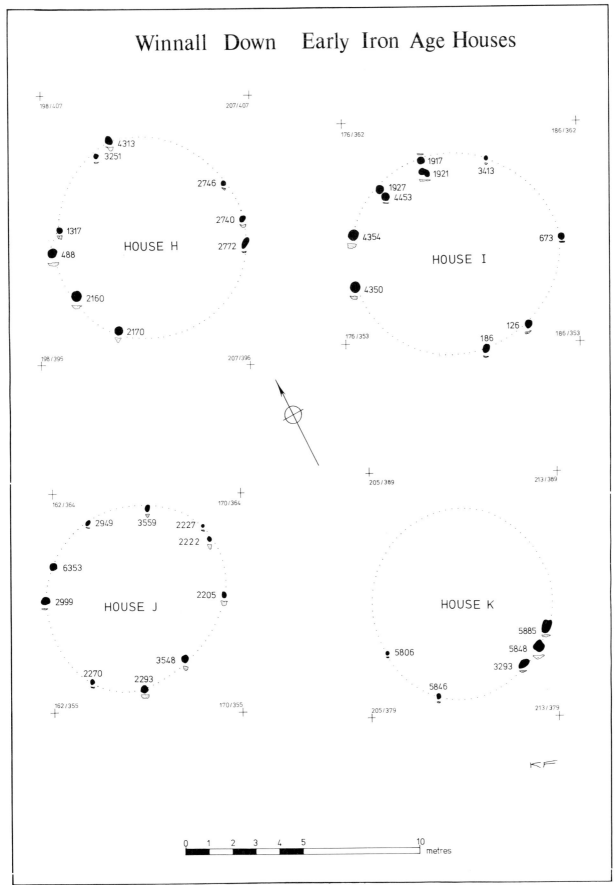

Fig 12.   Winnall Down: detailed plans of Early Iron Age houses, H, I, J and K.

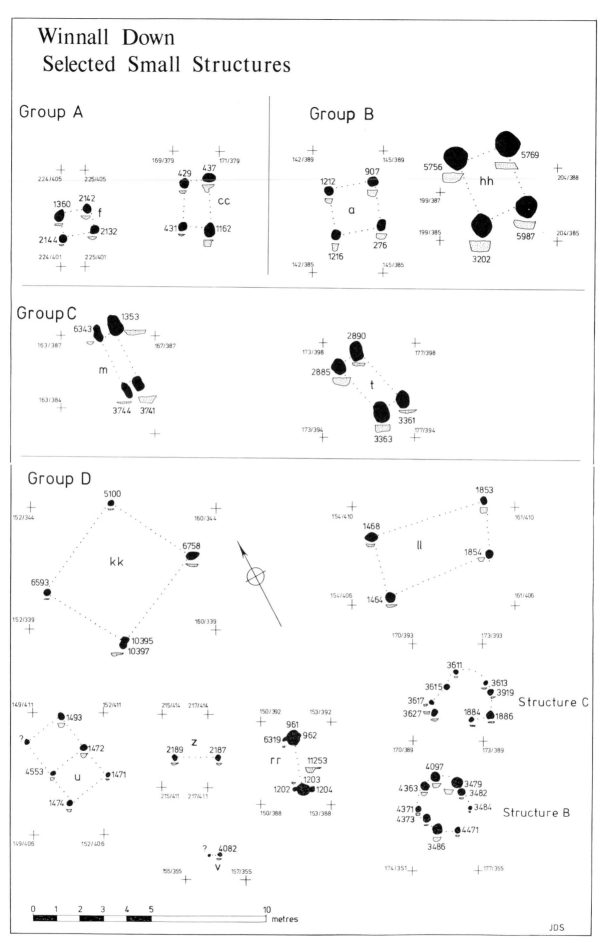

Fig 13. Winnall Down: plans of selected 2, 4 and 6 post structures and of structures *B* and *C*. Phase 3: *a*, *f*, *m*, *t*, *u*, *v*, *z*, *B*, *C*. Phase 4: *cc*, *hh*, *kk*, *ll* and *rr*.

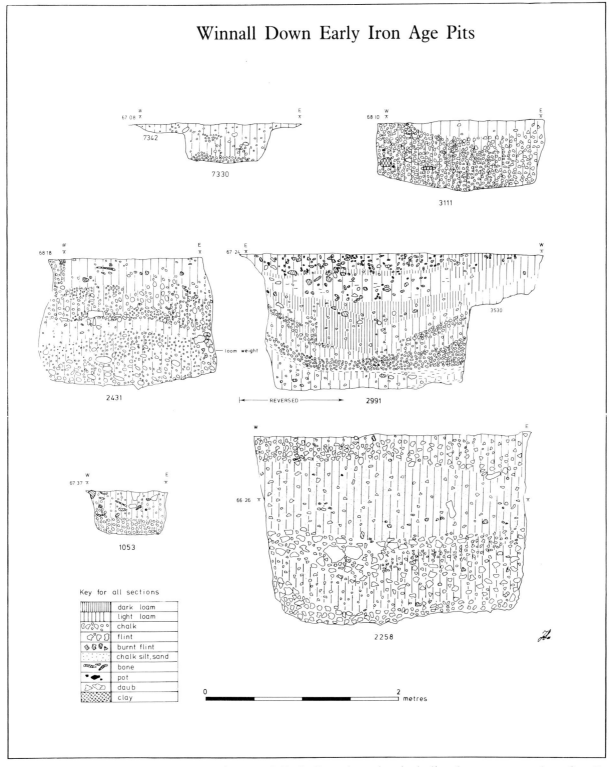

Fig 14. Winnall Down: sections of selected Early Iron Age pits, including key to conventions for all sections.

Features outside the enclosure

The most striking features outside the enclosure were the quarries. There seems to be no doubt that they were started during this phase but their full contemporary extent is not clear. A group of pits lay outside the southern end of the eastern side of the enclosure.

Human Remains (full details by Powell and Bayley in archive)

The fragmentary skeleton of an infant of less than one year, burial 266, was found in pit 5777. A collection of bones of a neo-natal infant was also recovered from segment M of the enclosure ditch (tabulated in Table 28 under the heading 'Odd Bones'). Another fragment of infant skull came from a different layer in 5M. There were 21 instances of isolated adult bones, occuring in 5A (5), 5B (2), 5C (2), 5FF (4), 5RR (3), pit 2258 (2) and singly in 5GG, 5J and pit 5797 and layer 10273 in quarry pit 7741.

Dating evidence

Most features were dated by pottery which included typical Early Iron Age forms of haematite-coated bowls, bipartite, tripartite and shouldered jars.

There are three radio-carbon dates associated with Early Iron Age pottery. In accordance with the editorial policy of the Hampshire Field Club all radio-carbon dates are expressed as uncalibrated years before present and are signified by BP.

HAR 2653:2560±80 BP was on animal bone from layer 4749, from segment 5FF of the enclosure ditch, about one third of the way up the ditch. It was associated directly with a shouldered jar (Fig 53.49), and sealed sherds of haematite-coated pottery.

HAR 2251:2540±90 BP was from a sample of charcoal, some of which was identified as twiggy maple (*acer* sp), from hearth 574 which was deposited in segment 5A of the enclosure ditch immediately above the primary silt. It was associated with a tripartite jar (not illustrated); a sherd of haematite bowl was in the layer above.

HAR 2194:2160±80 BP was on animal bone from pit 3111. The pottery from this pit, purely body sherds, is typical of the Early Iron Age.

HAR 2251 and 2653 indicate that the enclosure ditch 5 had been dug probably no later than the sixth century BC. Current opinion suggests that the Early Iron Age pottery forms associated with this phase could have continued into the third century BC (Cunliffe 1978). HAR 2194 suggests that this phase continued until some time in the third century.

The Radiocarbon Dates by Dr S J Shennan

The radiocarbon dates from Winnall Down Phases 3 and 4 were analysed by the methods described by Ward and Wilson (1978). They were treated as examples of Ward and Wilson's case II: dates obtained from different samples rather than replicates of the same sample. In calculating the sample variances it was assumed throughout that the sun-spot effect, which should be taken into account for short-lived examples, was not relevant.

The pooled mean for the three dates from Phase 3 is 2413.22 BP. The dates were tested to see if they were homogeneous.

$$T = 11.14 \text{ with 2 degree of freedom}$$

T is distributed as chi-squared; the result is significant at the 0.01 level. The dates are clearly not an homogeneous set, obviously because HAR-2194 from the pit is significantly later than the other two.'

The pooled mean of the dates from the ditch is 2550.87 BP. These are not significantly different from one another (T = 0.0115 with 1 df). The standard error of the mean date of the ditch is 69.55 years. The 95% confidence interval for the mean date of the ditch is (rounded) 2550±140 BP or 2690–2410 BP.

Phase 4. Middle Iron Age

An open settlement represented by circular houses mainly of gully construction, but also post-built, a rectangular structure, four-post structures and pits became established during the Middle Iron Age, (Fig 15).

Circular buildings (Figs 16 and 17)

As many as nine gully-built, and one post-built, structures may relate to this phase, although they cannot all be strictly contemporary.

House M, 14.7m diameter, with guly 0.4–0.8m wide, mean 0.6m, and 0.13–0.3m deep, mean 0.235. The gully straddled the entrance of the Phase 3 enclosure, and its relationship with the early feature was clearly determined in the fill of the south terminal of the enclosure ditch. The 2.6m wide entrance to the gully was on the east between two slightly expanded terminals. In the south terminal was the base of a jar in an early fabric and animal bones. The few other finds, mainly animal bone and burnt flint, were well scattered around the gully; there was a fragment of a greensand quernstone from the north side. Longitudinal sections showed a series of post-holes within the fill of the gully. Some reached to the base of the gully. An internal post-ring, M1, of 11–11.5m diameter can be postulated, consisting of sixteen irregularly-spaced and shaped post-holes, with an apparently recessed entrance represented by post-holes 85 and 1185. Between the post-ring and the gully were stake-holes. Structure M1 cannot definitely be associated with house M.

House N, 11.75m diameter, had been constructed across the north-west corner of the earlier enclosure ditch and some of the quarry scoops. The gully was 0.5m to 1.66m wide, mean 0.97, and 0.36–0.79m deep, 0.56 mean. The 3m-wide entrance faced east and contained an off-centre post-hole, 1224. Considerable effort had been expended on this structure, so that the bottom of the gully reached firm chalk rather than the soft fills of earlier features. Only where the gully crossed enclosure ditch 5 was chalk not reached. The complex nature of the archaeology around house N meant that it was not possible to excavate any longitudinal sections. Animal bones, including the skull of a dog, dominated the finds in the gully immediately south of the entrance. Where the gully cut through the enclosure ditch there was a large number of finds of all forms, some of which may have been residual from the ditch. There were further artifact concentrations opposite the entrance and 5m west of the northern terminal.

The large beehive pit 6038, dug through earlier features, was within house N. It was 1.47m deep, and 1.50m wide at the top, with a volume of 2.14m^3. There were 121 sherds of pottery, weighing on average 11g, compared with 16.3g for the average weight of sherds in this phase. The overall density of pottery was 57 sherds per m^3, which is fairly high. There were four fragments of greensand quernstone, animal bones, a piece of slag and at least 7,863 flint lumps of which 3,821 were burnt, the reminder being small nodules.

House P, diameter 10.2m, gully up to 0.1m deep, mean 0.8m, and 0.12–0.53m wide, mean 0.3m. A little over half of a complete circle survived, sufficient to show that the feature cut house E and had an east-facing entrance 3m wide. This was a shallow gully and the apparently missing section could have been eroded. The only finds were two intrusive medieval sherds.

House R (Fig 18), 11.8m diameter, gully 0.02–0.16m deep, mean 0.077m, and 0.2–0.6m wide, mean 0.303. The entrance appeared to be on the east side. Longitudinal sections did not reveal post-holes. The gully was superimposed on the rectangular structure D. Finds, including pottery, bone, flint flakes, burnt flint and one piece of slag, were fairly evenly distributed in the gully. Pit 447 in the north-east corner was stratigraphically earlier than house R and cannot be related to the gully.

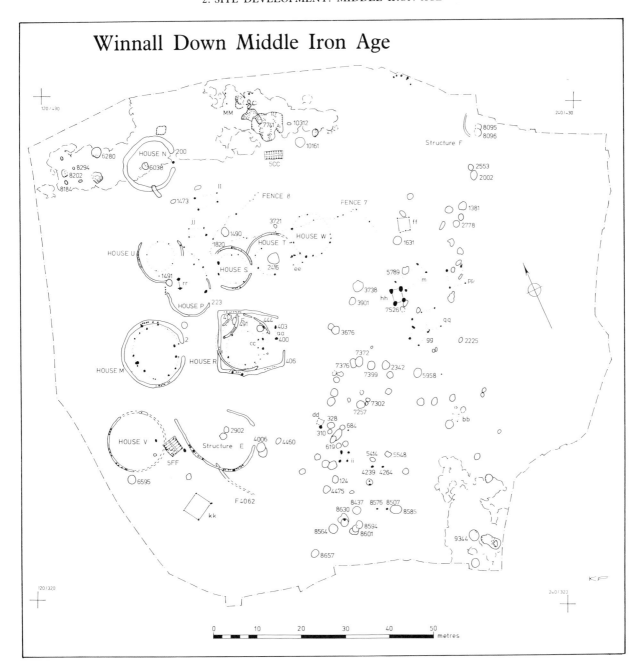

Fig 15. Winnall Down: Middle Iron Age. Plan of all features belonging to Phase 4.

Immediately inside house R an irregular circle of small stake-holes, R1, was detected. Structure R2, diameter 7.5m, was an irregular circle of six posts centred to the south of both R and R1. Neither R1 or R2 can be definitely related to R.

House S, the smallest of the penannular hut gullies, with a diameter of 9.7m, cut house T. It was incomplete, several metres of the west side having been eroded. It was 0.23–0.44m wide, mean 0.31, and 0.06–0.22m deep, mean 0.12. There was one sherd of pottery. Longitudinal sections revealed post-holes. The entrance faced east and was 1.6m wide. Within was a possible arrangement, S1, of six differently-sized and shaped post-holes. A few stake-holes were discovered inside the entrance.

A 10m arc was all that survived of house T, which had a diameter of 10.5m and was up to 0.07m deep, mean 0.0425, and 0.2–0.3m wide, mean 0.245. Longitudinal sections again revealed post-holes in the fill of the gully; the circle may have been completed by five

shallow post-holes. The entrance may have been the 2m wide gap between post-holes 4111, 4196 and post-holes 2821, 2823. There may have been an internal arrangement of at least four posts, structure T1. There were no finds. At roughly the centre of the arc was a large cylindrical pit, 2416, which was 2.26m deep, 2.39m in diameter, and had a volume of 6.096m^3. It was the largest Middle Iron Age pit on the site. The thirty small sherds recovered had an average weight of 10.25gm and occurred at the rate of 5 per m^3. The other main finds were the complete greensand upper stone of a rotary quern, the skeleton of an infant less than twelve months old, burial 143, and at least two other infant burials.

House U was represented by two arcs of gully which provided an approximate diameter of 11.4m. The lengths of gully were 0.27–0.4m wide, mean 0.335, and 0.04–0.14 deep, 0.075 mean. The two arcs, if joined, would not have formed a circle and it is possible that they belong to separate structures (or are similar to structure E), but are here interpreted as a single feature. The only

Winnall Down
Middle Iron Age Houses

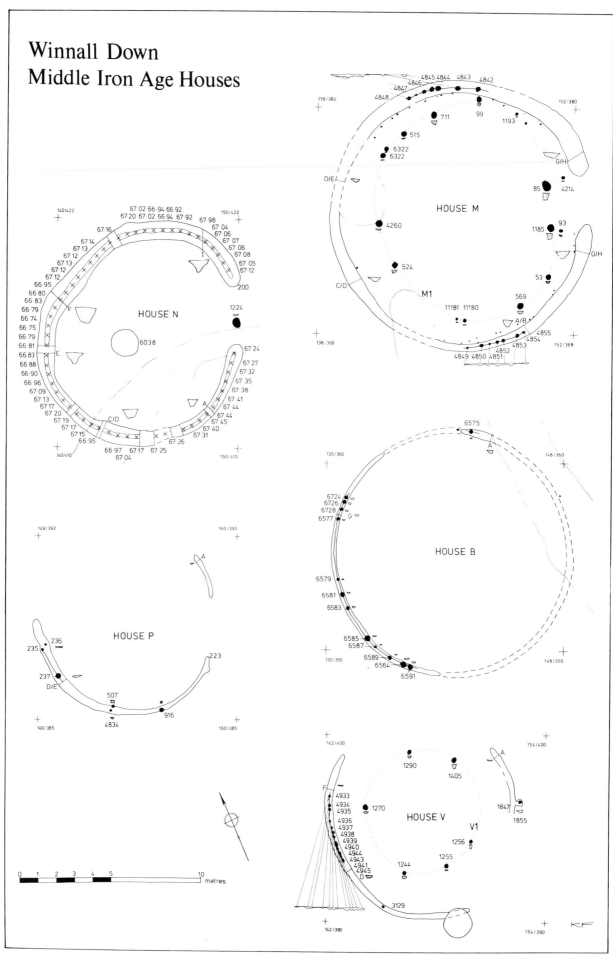

Fig 16. Winnall Down: detailed plans of Middle Iron Age houses B, M, N, P and V.

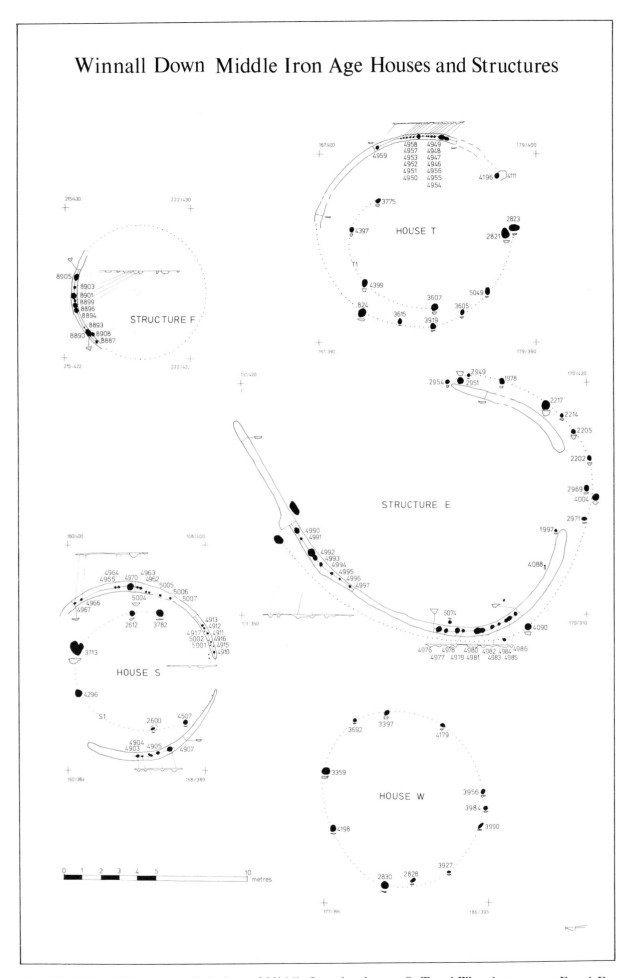

Fig 17. Winnall Down: detailed plans of Middle Iron Age houses S, T and W and structures *E* and *F*.

finds were animal bone and one pottery sherd from the west side. Post-holes were visible in the longtitudinal section. House U was cut by pit 1491. A post-ring of six posts, U1, can be detected within house U. The diameter of U1 was 6.5m.

Structure *E* consisted of gullies 1973 and 1989 and looked in plan like a question-mark. It must be assumed that gullies 1973 and 1989 were associated. The open circle had a diameter of about 12.5m. 1973 was 7.5m long, 0.35m deep and 0.51m wide. It contained a considerable amount of pottery, including a saucepan (Fig 65.54) and cut through the Neolithic feature 1972. 1973 and 1989 were separated by a gap of 4m. Gully 1989 was 0.31–0.55m wide, mean 0.455m, and 0.1–0.26m deep, 0.176m mean. Its stratigraphic relationship with 4062 was unclear. The bone, pottery and flint flakes were fairly evenly distributed, although there was considerably less in the westernmost six metres which did contain two iron nails. Longitudinal sections again revealed post-holes in the fill of the gully.

House V was 13m in diameter and less than half was preserved. It cut through the top of the Early Iron Age enclosure ditch where it was not easily traced. The gully was 0.04–0.12m deep, 0.098 mean, and 0.25–0.4m wide, 0.388 mean. The few finds were regularly scattered through the extant section of the gully in which, originally, posts had stood. It may have had an entrance of 4.5m width which would have faced north.

Structure *F* was in the north-east corner of the site, isolated from other similar features. An arc of 5.65m length was 0.23–0.28m wide, 0.267m mean, and 0.11–0.15m deep, 0.14 mean. The diameter would have been about 9m. The only finds were one fragment of Iron Age pottery, one Roman sherd and two medieval sherds. It is allocated to the Middle Iron Age by analogy of form with the other features of which four, on ceramic grounds, are fairly certainly Middle Iron Age.

House W was circular, 9m in diameter, and consisted of eleven irregularly-spaced shallow post-holes. There were no finds in the post-holes.

Rectangular structure *D* (Fig 18)

This rectangular, ditched structure measured 15.25m by 14.0m externally with an internal area of 178m². The entrance was on the east and measured 7m in width; post-holes 400 and 403 may have been a gate. The gully was 0.2–1.1m wide, mean 0.66, and 0.06–0.4m deep, mean 0.24. Finds of all forms were more densely distributed along the south side than elsewhere. The gully was clearly designed to support posts. The north-west corner of the enclosure was circumscribed by gully F 491 which was 0.44–0.5m wide and 0.32–0.4m deep. It was clearly a foundation trench for a post-built structure; pottery, daub and two fragments of green-sand, probably from querns, were in the fill.

Inside F 491, and cutting through the upper fill, was an oval pit, 413, measuring 1.6m by 1.14m, filled with many burnt flints and with a deposit of chalk paste which could have been created by burning. Pit 413 seems to have contained a fire.

The four-post structure *aa* stood within the rectangular enclosure D, as it did within house R, which is stratigraphically later than D.

Four-post structures

Sixteen possible four-post structures may have belonged to the Middle Iron Age. There was no clear concentration. They can be assigned to the groups outlined above (p13) as follows:

Group A – *bb*, *cc* and *dd*
Group B – *aa*, *ee*, *ff*, *gg*, *hh* and *ii*
Group C – *jj*
Group D – *kk*, *ll*, *mm*, *nn*, *pp* and *qq*

Post-holes 961 and 1203 may have formed a two-post structure (*rr*).

Pits (Fig 19)

More than eighty pits were dug in the Middle Iron Age. Two were rectangular with flat bottoms, forty-one were beehive-shaped, twenty-five were cylindrical and others were circular, ovoid, or rectangular in plan with a range of different profiles. When analyzed by volume five different volumetric ranges emerged.

Group 1, up to 0.8m³, consisted of twenty-three irregularly shaped features, more like scoops, with only 1381, 2553, 3721 and 5414 resembling pits. Nearly all these features contained bone and pottery, less than half contained flint, and only seven contained daub or baked clay. Other finds included a whetstone made of sandstone, from pit 122 (Fig 66.15).

Group 2, 0.81m³–1.6m³, consisted of twenty-six pits which were all cylindrical or beehive-shaped apart from the less regular feature 4460. Some of the pits appeared to be recut (*eg* 124, 310 and 328). The range of finds from these pits was greater than from the Group 1 pits and included more examples of flint, daub, baked clay, three examples of human bone and occasionally quernstones and loomweights. Iron sickles were found in pits 7525 and 2342 (Fig 44.31 and Fig 45.33). Artifacts did not occur throughout the complete fill of all pits; there were none in the middle of 1490, and in 310 there were finds only in the upper fill while in 8657 they occurred only in the bottom layers.

Group 3, 1.61m³–2.8m³, comprised seventeen cylindrical or beehive-shaped pits and the straight-sided rectangular pit 5548. Several pits showed signs of having been cut (*eg* 4006, 5548, 8594 and 8601). They contained a large range of artifacts including six instances of human bone and also examples of worked animal bone and antler, iron and bronze objects. All but five contained fragments of loomweights and quernstones. Again there was a range of depositional histories. Pit 619 was filled with chalk rubble except for the upper layers which contained artifacts, while 3676 and 9344 contained no finds in their middle fills. Artifacts were recovered from just the top of 8437 but none from 8095 and 8096.

Group 4, 2.81m³–4.6m³, consisted of eleven cylindrical or bee-hive-shaped pits most of which contained, throughout all their fills, a wide range of artifacts. Suggestions of recuts were visible in 1631, 5958, 7257 and 6595.

Group 5, 4.61–6.1m³, comprised one rectangular pit, 640, and six cylindrical or beehive-shaped pits. A broad range of finds was discovered throughout these pits. Pits 2002 and 2416 showed signs of having been recut.

Three of the pits are described below, as the detailed study of the rubbish they contained sheds some light on their infilling processes, and possible activities in adjacent areas. The identification and location of specific activities is notoriously difficult on sites which have been flattened by subsequent agricultural activity. Pit 5548 contained evidence relating to a range of activities, including possibly burning or parching, weaving, and general domestic activities such as cooking. The rubbish in pit 6595 is indicative of animal butchery, and the material from pit 7399 clearly reveals that the pit was filled with rubbish derived from a context much earlier than the digging of the pit.

Pit 5548 (Fig 19) by R P Winham

All classes of artifacts and ecofacts were studied in detail, in terms of the perceived and recorded stratigraphy of the pit. This straight-sided, rectangular pit with stepped base was probably originally dug in the earlier part of the Middle Iron Age. The pit was located away from the settlement area which suggests that some of the rubbish, the 'domestic' refuse, was derived from a considerable distance. When abandoned it was left open and silted up with layers 5595, 5591, 5594 and 5593. On top of these deposits was a small patch of ash or charcoal, 5589, presumably deriving from a fire in the pit or from hearth material that had been thrown in. It was sealed by layer 5590. Layers 5590, 5593 and possibly 5589 were the residue from a burning process like corn drying or parching, as there was a significant correlation of

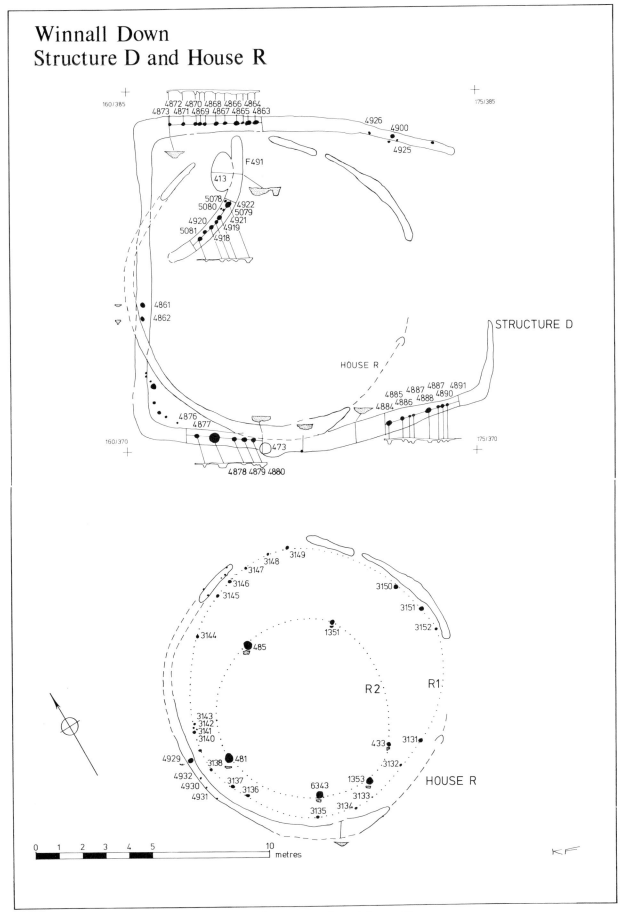

Fig 18. Winnall Down: detailed plans of structure *D* and house R.

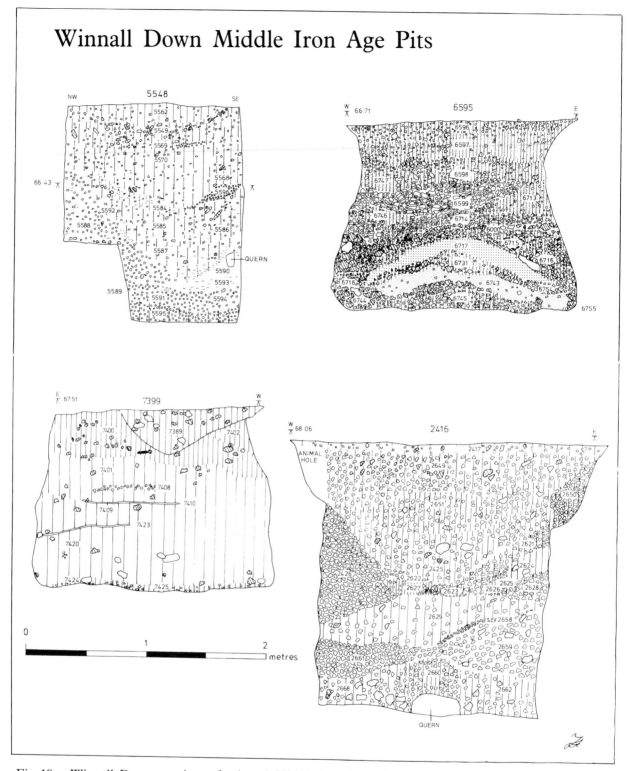

Fig 19.   Winnall Down: sections of selected Middle Iron Age pits. (For key, see Fig 14).

chaff waste and twig charcoal and a large quantity of weed seeds (Monk archive and Keepax archive).

The absence of almost any other form of artifact or ecofact in these layers suggests that these deposits were derived from a discrete activity. Loomweight fragments and cob in layers 5590 and 5593 suggest that weaving may have occurred away from the settlement zone.

Layer 5588 contained large quantities of daub, burnt flint, and pottery of saucepan type indicating adjacent domestic activity. Layer 5587 was a recut of 5588 and contained refuse-pottery, daub and burnt flint – indicative of domestic activity. The layers up to and including 5584 contained, in comparison with 5570, small numbers of pot sherds, but the sherds were larger and heavier. Layer 5584 contained very little pottery but a large number of charcoal fragments and burnt flints, suggesting it was derived from a specialised activity which included burning in its process.

Layers 5585, 5587 and 5588 contained much daub, perhaps indicative of considerable activity in a short period of time. Layer 5596 may relate to this phase of activity.

Layers 5568 and 5570 are similar in many respects – containing Roman pottery and a wide range of pottery fabrics. The sherds are small, abraded and numerous. Also found were many burnt flints and quernstone fragments (one other was in layer 55). Loomweights and daub were not present in quantity. The charcoal content of these two layers was very similar and reflected that of the 'shallow' scoops found elsewhere on the site. These artifact interactions are indicative of a shallow recut or the usual deposition of material from adjacent activities in the ultimate depression at the top of a pit.

Pit 6595 Animal bones by J M Maltby

Pit 6595, at the south-west of the site, was adjacent to house V. Its location may suggest a specialised activity in the area.

This beehive pit was 1.5m deep. The bottom chalk and loam layers 6745 and 6744 contained few, but large, sherds of pottery, some large animal bones and a large number of burnt flints. They were sealed by a deposit of daub, 6743, of varying thickness which contained 43 relatively large sherds weighing 62g. The chalk mould was found in 6743 (Fig 65.12). There was, with layer 6744, a concentration of large animal bones. In the loamy chalk above the daub, 6731, were two almost complete animal skeletons. One of a sow, probably a little over two years of age, was in the centre of the pit. All of the skeleton was recovered apart from the right fore foot. The right astralagus had a knife cut on its anterior aspect towards the medial and running in a medio-lateral direction. This mark may have been made during skinning, as the position of the burial suggests that no attempt was made to dismember the hind limbs. No other butchery was observed, however, and it is possible that skinning was abandoned at an early stage. The dog skeleton had been placed at the side of the pit and lay on its right side. All parts of the skeleton were recovered apart from the front feet. The animal was adult, probably female, and had a shoulder height of 0.456–0.457m. The left femur had been fractured at some stage of the animal's life, but the bone had reset, albeit distorted, and the animal had lived for some time after this trauma.

The two burials were sealed by a layer, up to 0.14m thick, of compressed, rammed chalk, 6717. This must have been a deliberate infill as the material was extremely compacted and contained one flint flake and a few animal bones on the east side. It was covered by 6716 which contained a few animal bones, two large pot sherds and part of an upper stone of a rotary quern. This was sealed by a layer of burnt flints, 6600, which contained 34 animal bone fragments and three sherds of pottery smaller than those found below. Above 6600 the number and size of finds, pottery and animal bones decline, apart from one large sherd in layer 6597 where there was a large number of small, eroded bone fragments and usually small sherds.

In all, 14 small fragments of animal bone were ivoried, and 15 showed some gnawing marks made by dogs. Cattle fragments were the most commonly identified followed by sheep/goat, horse, pig and dog. There was an unusually high concentration of horse and cattle. Most of the major limb bones were represented amongst the cattle bones but the tarsals, metapodia and phalanges were poorly represented. Butchery evidence in the form of knife cuts was found in several of the mandibles, scapulae, humeri, radii and os coxae, and some of the limb bones had been broken, probably for marrow extraction. The horse remains were less fragmented than the cattle but knife cuts were found in several of the bones.

It would appear that the lower part of the pit, particularly up to the rammed chalk of 6717, was deliberate rubbish backfill, a process which might have gone as high as 6600. Above the latter, the infill process included a mixture of natural weathering, 6599, and gradual rubbish and natural filling.

The density of large bones particularly in the lower layers may suggest that butchery of cattle and horse was taking place nearby, possibly on quite a large scale, since a minimum of twelve cattle were represented by mandibles in the four layers below 6717 (although this is conditioned by the time factor). Above 6717 ten cattle mandibles were scattered through the rest of the pit. This may partly explain the high proportion of cattle and horse bones in relation to those of sheep/goat and pig.

Pit 7399

Pit 7399 appeared to have been filled with burnt midden material; it was situated at the south-west corner of the Early Iron Age activity Area 3. In the bottom was a burnished sherd of a Middle Iron Age type which can only have arrived when the pit was open. Layer 7424, immediately sealing the lowest layer, contained much charcoal and was sampled for a radio-carbon determination of 2100±80 BP (HAR 2592). The next metre of fill was a deposit of grey-brown silty loam (field description) with layers of chalk (7408), sand (7410) and charcoal (7423). The general deposit contained a large quantity of broken Early Iron Age pottery, loomweights and quernstones. Monk's analysis of carbonised weeds and seeds indicates that they were a charrred waste product. The ashy, silty material is best regarded as an Early Iron Age midden redeposited in a Middle Iron Age pit. The ceramic evidence suggests that the redeposited material was fairly homogeneous but this cannot be considered a definitive statement.

Other structures

Bersu introduced the concept of the working hollow which he defined as "an irregular quadrangle with rounded corners, steep or sloping sides and a floor that is in general level. The floors are divided by shallow oval to circular depressions arranged in such a way that their edges often look as if they had served as sitting places; sometimes these 'sitting places' extend beyond the edge of the hollow" (Bersu 1940, 64). There are no clear cut examples of working hollows in Phase 4 although feature 7302 may just be one such example. It cut the beehive-shaped pit 7257 and was associated with a few adjacent shallow scoops. The quarries of the south-east and north-west were probably still in use in Phase 4, with possibly the emphasis being placed on the former group.

Two possible fences have been identified. Fence 7 consisted of 17 post-holes forming a total length of 37m. It was aligned east-west and turned through 60° to the south-east at its eastern end. Fence 8 was 18m long and comprised of twelve posts.

Human Remains (full details by Powell and Bayley in archive)

Eighteen complete or fairly complete burials are associated with Phase 4; one adult male, two definite and two possible adult females, an adolescent, two children and ten infants. There were 25 records of 'loose' human bone.

In the north-west quarry was a small burial area which, although difficult to date, is likely to belong to Phase 4 (Fig 20). The burials were: a 20–25 year old female, 508, in pit 8265; a child of about 12 years, 506, in grave 8294; a child of 8–9 years, 505, and a fragmentary infant 460 in grave 8184; infant burial 397 in scoop 6280. While actually unphased, infant burials 457 and 507 and infant bones 3555 may also relate to this burial area (Fig 21).

Another small burial area, at the south of the site, consisted of inhumations in three closely-spaced beehive pits (Fig 22). Adult male 500 and bones from infant 3563 were buried in pit 8564; adult female 574 was in the bottom of, and infant burials 470 and 531 towards the top of, pit 8630. Bones from an adult, 3566, and an elderly person, 3566a, in pit 8630 may be from burial 574, but have been tabulated separately. Infant burial 567 was in pit 8594.

Outliers to this group were adolescent male 174 in pit 4475 (from

Fig 20.   Winnall Down: view of Middle Iron Age burial area in the quarries at the north-west of the site. Scales 2m. (Photo: J Lockett).

which pit also came a considerable number of other adolescent bones probably from one individual, 3544–3546), and adult skull fragments 3547. Neo-natal infant 156 and adult bones 3576 came from pit 4006, infant 487 from post-hole 8547, and infant 488 from post-hole 8576. Post-hole 8547 was cut by the Phase 6 ditch 678 and 8567 was in a comparable but not observable stratigraphic relationship. Male 174 was the only burial with grave goods, which consisted of personal ornaments in the form of a shale bracelet on the left forearm (Fig 66.16) and a bronze thumb ring on the left hand (Fig 41.4).

Infant burials 159 in grave 4239 and 161 in grave 4264 cannot be securely dated to this phase but may belong to the periphery of this second cemetery. Also insecurely dated were infant fragments 3517–3518 from post-hole 142 and infant fragments 3565 from pit 8585. Adult fragments 3529 and infant bones 3530 were found in gully 1989 and adult fragments 3574 in pit 684.

Elsewhere on the site, adult female 35 was in grave 2020 on the east and cut into the Phase 3 enclosure ditch, and a 17–25 year old female, 629, was in grave 10312 at the east of the northern quarries (Fig 23). Complete infant 143 and bones of two (possibly six) others, 3534–3535 and 3536–3539, were in pit 2416. Pit 7372 contained part of an infant, 420, and both adult and infant bones, 419 and 3578.

Scattered infant bones were also recorded from pits 1473, 2002 and 5789. Adult bones were also in segment CC of ditch 5, linear feature 2778 and pits 1491 and 3901 (2). Part of a 17–25 year old was in pit 5548.

Dating evidence

The pottery from this phase lies within the southern British saucepan pot tradition and is in the style of Cunliffe's St Catherine's Hill-Worthy Down Group (Cunliffe 1978). The saucepan tradition seems to start in the third century BC and last into the first century BC.

Seven radio-carbon determinations were obtained.

HAR 2252:2140±80BP was from oak and ash charcoal of large timbers in the top layer of pit 3738 and was associated with a wide-mouthed jar.

Winnall Down Middle Iron Age Burials

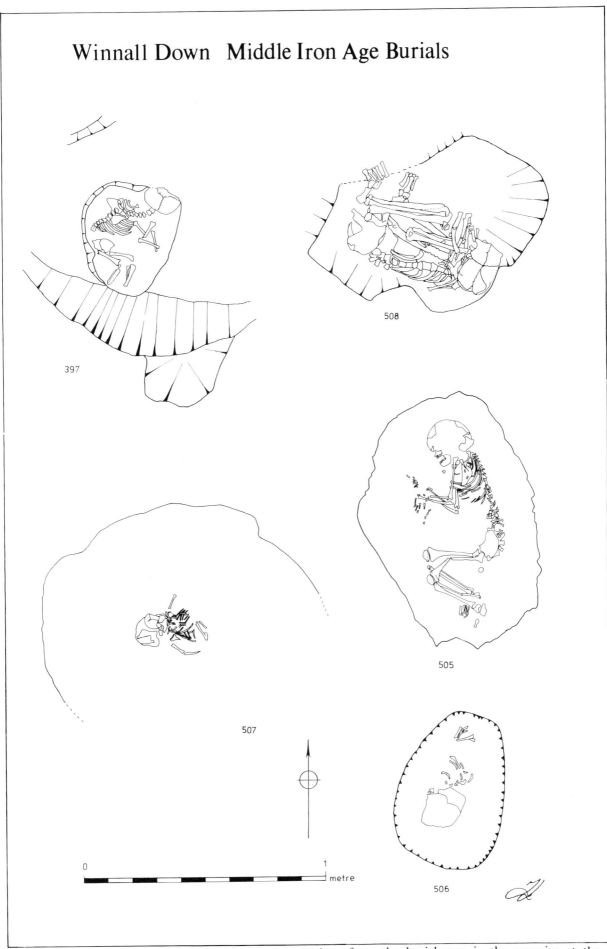

397

508

507

505

506

0   1
metre

Fig 21. Winnall Down: Middle Iron Age inhumations from the burial area in the quarries at the north-west of the excavation.

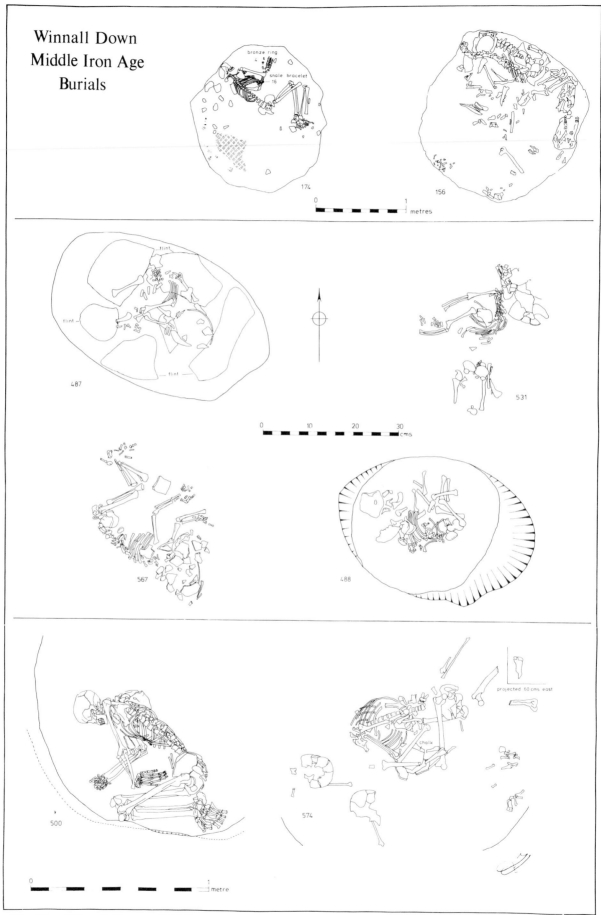

Fig 22.   Winnall Down: Middle Iron Age inhumations. Burials 500, 531, 567 and 574 were from the southern burial area; burials 156, 174, 487 and 488 were outliers.

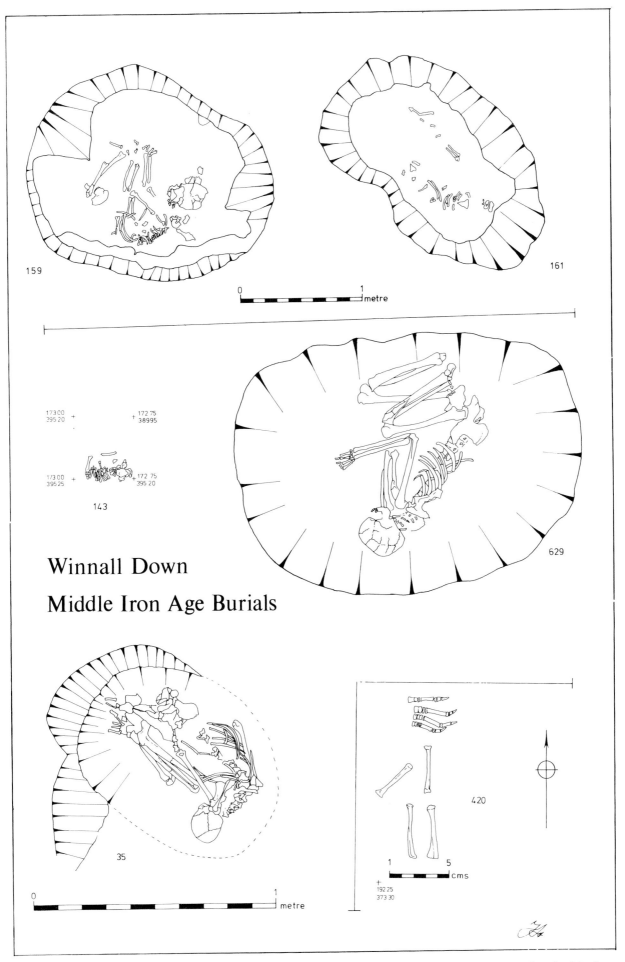

Fig 23.   Winnall Down: Middle Iron Age inhumations. 159 and 161 may have been associated with the southern burial area. Burials 35, 143, 420 and 629 were from diverse contexts across the site.

HAR 2591:2190±60BP was on charcoal from the bottom of pit 5789. The pit contained a range of pottery including simple and round-bodied bowls, bipartite, bead-rim, and narrow-mouthed jars, as well as some haematite-coated sherds. There is clearly a residual element within this pit.

HAR 2592:2100±80BP was on charcoal from pit 7399 which was filled with material derived from an Early Iron Age midden.

HAR 2938:1990±70BP was on bone from human burial 500 which was in the middle of pit 8564 and sealed deposits containing saucepans and a round-bodied bowl.

HAR 2195:2070±80BP was from human burial 35 which had been inserted into the Early Iron Age enclosure ditch.

HAR 2980:2150±80BP was from burial 574 in grave 8630 and was associated with a saucepan.

HAR 2937:2250±90BP was from burial 629 in grave 10312.

Comments on the Radio-carbon dates
by S J Shennan

The pooled mean for the seven dates from this phase is 2124.66BP. The dates were tested to see if they were significantly different from one another.

T = 5.135 with 6 df; not significant at the 0.05 level. The dates form an homogeneous set. The mean date for Phase 4 is 2124.66BP, with a standard error of 34.44. The 95% confidence interval for the mean date of Phase 4 (slightly rounded) is 2125±70BP, or 2195–2055BP; in other words there is a 95% probability that the mean date for Phase 4 lies within these limits.

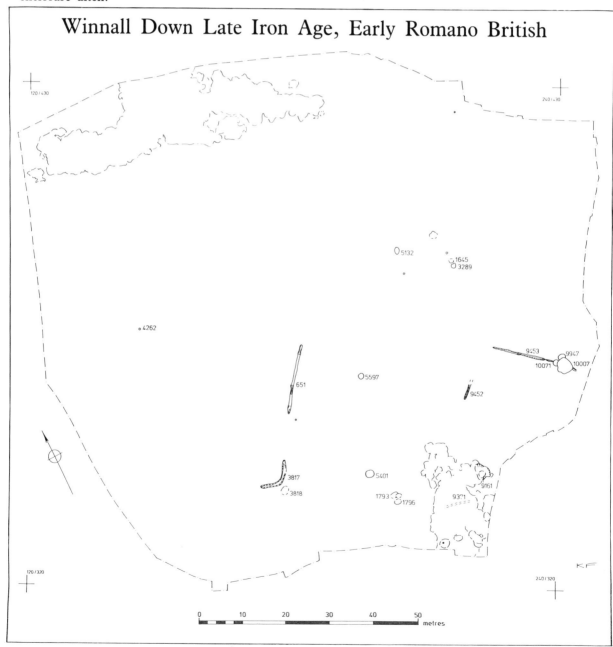

Fig 24. Winnall Down: Late Iron Age/Early Romano-British. Plan of features belonging to Phase 5.

Phase 5. Late Iron Age–Romano-British (Figs 24 and 25)

Phase 5 consisted of a few features which were stratigraphically earlier than Phase 6 features or were regarded on ceramic grounds (M Fulford and C Young, pers com) as being slightly earlier than Phase 6.

The only relevant features were ditches/gullies, pits, scoops and post-holes.

Ditch 651 was a small narrow ditch 16m long. It was between 0.34m and 0.65m wide (mean 0.47m) and 0.09m to 0.17m deep (mean 0.13m) with sloping sides and a flat bottom. Ditch 3817 was a possible continuation of 651 and had sloping sides and a flat bottom. About 9m survived which included a 90° bend. It was 0.70m to 1.04m wide and 0.20m to 0.33m deep. Ditch 9371 had been badly damaged by later features, but could be traced for a length of 5m. It appeared to have sloping sides and a flat bottom. It was in the order of 0.25m wide and 0.20m deep. Ditch 9452 was 3.6m long with sloping sides and a flat bottom. It was 0.39m wide and 0.12m deep. Ditch 9453, 20m long, was cut by pit 10007. It was of irregular profile with the width ranging from 0.25m to 0.60m and the depth from 0.05m to 0.22m.

There were eight scoops and twelve pits. The majority were to the south-east of the Phase 3 enclosure ditch 5. Pits 1645, 3289 and 5732 were grouped together 50m north of the southern concentration. Pit 5597 was an eroded beehive. The 10007 complex was reminiscent of a working hollow but the remainder were generally irregular circular or oval pits with flattish bottoms. There were no dimensions available for 10071 but seven pits had Group 1 volumes of less than 0.8m³, two had Group 3 volumes of 1.61m³–2.8m³ and there were one each of volumetric Groups 4 (2.81m³–4.6m³) and 5 (4.61m³–6.1m³). The total estimated storage capacity was a little under 14.5m³ and the number of sherds per m³ was calculated to range from 12.8 to 487. It was the smallest pit, 3289, which produced the greatest number of sherds per m³, although 10007 contained more actual sherds than any of the other pits.

Four post-holes may relate to Phase 5. The only human remains were the right femur of an infant in pit 1645. With so few features spatial analysis had no validity. Charred cereal fragments included spelt.

If Phase 5 can be separated as a coherent phase from the later Phase 6, its period of activity would have been during the first half of the first century AD.

Phase 6. Romano-British (Fig 26)

A series of four enclosures linked by a track and associated with other ditches, pits and post-hole structures were the essential components of Phase 6. About thirty ditches, some recut, some showing no signs of stratigraphic relationships, were dug during the century or so that this phase lasted (Fig 26).

Rather than discuss in detail the individual ditches, a possible sequence, indeed the most likely sequence, is illustrated in Fig 27 and sections of the ditches in Figs 28 and 29. The full details and justification for the proffered sequence are in the archive.

The Ditches

Ditches 8083 and 8923 had an east-west orientation and were cut by the ditches of enclosure A: two factors which suggest that 8083 and 8923 belong to the earliest period of this phase, period i. The relationship of the former ditch and the quarries was not clear. 8083 was cut by ditch 1300 and its recuts 8822 and 2199. 8088 cut ditch 8822. All these activities belong to period i, before enclosure A was constructed. Ditch 2022 was cut by ditches 9805 and 9806 and is presumed to belong to period i. It is possible that enclosure D belongs to this first period but it seems more likely to be associated with the north-south flanking ditches of the periods ii-v. Thus, in period i, the ditch system seems to relate to a track and field system to the north and east of the excavation.

Period ii saw the commencement of the enclosure system proper with a linking track running down the east side. In this period were enclosure A, possibly with its southern side being completed by an unrecorded ditch or a post fence, and its east side by either of those forms or by a fence or hedge on the extant portion of the Early Iron Age enclosure, ditch 5, and enclosure D at the south.

In period iii the system of enclosures reached its greatest elaboration with enclosures A-D being in use. This must imply that preceding earthworks, with hedges or fences, were utilised in subsequent periods.

In period iv enclosures A and B were combined and there were further recuts in enclosures A and C and in the ditches of the track.

In period v enclosures A and B were separated by 1308, a recut of various ditches from periods 3 and 4. Ditches 4637 and 1300 south were small and shallow and may relate to a subsequent period of activity.

The enclosure system covered a minimum area of 3500m² and a fifth enclosure to the south is discernible on aerial photographs. The enclosures had various entrances and gaps, frequently linking them to the track on the east, sometimes providing access to the apparent open areas to the west and sometimes linking one enclosure with another.

The north side of enclosure D was defined by ditch 678. Child burials 487 and 488 were discovered during its excavation. The former burial was cut by the ditch and the latter burial is assumed to be in the same stratigraphic relationship. The burials belong to Phase 4 rather than Phase 6 and therefore are not foundation burials. Inserted into the period iii ditch, 6732, on the west side of enclosure D was an inverted narrow-mouthed jar.

Within each enclosure were only a few shallow pits and scoops, except in enclosure C where there was a small concentration of these features.

Enclosure C was the only enclosure to provide evidence for an internal revetment, with a series of large post-holes, Fence 9, on the east side of ditch 660.

Pits (Fig 30)

Thirty-seven measurable pits were allocated to this phase. There were also traces of about five others. Six were rectangular, eleven cylindrical and twenty were sub-circular with rounded bottoms. They were generally shallow (78% were 0.5m deep or less) and of small volume (95% less than 1m³). There was no regular pattern to their distribution and they occurred both within and without the enclosures. There was perhaps a slight concentration within enclosure C and a group at the west junction of enclosures A and B.

Rectangular post-built structures (Fig 31)

Structure G, between enclosure A and ditch 9806 which it cut, measured 3m east-west by 2.3m north-south and had a central

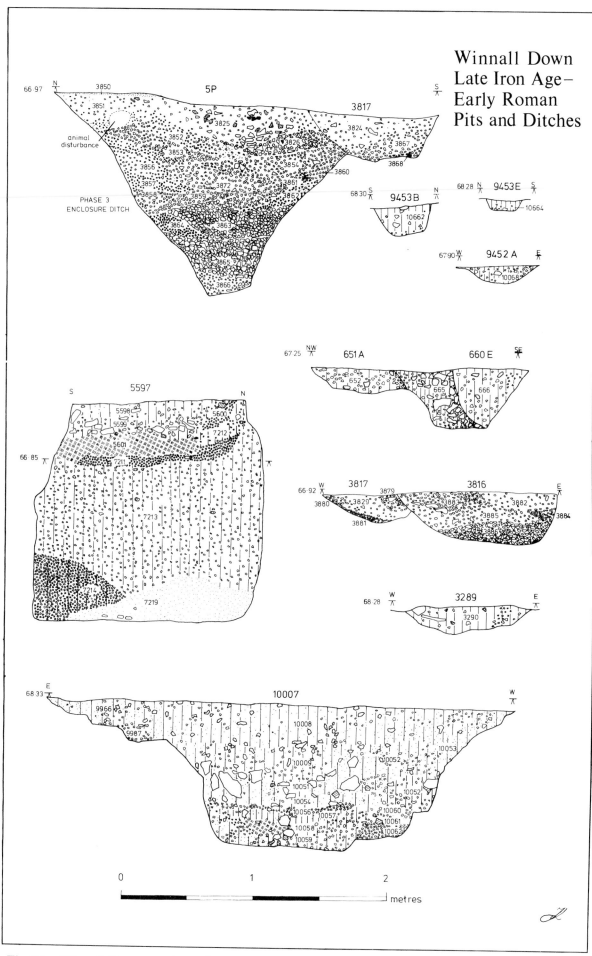

Fig 25.   Winnall Down: sections of Late Iron Age/Early Romano-British features. Pits 3289, 5597 and 10007; ditches 651, 3817, 9452 and 9453.

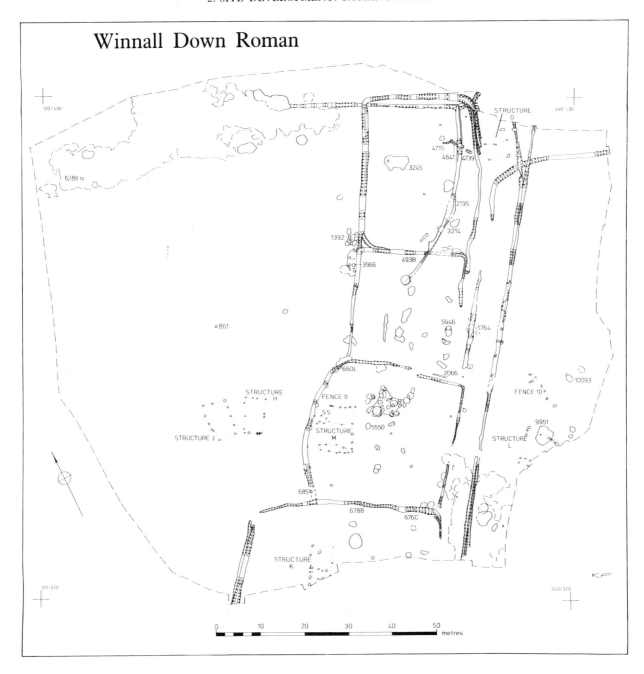

Fig 26.   Winnall Down: Romano-British. Plan of all features belonging to Phase 6.

division. The east side was erected in the fill of ditch 9806. There was no evidence for a post-hole at the north-west corner.

Structure *H*, west of enclosure C, was 3m north-south and 1.8m wide. There were more posts on the short sides and only central posts on the long sides. Possible entrances were in all but the west side.

Structure *J* was 2m west of *H* and on a slightly different alignment. It measured 3m by 2m, with an internal division.

Structure *K*, in enclosure D, was only partially excavated. It was at least 6m north-south and 2m east-west. Between post-holes 9048/9049 and 9093 there may have been an entrance leading onto a central cross passage. A sherd of Roman grey ware, Fabric 6, was in post-hole 8674.

Structure *L* was to the east of the track and is dubious. Its minimum measurements were 3m by 3.1m.

Structure *M* comprised four lines of posts, 8m–10m in length, which ran east from fence 9, the revetment inside ditch 660. The east side of these fences could easily have been closed to form either a building or a series of animal pens.

Four-post structures

There was one four-post structure. Structure *SS* stood in enclosure C and had sides of 1m length. It was built of small posts.

Fence

Fence 10 was 13m long, of seven posts and was east of the track.

Winnall Down
Early Roman
Enclosures

Sections on Fig. 34			Sections on Fig. 35		
1	8083 C		3	8923	8088 A
2	8088 CB		6	1300 D	2199
4	8822 B	1300 J/K	10	1643 G/H	4637 4607 B
5	8822 B	1300 A	18	6732 D	
7	2022 B		19	9805 A	
8	8082 EF		20	1643 5K	
9	1643 HI	4637 B/C	21	1308 F	
11	9806 A		22	1643	
12	9805 B		23	4679 F/G	
13	2761 B 1308 B	471 H	24	4679 I	
14	9450 A 9451 A	9452 A	25	660 F	
15	9397		27	660 D	
16	678 C		29	8584	
17	6740 6718	6732 B	30	6732 D 6740 D	
25	1135 I/H		32	2761 E 493 Z	
28	560 A 560 B 560 C	685	33	10629	
31	881 A 8818 A		34	2066	
			36	9936	
			35	7513 C/B	
			37	7513 E / F	

New cut each stage

0 10 20 30 40 50
metres

Subphases
a | b | c | d

I
II
III
IV
V

8088
8083
8923
8822
2022
2199
1300

9806
4607
9914
9451
9397
8082
471
678
6740

9805
1643
4679
493
1135
9452
9136
8584
660
6732
8818

8817
2761
2066
10629
7513

4637
1308
7513

A B C D

JDS

Fig 27.   Winnall Down: schematic plan of Roman enclosures in probable chronological sequence.

Winnall Down

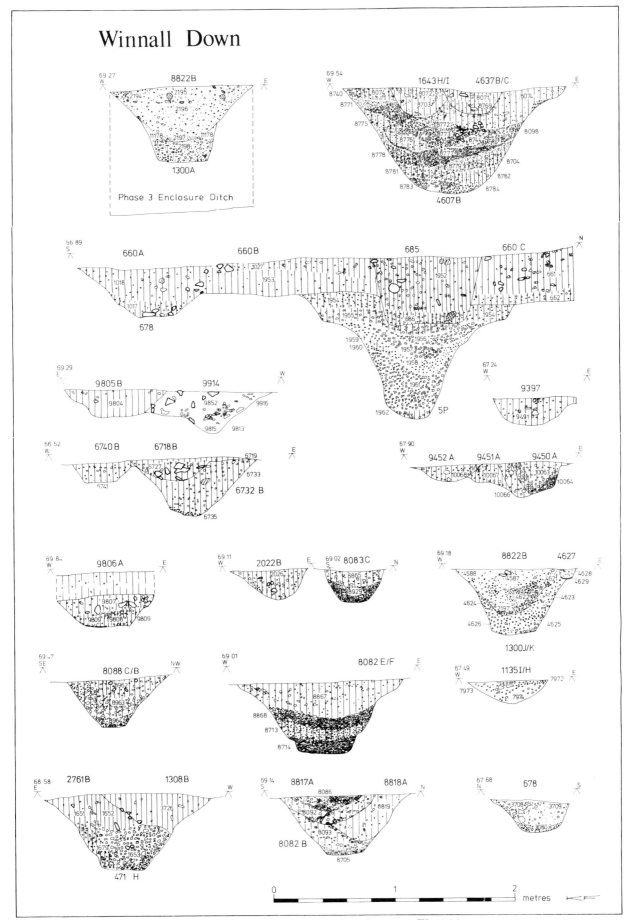

Fig 28.   Winnall Down: sections of Roman ditches. (For key, see Fig 14.)

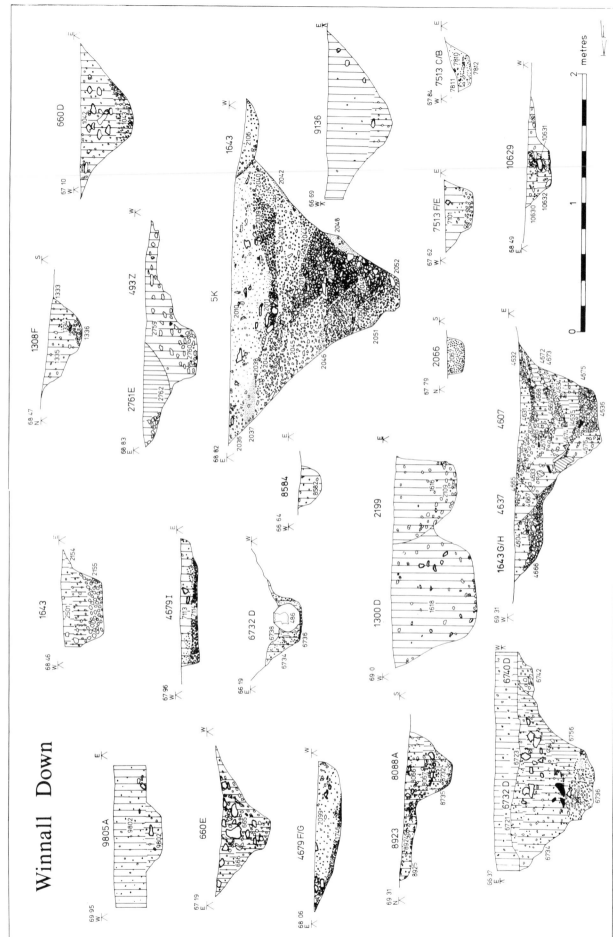

Fig 29. Winnall Down: sections of Roman ditches. (For key, see Fig 14.)

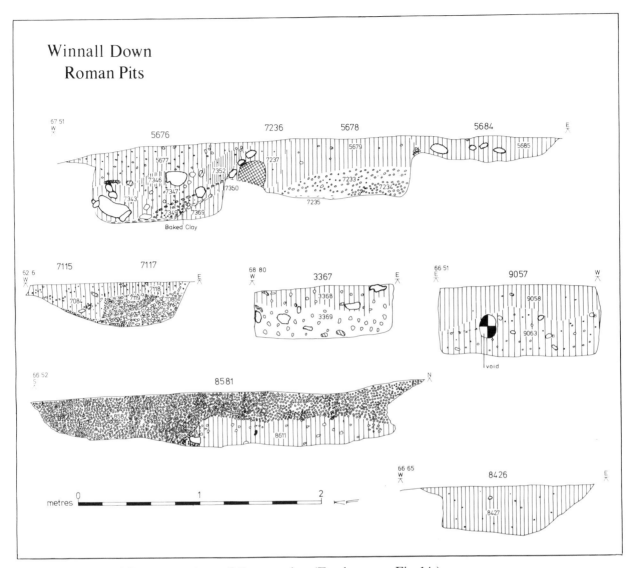

Fig 30. Winnall Down: sections of Roman pits. (For key, see Fig 14.)

Table 3. Unphased features ordered in feature types.

	No	% of unphased features	% of feature type	% of all features
Post-holes	1078	66	53	30
Scoops/Shallow scoops	362	22	71	10
Stake-holes	67	4	60	2
Pits/Quarry pits	97	6	27	3
Other (Ditches, posts, slots, graves, ruts)	27	2	5	1
	1631	100		46

Human remains (Fig 32. Full details by Powell and Bayley in archive)

There were only five complete burials from this phase. Burial 126, whilst fragmentary, was of a child aged 5–6 years and was in grave 685. Infant burial 398 was in grave 6289, infant 489 in segment B of ditch 678, where there was also a fragmentary infant, and infants 495 and 509 were in scoop 8581. The latter two were located just south of the southern Phase 4 burial area. Cremation 133 was in a damaged pot in scoop 3966.

Phase 7. Medieval (Fig 33)

The medieval evidence on the site was limited to two ditches. Ditch 1100 was 132m long. It ran from the south-east corner of the site in a northerly direction for 82m before turning through almost a right angle to run westwards. It was between 0.34 and 0.65m wide, mean 0.47, and 0.04–0.2m deep, mean 0.11. It

Winnall Down Roman Structures

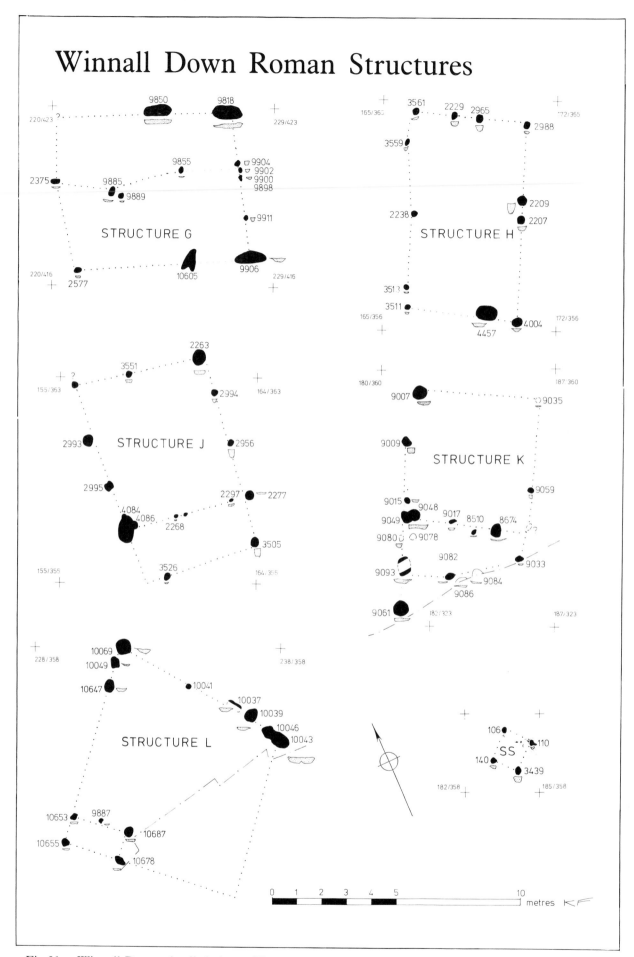

Fig 31.   Winnall Down: detailed plans of Roman structures *G*, *H*, *J*, *K* and *L* and four-post structure *ss*.

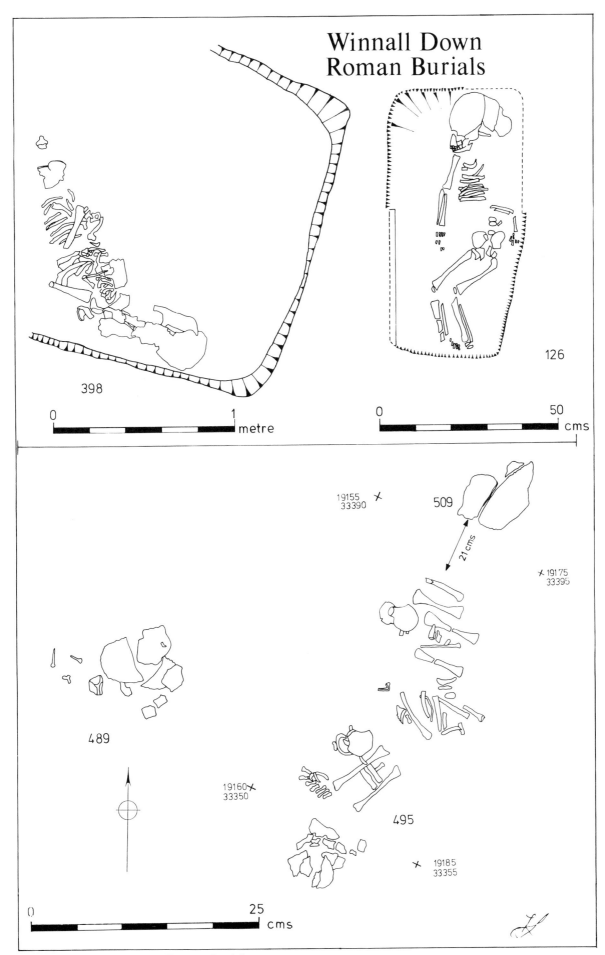

Winnall Down
Roman Burials

398

126

0   1
metre

0   50
cms

19155
33390

509

21cms

× 19175
33395

489

19160×
33350

495

× 19185
33355

0   25
cms

Fig 32.   Winnall Down: Roman burials.

Winnall Down Phase 7 and Unphased

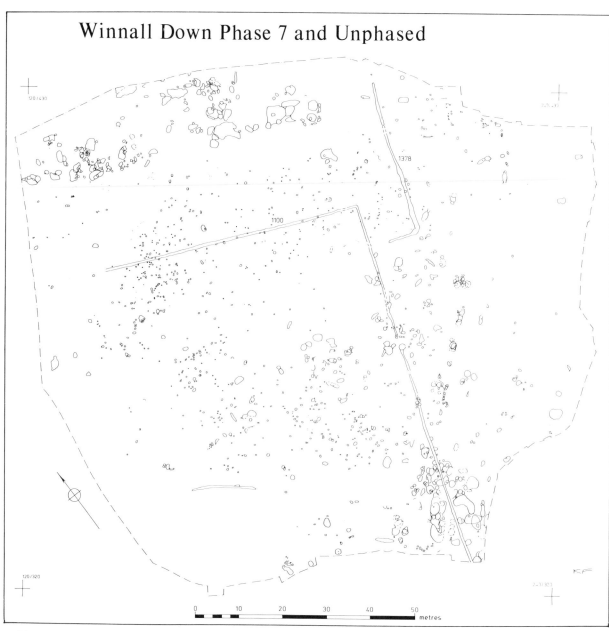

Fig 33. Winnall Down: plan of Phase 7 and unphased features.

Fig 34. Winnall Down: view of the quarry area in the south-east of the site, from the north. Scales 2m. (Photo: J Lockett).

Fig 35.   Winnall Down: view of the quarries in the north-west, showing house N in the foreground and the Early Iron Age enclosure ditch right foreground. View from west. Scales 2m. (Photo: J Lockett).

reached its maximum proportions in the middle of the northern alignment.

Ditch 1378/8866 started just south and east of the corner of 1100 and ran east for 6m before turning through a right angle to continue north for 33m. It was 0.43–1.1m wide, mean 0.61, and 0.04–0.18m deep, mean 0.1.

Unphased features (Fig 33)

There are 2,274 features which cannot be directly phased but, of these, 643 are provisionally allocated to different phases on spatial and other grounds. The remaining 1,631 unphased features are tabulated (Table 3, p39).

Probable quarry scoops

The scoops are mainly located in the areas of extensive quarry digging at the south-east and north-west corners of the site (Figs 34 and 35). It seems that the latter was started in the Early Iron Age and continued into the Middle Iron Age. Extensive sections of the north-west area were recorded, but there had been so much re-digging of features that it proved impossible to develop a detailed stratigraphic and chronological sequence. An estimate of the extent of these areas in Phases 3 and 4 is shown in the relevant figures. A plan of part of the area in the north-west is shown in Fig 36 and typical sections in Figs 37 and 38. The area in the south-east was of different character and the scoops and recuts generally smaller than those in the north-west (Fig 39).

Part of the north-west quarry area is demonstrably early. The Early Iron Age enclosure ditch cut some of the scoops and pits, the Phase 4 house 200 cut others, and the radiocarbon dates for some of the intrusive human burials again indicate that they were inserted into pre-existing scoops during the Middle Iron Age. It therefore seems that a large portion of the north-west area was already quarried by the Middle Iron Age. In the south-east, some of the Middle Iron Age pits appear to be contemporary with, or even earlier than, the scoops, but the scoops are earlier than the

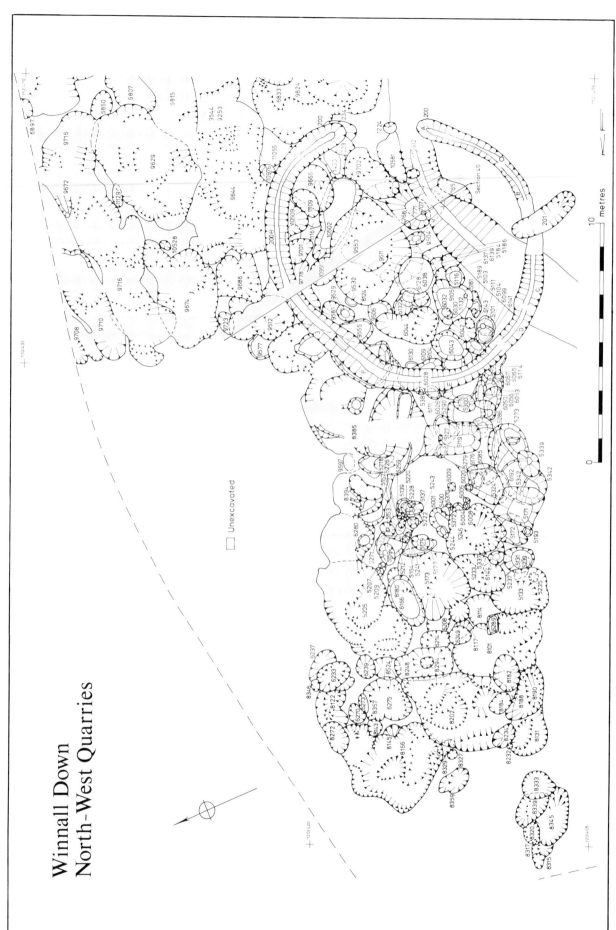

Fig 36. Winnall Down: plan of part of the quarries at the north-west.

Winnall Down

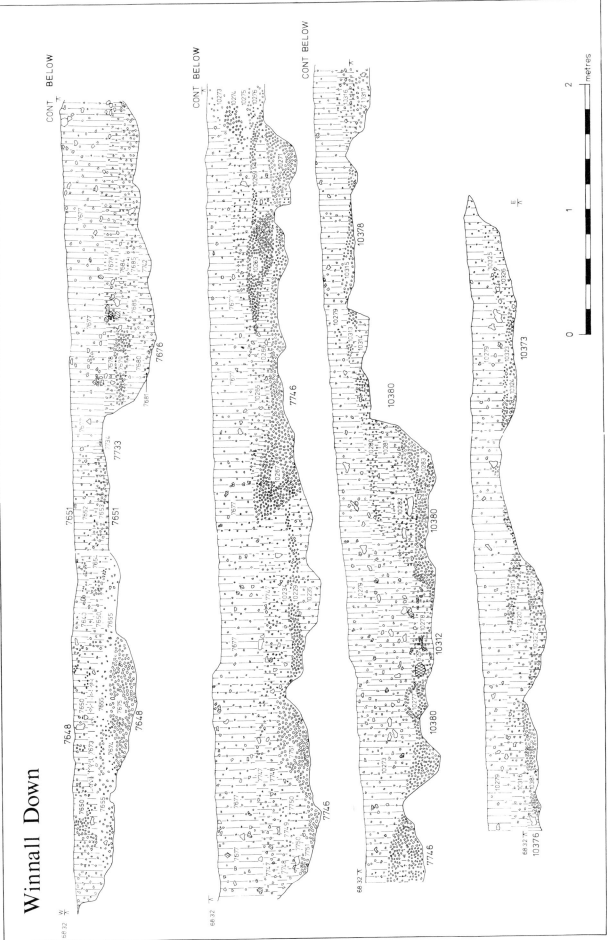

Fig 37. Winnall Down: sections of quarries at the north-west. (For key, see Fig 14.)

Winnall Down

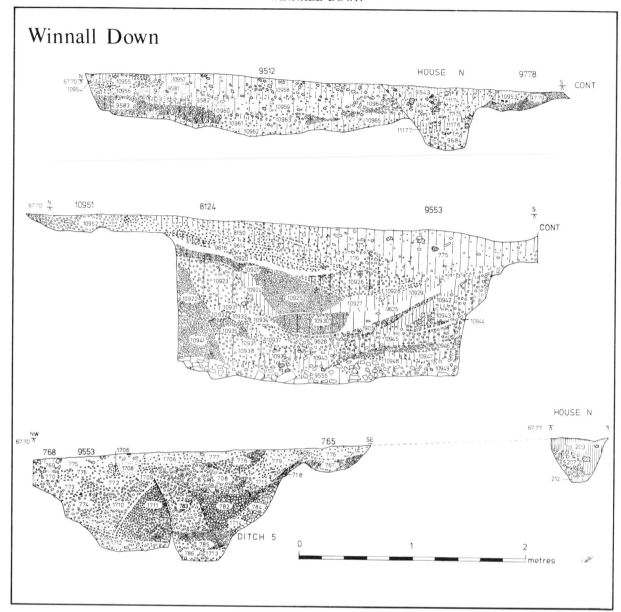

Fig 38.   Winnall Down: sections across part of the north-west quarry area and house N. (For key, see Fig 14.)

Phase 6 ditches. Thus a date perhaps towards the end of the Middle Iron Age might be acceptable for the scoops at the south-east of the site.

Possible Structures

The only other unphased or insecurely-phased structures to which attention must be drawn are structure *G* (Fig 31), which has been allocated to Phase 6, and features 4641, 4739 and 4715 (Fig 40). The latter three features are a series of post-holes in gullies which, between them, cut both the Early Iron Age enclosure ditch and a Phase 6 enclosure ditch. 4641 and 4739, especially, resemble the constructional techniques utilized at the Anglo-Saxon sites of Chalton (Addyman 1972, Addyman and Leigh 1973) and Cowdery's Down (Millett 1980) in Hampshire. One sherd of residual Iron Age pottery was in 4715. These features and possibly structure *G* may relate to a post-Roman phase of occupation, although this is clearly impossible to prove.

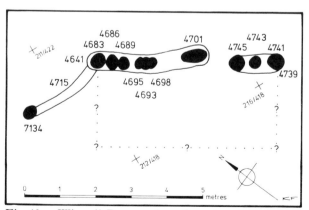

Fig 40.   Winnall Down: plan of unphased features 4641, 4715 and 4739.

Winnall Down   South-East Quarries

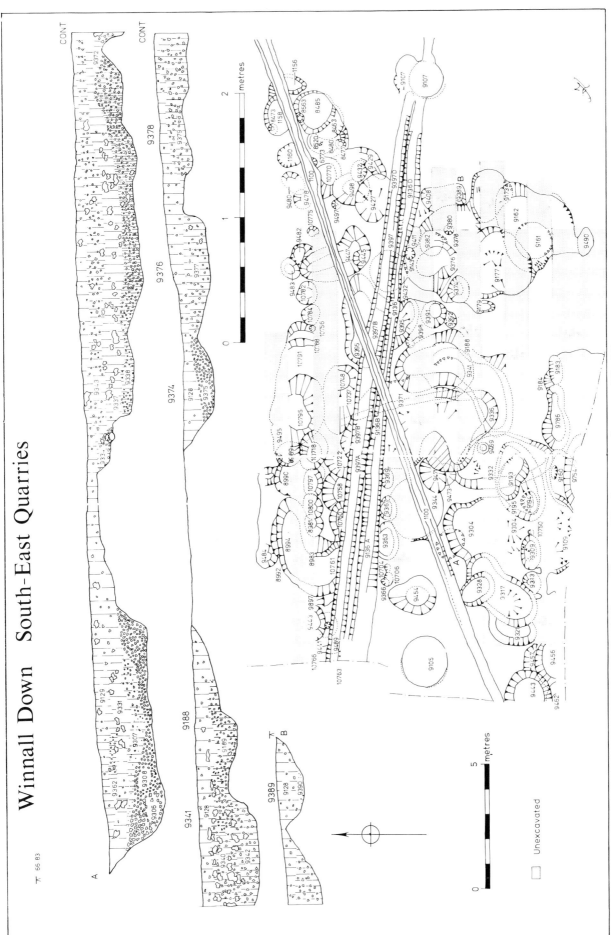

Fig. 39.   Winnall Down: plan and sections of quarries in the south-east. (For key to sections, see Fig 14).

Chapter 3
The Finds

Finds of metal by R P Winham with contributions by C Catling, D F Mackreth and W H Manning

Table 4 summarises the distribution of metal objects by phase.

Bronze

Coin by C Catling

Antoninianus of Tetricus II, AD 271–273
Obverse: Crowned and draped bust. Legends:
CPIU ESU TETRICUS CAES. Reverse:

Pontifical instruments. Legends: PEITAS AUGG (Mattingley and Sydenham 1972, No 254). Unphased, quarry pit 9127. Not illustrated.

Brooches by D F Mackreth (Fig 41)

1. Hod Hill Type. Only the lower bow survives. It is flat and lozenge-shaped, the upper point of which was cut off by the upper bow, now missing, and the lower by the foot-knob which has a weak cross-moulding above. The catch-plate is damaged. Not enough of the brooch survives for useful parallels to be given. The Hod Hill type has yet to be proved to have been imported into Britain before the Roman Conquest, but arrived then in considerable numbers and in all its varieties. The type was probably very nearly at the end of its manufacturing life by *c* AD 45, was going out of use by *c* AD 60, and was only rarely worn by *c* AD 70, as

Table 4. The distribution of metal objects by phase. NP = Not Phased.

	Object	Phase 3	4	6	7	NP	TOTAL
Bronze	Coin	–	–	–	–	1	1
	Brooches	–	1	1	–	1	3
	Rings	–	2	1	–	–	3
	Pins	–	1	2	–	–	3
	Miscellaneous	–	2	2	–	2	6
Speculum	'Collar'	–	1	–	–	–	1
Lead	Dish	–	–	1	–	–	1
Iron	Brooches	–	2	–	–	–	2
	Tweezers	–	1	–	–	–	1
	Ring-headed pin	–	1	–	–	–	1
	Key	–	1	–	–	–	1
	Timber 'dog'	–	1	–	–	–	1
	'Goads'?	1	1	–	–	–	2
	Ard point	–	–	1	–	–	1
	Plough bar	–	–	1	–	–	1
	Blades	–	6	1	–	2	9
	Strips/bars	–	2	3	–	6	11
	Miscellaneous	5	7	5	–	6	23
	Nails	3	14	78	4	25	124
		9	43	96	4	43	195

the small number of examples known from the area taken into the Province in the north of England from AD 72 show. Phase 6 grave 6289, infant burial 398.

2.   Plate Type. In the centre is a sunken recess with a central hole and a bordering ridge with traces of beading. Around the recess are six equally spaced smaller ones each with a central hole and, in three cases, these hold rivets. Between each of these recesses is the faint trace of a leaf stamp. The outer edge of the plate is alternatively round and pointed to suit the sequence of recesses and leaves. The pin is hinged.

Each recess once held a bone boss (Riha 1979, 184, Taf 59, 1567), the central one having a raised border. The type is usually tinned or silvered. The brooch is probably an import from the continent and few have been found in Britain. Specimens come from Wappenham, Northants (Ward 1911, 259, Fig 74.1), Holbrooks, Old Harlow, Herts (Harlow Museum C207) and Brampton, Norfolk (excavations, Dr A K Knowles), but none seems to be dated. On the continent, examples come from Mandeure (Jeanin and Lerat 1957, 23, Pl VIII.143), Vindonissa (Ettlinger 1973, 110, Taf 12,12), Petit Creusot (Feugère 1977, 125, Pl 16.99), and Augst (Riha 1979, 184, Taf 59,1567). The last was found with pottery belonging to the late first and second centuries as well as an Augenfibel and two Hod Hill types which would normally be dated c AD1 – c AD 60. The period during which a silvery finish was commonly applied to brooches cannot be closely dated, however the use of leaf-stamps is known on Aucissa variants (Frere 1954, 140, Fig 23.1), and on an example of Ettlinger's Type 10 (Ettlinger 1973, 57, Taf 5,1). These brooch types belong to Augustan into Claudian times in manufacture and use, and may indicate the period to which the present brooch belongs. Phase 6, ditch 493.

3.   Nauheim Derivative, 98mm long. One coil of the spring survives as well as part of a 'plug' through the spring. There is no sign in the corrosion under the head of the bow to suggest an internal chord and there is a possibility that the chord had been external (Ettlinger 1973, 35, Taf 2,5). The section of the upper bow is flat behind and on the sides, with a rounded front and with the rear corners slightly rounded. Although distorted, the bow clearly had a recurve and the pin would originally have run virtually straight from the catch-plate return to the back of the spring. The catch-plate has three circular holes arranged in a vertical line.

The length of the brooch, the recurve and the narrow catch-plate with its piercings cannot be paralleled amongst brooches which would normally be considered to have been made in Britain. However, the recurve and the type of catch-plate are characteristic of brooches made on the continent and belong not only to this type, but occur also on the continental equivalent of the Colchester type (Riha 1979, 66, Taf 4,142; 66, Taf 5,161; 67, Taf 6,184. Lerat 1956, 8–9, Pl II.56) as well as the Langton Down type (Riha 1979, 95, Taf 16,392; Brodribb et al 1968, 95, Fig 27.6) although infrequently on the latter. Close parallels for the present brooch are hard to find. However, the general characteristics are reflected to a greater or lesser degree in one from St Bertrand-de-Comminges (Gavelle 1962, 206, Fig 6.6) which has a broader bow, but with the recurve and the pierced narrow catch-plate. A Gallic variant of the Kragenfibel also had the recurve, which, in any case is to be expected in this type, and a vertical row of circular holes in its catch-plate, from the Saône at Bordes (Feugere 1977, 88, Pl 4.22). A Nauheim Derivative from Dangstetten (Fingerlin 1972, 217, abb 9,8), made of iron, is particularly close while another from the same site (Fingerlin 1972, 217, abb 9.6) has a slacker profile, and both have solid catch-plates.

The last two, like the present specimen, should be regarded as the immediate descendants of the Nauheim proper and, on the continent, are late versions of a type called the Drahtfibel. Their appearance at Dangstetten places them certainly in the earlier Augustan period (Fingerlin 1972, 213–7). Werner remarked that there had been a long tradition of using thin-sectioned metal for brooches (Werner 1955, 179) but declined to discuss them. He placed the Nauheim in the second half of the first century BC, but

de Navarro has summarized more recent dating and discussion and concludes that it should start in the first half of that century (de Navarro, 1972, 317–9) but he, as well, declines to discuss the Drahtfibel. In the present case, it is perhaps wiser to draw attention to the recurved bow and the pierced catch-plate, and recall the occurrence of these features on Augustan and Tiberian brooches, and to consider that it stands more correctly in the period from c 25 BC into the first century AD. The use of circular piercings in the catch-plate rather than fretting suggests that the brooch may not be at the beginning of this time range. From topsoil.

Other Bronze Objects by R P Winham (Fig 41, unless otherwise noted)

4.   Ring 20mm diameter, 5mm wide, made of a coiled strip. Found on proximal phalange of thumb on left hand of skeleton, associated with shale bracelet. Phase 4 pit 4475.

5.   Circular ring 15mm diameter. One quarter missing. Probably cast. Phase 4 pit 9344.

6.   Sub-circular ring 21mm by 24mm, with overlapping ends. Phase 6 scoop 5833.

7.   Pin, hollow-headed, point broken. From Phase 4, layer 3810 of Phase 3 enclosure ditch 5.

8.   Pin, round-headed. Phase 6 ditch 6718.

9.   Twisted, spiked hook with looped head. ?Bent ring-headed pin. Phase 6 feature 6732.

10.   Incomplete, thin disc with a central hole and three concentric grooves and ridges. Similar to a moulded bronze disc from Portchester that was attached to a second disc through a central opening, and probably part of a harness fitting (Cunliffe 1975, 202–3, Fig 110. 23). Another similar disc from Maythorpe Roman fortress (Frere and St Joseph 1974, Fig 27.33) is recorded as possibly the centre of a belt-plate or stud from helmet or breastplate. Phase 6 enclosure ditch 9805.

11.   12 mm diameter disc pierced by two holes, one with stud attached. Phase 4 pit 5601.

12.   Buckle or strap attachment 24mm long with knobbed ends and a central part shaped into three arches, the central one being about twice the size of the outer two. Phase 4 pit 3901.

13.   Flat, circular ring formed of two rings with a central ? fibrous, core. The edges of one ring are folded under the other for attachment. Unphased, from topsoil.

14.   82mm length of semi-cylindrical tube (Fig 42). Unphased, pit or large post hole 5507.

15.   Triangular fragment (Fig 42). Phase 6 ditch 8088.

Speculum (Fig 42)

16.   Fragment of circular band with part of a catch indicated on one terminal, shaped out of a raised decorative band. Two other such bands are present on the remaining parts, perhaps the end of a 'collar' as found at Dorchester (Megaw 1971, 148 Fig 3). R Tylecote reports that the tin content is somewhat less than that normally expected for speculum (25–30% Sn). It is a cored, cast copper base alloy with a good deal of the alpha-delta eutectoid, ie, between about $\frac{1}{3}$ to $\frac{1}{2}$ of the area, which puts it in the range 15–20% equivalent tin. The hardness is 158 HUI which would make it about 16–17% Sn. This metal is brittle and is usually used in purely decorative contexts such as bells and mirrors (J Bayley pers com). Phase 4 pit 7372.

Lead (Fig 42)

17.   Small circular shaped dish approximately 52mm diameter

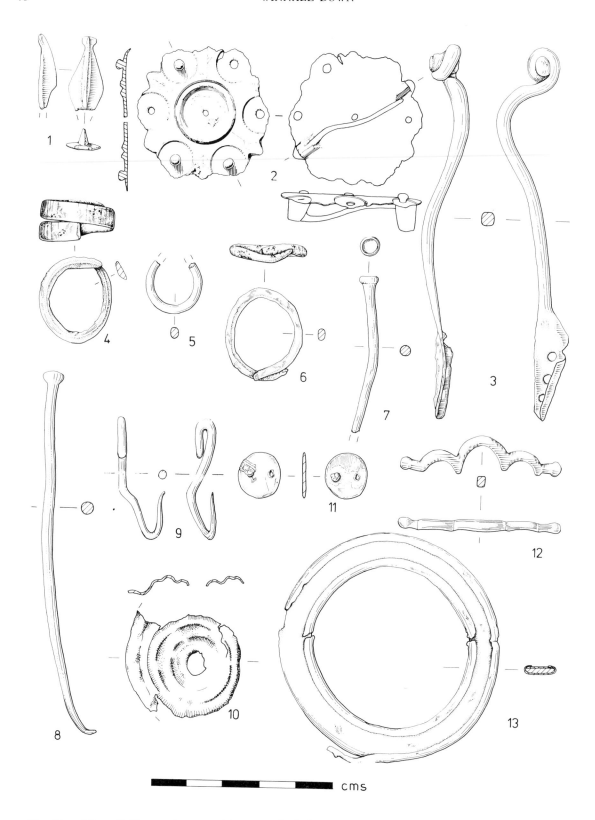

Fig 41.   Winnall Down: bronze objects, scale 1:1.

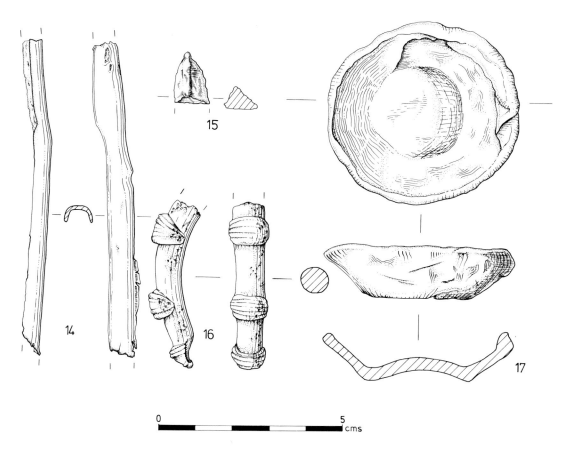

Fig 42.   Winnall Down: bronze objects 14–15, speculum 16, lead 17; all scale 1:1.

and 13mm high. Base indented, probably by thumb, and edges irregular, and folded in places. Roman, ditch 6718.

Iron (Fig 43–49)

Brooches by D F Mackreth

18.   La Tène I or II. The spring has eight coils and the chord is external and placed behind the coils. The bow has an oval section and has a fairly high arched profile. The lower part, with the catch-plate, is missing but the end of the foot is corroded onto the front of the bow. Although the brooch could be described as being a La Tène I, as the foot is not joined to the bow, it may be that there was once a collar which bound the foot and bow together thus making the brooch a La Tène II. Typologically, as a La Tène I, it is late in the series, as the foot runs a long way up the bow and, hence, it is possible that there would have been little real difference in date between it, in this form, than if it had been a La Tène II. It should be noted that the bow and feet, be the brooch La Tène I or II, do not conform with the flattened bow and restricted foot described by Harding as characteristic of the British series of these types (Harding 1974, 170–2, 187–8). Cunliffe devotes little space to discussion of the development of brooch types in the Iron Age, but his date for the change-over from La Tène I to II is, by implication rather than by statement, different from Harding's view which gives the change-over as being near the end of the third century BC (Harding 1974, 187), while Cunliffe allows some La Tène II brooches to be present in the fourth or third century BC (Cunliffe 1974, 37–8). It is not clear if the development of brooches in Britain during early and middle La Tène times runs parallel with that on the continent.

Attention has already been drawn to the differences between the present specimen and Harding's series and it may be pertinent to draw a parallel between this brooch and some La Tène III specimens in which there is a skeuomorph collar and a groove which marks the original division between foot and bow. These later brooches occur both on the continent (Ettlinger 1973, 48, 53, Taf 3,7 and 9) and in Britain: Great Chesterford (Stead 1976, 406, Fig 3.3) and one from the Thames (Fox 1958, 66, pl 40 a). In all these it is clear that it is the La Tène II precursors which are being followed, but in each case the collar, and therefore the position of the end of the foot in the La Tène I, is on the crest of the arch of the bow. It would seem that here can be seen what is happening on the continent, where bows high in proportion to their length are perhaps to be expected. No close dating is at hand for the present brooch, coming as it does from Britain, and a wide time range is suggested, probably centering on the third century BC, with the possibility that it might date back into the fourth century if it is a La Tène I, but possibly going forward into the second if it is a La Tène II. Phase 4 pit 7257.

19.   Nauheim Derivative. The spring has the usual four coils and internal chord. The bow has a thin rectangular section and most of the catch-plate is missing. There is little that can be said about such a small and fragmentary iron brooch as it has no distinguishing features. The use of iron for brooches appears to be common only in the earliest Roman period and this is a reflection of its use in the pre-Roman Iron Age. The terminal date for Nauheim Derivatives appears to be towards the end of the first century AD, and in default of any marked diagnostic characteristic, the present example should probably be dated to the period c 25–75 AD. Phase 6 scoop 7278.

Other Iron Objects

20.   Tweezers, broken, with points incurving. Phase 4 pit 7257.

21.   Ring-headed pin, 120mm long, straight-necked. Phase 4 pit 122.

22.   Key? from slide lock, end broken. Phase 4 pit 175.

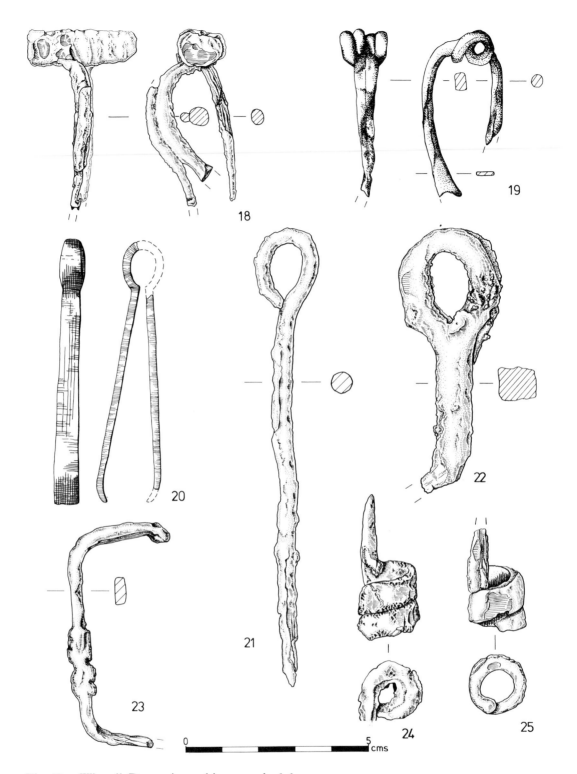

Fig 43. Winnall Down: iron objects, scale 1:1.

23. Timber dog, 52mm span between terminals, one of which is broken. Both terminals displayed slight traces of unidentifiable replaced wood. Phase 4 pit 1095.

24. Double-coiled ring with complete point, an animal goad. Phase 3 pit 5777.

25. Double-coiled ring with broken point, a goad. Phase 4 pit 1095. Nos 24 and 25 are almost identical to an object found in a mixed layer at Maiden Castle (Wheeler 1943, 288, Fig 97.4) and interpreted as an ox-goad of a type familiar on Roman sites, such

as Woodcuts and Rotherley. A different form is present at Ructstalls Hill, Basingstoke (Oliver and Applin 1978, 77, Fig 25.23). The use of such objects as goads seems generally accepted, as at Gussage All Saints (Wainwright 1979), but they may also have functioned as binding ferrules.

Ploughshare and bar by W H Manning (Fig 44.26–27)

26. Ploughshare (length 143mm) with a solid, tapering tip of D-shaped cross-section which continues into a solid, flanged socket of slightly oval cross-section.

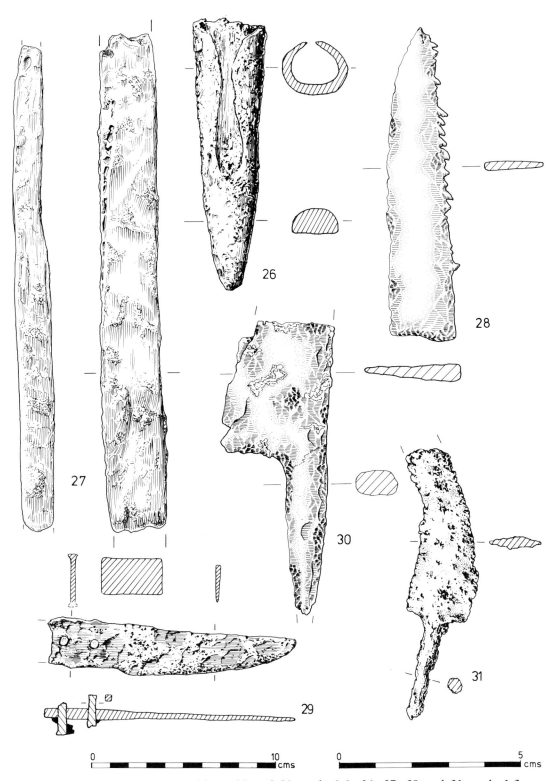

Fig 44.   Winnall Down: iron objects 28 and 30, scale 1:1; 26, 27, 29 and 31, scale 1:2.

Shares of this type were used to protect the tips of wooden bar-shares (Manning 1964, 62). They first appeared in the middle centuries of the Iron Age, the earliest datable example probably being that from Phase 1 at Gussage All Saints (Wainwright 1979, 104, Fig 80.1084) which is of the fifth-third century BC. Another from Phase 2 at the same site can be assigned to the third-second century BC (Wainwright 1979, 105, Fig 81.1022). They are not uncommon finds and a complete list is given by Rees (1979, 51). These early tips are all small and lack the very solid point seen in

our example; this is a feature which first appears at the very end of the Iron Age or early in the Roman period. The most comparable examples to ours are those from Woodcuts, Dorset (Pitt-Rivers 1887, 76, Pl XXV 9 and 12; 82, Pl XXVI 7), which are most likely of first century AD date. Another from Coygan Camp, Carmarthenshire (now Dyfed) may date from as late as the end of the third century AD, suggesting that in some areas the type had a very long life (Wainwright 1967, 104, Fig 30.1).

27.   Bar (length 26.4cm) with straight sides and a rectangular cross-section; broken at one end. The complete end is carefully rounded.

The function of this piece is not obvious from the surviving fragment, but there is no reason to suppose that it was connected with the ploughshare with which it was found. The section makes it virtually certain that it was not part of the shaft of a coulter, and whilst it *could* have been the end of a bar-share these usually had a square cross-section. Nor is it likely to have been the butt of a struck tool such as a large chisel, for the rounded end is quite unsuited for this purpose. Although functions could be suggested for it they would be too speculative to be of any real value.

28.   Saw blade fragment (details from x-ray). Phase 4 pit 7257.

29.   Knife blade, 94mm long, complete; and broken handle remaining 40 mm long, with two rivets indicating a minimum thickness of 21mm. There are extensive traces of iron replaced wood on the upper part of the knife blade. The wood appeared to be diffuse, porous with homocellular rays a few cells wide, faint spiral thickening and simple perforation plates. A commonly occurring family with these features is the Rosaceae, sub family Pomoideae (cf Hawthorn; Keepax archive). Phase 4 pit 7372.

30.   Tang, with sub-rectangular section, and portion of blade of knife or sickle. Phase 4 pit 7257.

31.   Tang, with circular section, and broken blade of knife or sickle. Phase 4 pit 7525.

Figure 45

32.   Complete handle, 77mm long, and much corroded blade of knife or sickle. Unphased quarry pit 9127.

33.   Socketed sickle or bill hook. Phase 4 pit 2342.

34.   Socketed sickle or bill hook with nail or rivet in place in socket. Phase 4 pit 9105.

Figure 46

35.   Socketed sickle or bill hook with nail or rivet through socket. Phase 6 ditch 8083. The general contemporaneity of riveted-handled and tang-handled blades should be noted – as was the case at Gussage All Saints, Phase 1 (Wainwright 1979, 105, Fig 80).

36.   Iron bar 45mm long, 9mm wide, 4mm thick. Phase 4 pit 1631.

37.   Iron bar 35mm long, 15mm wide, 1mm thick strip with edges thickened to 3mm. Phase 6 ditch 9806.

38.   Iron strip 35mm long, 18mm wide, 1.5mm thick strip. Phase 6 ditch 678.

39.   Binding strip 137mm long, 17mm wide, 3mm thick. Rounded at one end, with two definite and two possible rivets. Broken at the other end adjacent to a rivet. Phase 4 pit 3901.

40.   Curved, ovoid sectioned strip, 39mm in length, 8mm wide and 4mm thick. From spit of ploughsoil, layer 4614.

41.   Thin bar, 175mm long, with one end formed into a T-shape. Unphased, post-hole 5966.

Figure 47

42.   Much corroded bar, 95mm long, maximum width 14mm. From spit of ploughsoil, layer 4606.

43.   End fragment of bar with slightly curved cross-section. 73mm long, 32mm wide and 4mm thick. Phase 6 pit 5676.

44.   Curved strip, bent and flattened at one end, with hole for attachment. The other end is broken and also flattened out. Phase 6 ditch 4607.

45.   Loop-headed spike, 179mm long, with twisting, square-sectioned shaft (based on x-ray). Phase 4 scoop 9304.

46.   Looped fitting with holes through both terminals for securing. Unphased scoop 5239.

47.   Strip, about 10mm wide, bent to form a ring with overlapping terminals; ferrule. Phase 6 ditch 660.

48.   U-shaped loop; one terminal grooved for hafting onto wood. Hole through apex. ?Hook. Phase 3 pit 2431.

49.   39mm length of semi-cylindrical tube. Phase 6 scoop 7256.

50.   Bar fragment with slight curvature at one end. Phase 6 ditch 660.

51.   Indeterminate fragment. From subsoil layer 4620.

52.   Indeterminate fragment. Phase 4 pit 175.

Figure 48

53.   Nail 28 by 7mm, with rectangular head, 18 by 4mm. Phase 3 scoop 8166.

54.   Nail 34 by 4mm, with rectangular head, 11 x 4mm. Phase 3 scoop 8166. A nail shank (not illustrated) came from scoop 6292, Phase 3.

55.   Nail 35 by 7mm, with rectangular head, 14 by 5mm. Phase 4 pit 8585.

56.   Nail 44 by 4mm, with irregularly circular head, 17mm diameter. Phase 4 pit 447.

57.   Nail shank, square sectioned, 48 by 4mm. Phase 4 house U gully 1414.

Eleven other nails came from Phase 4 contexts. One each from pits 1095 (with unidentifiable replaced wood traces), 1631, 5548, 7372, 8594 and two from 5789; one from ditch 201, two from ditch 1989 and one from post-hole 3202.

58.   Shoe nail, 17 by 4mm with cowl-shaped head, 8mm diameter. Phase 6 ditch 660.

59.   Nail, 25 by 4mm with sub-rectangular head 9 by 5mm. Phase 6 scoop 1392.

60.   Nail, 29 by 3mm, with irregularly circular head, 8mm diameter. Phase 6 ditch 8817.

61.   Nail, 62 by 6mm, with circular head, 6mm diameter and circular sectioned shank. Phase 6 ditch 6732.

62.   Nail, 30 by 5mm, with a head that is T-shaped when viewed from the side, and a rectangular top, 9 by 6mm. Phase 6 ditch 678.

63.   Nail, 58 by 6mm, with sub-circular head 14mm diameter and shank bent at right angles. Phase 6 scoop 7256.

64.   Nail, 52 by 4mm, with a sub-rectangular head, 14 x 12mm. Phase 6 ditch 8817.

65.   Nail, 58 by 5mm, point broken, with sub-circular head 14mm diameter. Phase 6 ditch 8817.

66.   Nail, 60 by 5mm with incomplete, sub-circular head 11mm diameter. Phase 6 ditch 660.

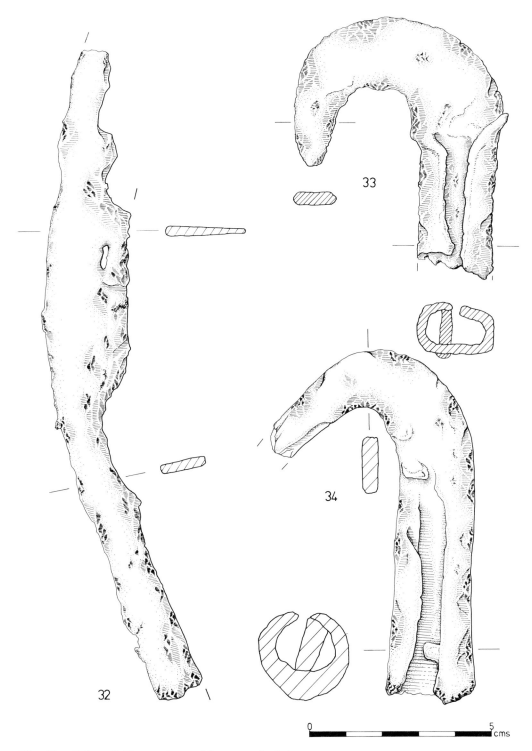

Fig 45. Winnall Down: iron objects, scale 1:1.

67. Nail, 60 by 4mm, point broken, with sub-circular head 14mm diameter, and bent shank. Phase 6 ditch 1308.

68. Nail, 60 by 3mm, with circular head 14mm in diameter. Phase 6 scoop 5550.

69. Nail shank, 77 by 7mm, rectangular sectioned. Phase 6 pit 3214.

70. Nail, 88 by 5mm, with circular head, 6mm diameter, and circular sectioned shank. Phase 6 ditch 6732.

71. Nail, 120 by 6mm with sub-circular head, 20mm diameter. Phase 6 ditch 8817.

Sixty-four other nails came from Phase 6 contexts: one each from pits 2022, 5623, 5676 and 7274; one each from ditches 493, 2066, 2199, 2761, 6718, 9136, 9805, 9806; two each from ditches 471, 660, 678, 1308, 4607, 6732, 8082, 9914 and twenty-two from ditch 8817. Fourteen came from scoops, one each from 5946, 7117, 7221, 7302, 9951, 10093; three from 7215 and five from 7256.

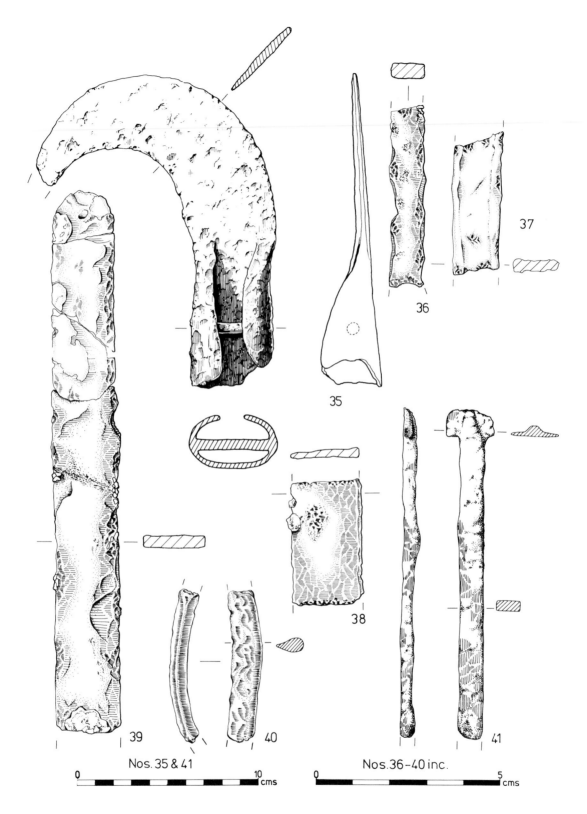

Fig 46.   Winnall Down: iron objects 36–40, scale 1:1; 35 and 41, scale 1:2.

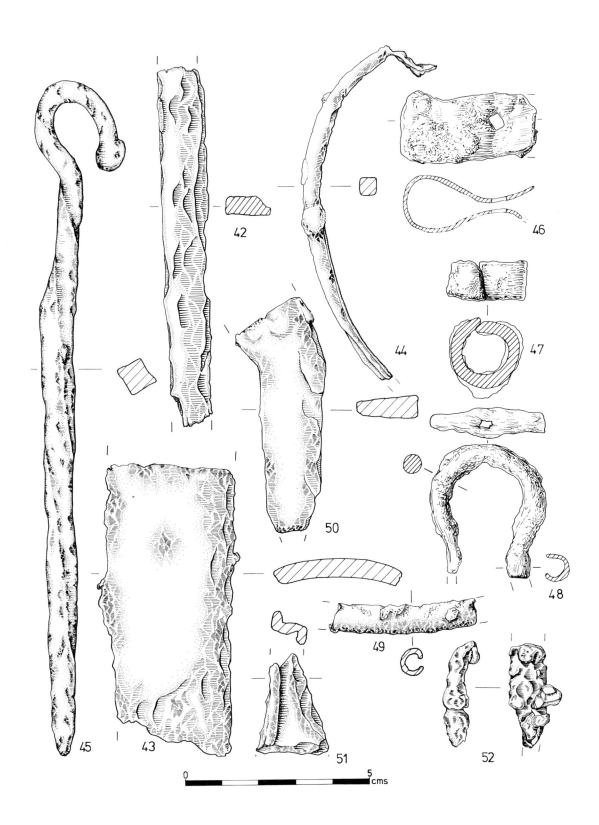

Fig 47. Winnall Down: iron objects scale 1:1.

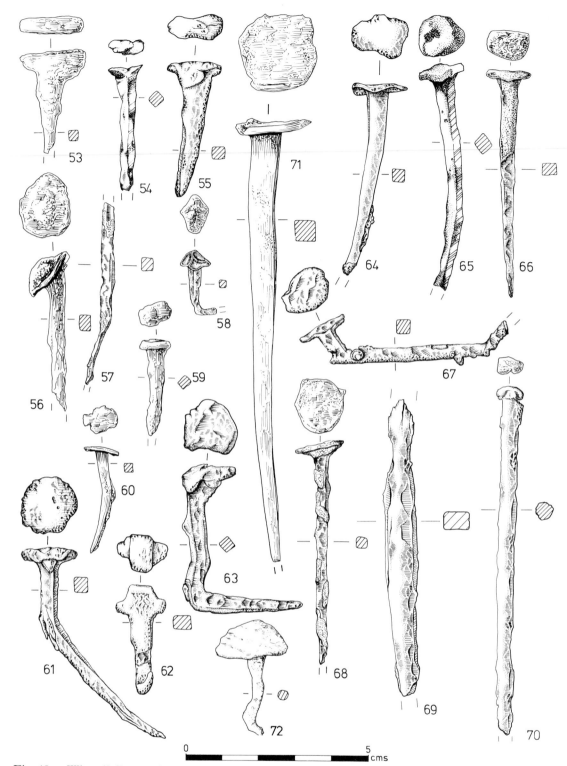

Fig 48. Winnall Down: iron nails, scale 1:1.

72. Nail, 26 by 4mm with irregular, sub-rectangular head 18 by 8mm, Phase 7 ditch 1100.

Three other nails came from Phase 7 contexts, one from ditch 1100 and two from ditch 1378.

Twenty-five nails came from unphased contexts: one each from pits 8634, 6211, 6618; from postholes 138, 6677, 9850 and from scoops 5879, 6651, 9919; two from scoop 9127 and fourteen from the topsoil.

There were, in addition to the finds illustrated, eighteen other finds of iron, seven from the topsoil – a fragment, two strips, a twisted strand, a knife, a horse shoe fragment and a semi-circular loop. The remainder are all indeterminate objects or fragments: one from an unphased scooop, 5239; four from Phase 3 contexts – one from pit 3670, one from enclosure ditch 5 layer 4584, and one each from scoops 8153 and 9629; five from Phase 4 contexts, one each from pits 3738, 7399 and two from pit 313, and one from gully 406; and one from a Phase 6 ditch, 6732.

The Pottery by J W Hawkes

Introduction

The report is presented in four sections. This introduction outlines the objectives and the methods employed by the M3 Archaeological Rescue Committee in its pottery analysis programme. The pottery itself is ordered by phase within the period divisions 'Prehistoric', 'Roman' and 'Medieval'; discussion is, as far as possible, separated from the descriptive data and is offered both as specific comment on individual phases and as a general summary of the period assemblage as a whole. The pottery was sorted by Ingrid Clifford and Charlotte Matthews, and the procedures devised by Jane Ross.

The use of a computer based recording system (Fasham *et al* 1976, Fasham and Hawkes 1980) has resulted in the availability of large quantities of primary and synthesised data; selection for inclusion in this report being based on the guidelines laid down in the Frere report (DoE 1975) and on the relevance of such data to the specific objectives of the MARC3 pottery programme, which may be summarised as follows:

1)   Quantification – to establish the proportion of different types of vessels, fabrics and decorative traits in use at any one time, and to examine how these proportions change through time;

2)   Phasing – to augment the excavated sequence in providing a chronology for the site;

3)   To try to establish from the presence or absence of imported vessels, tempering agents, decorative motifs *etc*, aspects of the economic situation of the site at any one period and the extent of external contacts, and to examine how these patterns change through time;

4)   To compare pottery from sites of the same period to determine differences or similarities in pot assemblages at different sites, and to formulate hypotheses to account for these differences and similarities;

5)   To examine the spatial distributions within a site's assemblage of particular pottery types, fabrics and decorative motifs, and to formulate hypotheses to account for particular distribution patterns.

Objectives 1, 3 and 4 are considered in the pottery section, and objective 5 is incorporated elsewhere in the excavation report; objective 2 is integral to both sections.

Method

The pottery was sorted into fabric groups on the basis of visible inclusions, counted, weighed and the results entered on the computer. Featured sherds (*ie* rims, bases and decorated sherds) were individually drawn, described and classified where possible. The computer records and the drawings together with the results of the computer analyses and the form and fabric type series are the basis of the level III pottery archive.

The fabrics identified by this visual classification often rely on small variations which may not be consistently identifiable for the entire assemblage, particularly for groups with a high proportion of fragmentary material. For the purposes of this report they have been assigned to groups on the basis of their principal inclusions, and detailed fabric descriptions together with a series of type sherds are to be found in the archive. A very limited programme of thin-section analysis was not sufficiently extensive to enable fabrics to be grouped on a petrological basis as at Winklebury (Smith 1977) and, as a consequence, individual fabrics and fabric groupings probably define variations in manufacturing technique and do not necessarily represent geographically distinct production centres. The vessel form type series is based not only on material from Winnall Down but also on pottery from the nearby 'banjo' enclosure in Micheldever Wood (Hawkes in prep).

Phasing

Phasing has been achieved by the adoption of a form/fabric approach for the pottery, supplemented by the excavated sequence where direct stratigraphical relationships exist. Within the period 'Prehistoric' four phases can be discerned: Phase 1, Neolithic is considered elsewhere (Fasham 1982); Phase 2, Bronze Age; Phase 3, Early Iron Age, is an assemblage associated with the enclosed settlement and is best typified by Cunliffe's (1978, 35–37) West Harling – Staple Howe/Kimmeridge – Caburn groups; Phase 4, Middle Iron Age, has affinities with the St Catherine's Hill – Worthy Down style of the southern British saucepan pot tradition (Cunliffe 1978, 46), and is related to the open settlement period. Phase 5 and Phase 6 cannot practicably be distinguished and are treated together as 'Roman'. Throughout all periods of the site fabrics alone have proved an unreliable guide to chronology, and their use for phasing has been avoided wherever possible.

Reliability

The reliability of data presented in archaeological reports is seldom considered, but the use of quantitative analyses obliges some assessment of the level of accuracy achieved. A particular problem in dealing with large quantities of pottery is the consistent identification of fabrics. Some assessment of the scale of the problem may be made by reference to the form/fabric correlations, Fig 49. Obviously early fabrics occurring as late forms and *vice versa* must represent the minimum error, here about 5%, and it

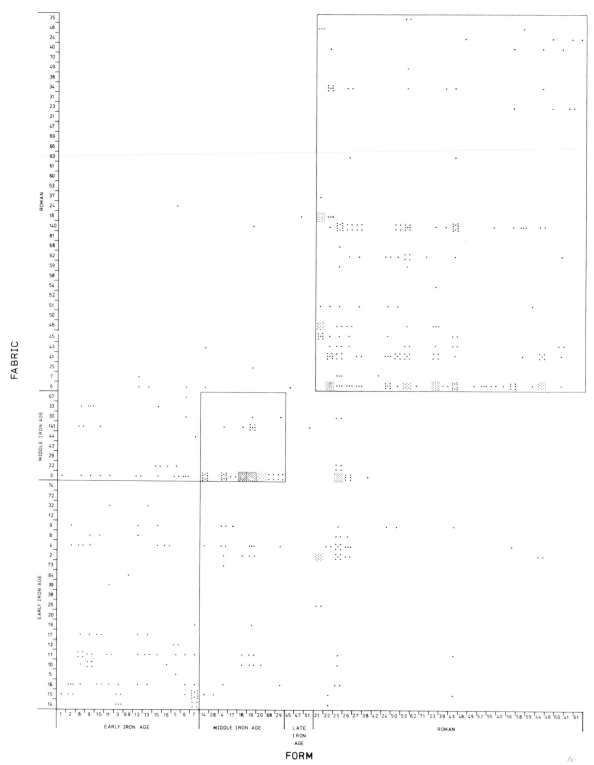

Fig 49.   Winnall Down: pottery – form/fabric correlation.

is intuitively obvious that confusion between subjectively similar fabrics will be higher still. Although no formula exists to calculate this figure, a 'standard deviation' of ±10% including computer input errors would not seem unreasonable, and no attempt should be made to interpret smaller variations in the data.

A further problem arises in calculating the amount of pottery either residual or intrusive. The distribution of fabrics by phase, Fig 50, shows between 10–15% of the Prehistoric pottery occurring in Phase 6 contexts, and a slightly smaller proportion of the Roman pottery occurring intrusively in the upper fills of pre-Phase 5 features. Estimates for phases

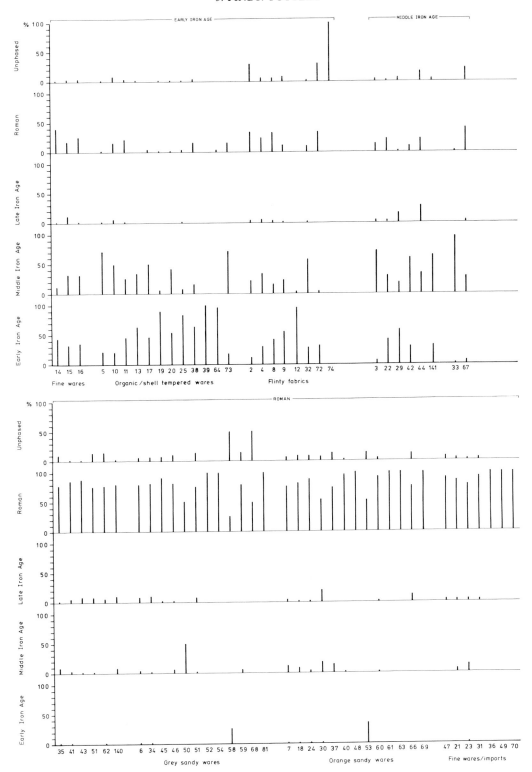

Fig 50. Winnall Down: pottery – fabrics by phase.

within the Iron Age are unreliable, and reflect the difficulty of assigning individual fabrics to a particular phase. A more reliable figure is provided by vessel forms. From a total of 105 diagnostically early Iron Age vessels, only 56 (53%) occur in Phase 3; there is a minimum of 190 Middle Iron Age pots of which 135 (71%) occur in Phase 4 contexts.

The Prehistoric Pottery

Fabrics

Thirty-four fabrics are associated with the pre-Roman occupation of the site. These fabrics are arranged in groups according to their principal inclusions (Table 5) and are described in summary form only. Full fabric descriptions are in the archive. Two fabrics are restricted to one phase only: fabric 1 is exclusive to the Neolithic ring ditch (see Smith in Fasham 1982), and fabric 12 is described in the Deverel-Rimbury section of Phase 2. The remaining fabrics belong to a continuum beginning in the Late Bronze Age and lasting until the Late Iron Age. Petrological examination of 23 fabric samples by Mr S Wandibba, Department of Archaeology, University of Southampton, suggests that the main inclusions of quartz and glauconitic sands or flint could all have been obtained relatively locally, although sources

Table 5. Pottery: Later Bronze Age/Iron Age fabrics.

GROUP	FABRIC	SHERDS	
		No	Wt in grams
1. FINE WARES			
Organic + Flint + Grog	14	131	946
Organic + Fine Flint	15	169	2737
	16	288	5076
		588	6759
2. ORGANIC-TEMPERED FABRICS			
Fine Organic	17	70	797
	19	123	649
	64	27	167
Coarse Organic	38	17	137
	39	9	476
	73	14	150
Briquetage	28	103	740
Flint + Organic	13	113	744
		476	3860
3. SHELL-TEMPERED FABRICS	20	46	550
	25	342	7723
	29	53	658
		441	8931
4. FLINT-TEMPERED FABRICS	3	2470	42832
Fine/Medium Flint	4	836	9093
	8	492	4892
	9	134	1008
	11	360	3547
	22	298	5083
	33	72	1449
	42	19	414
	72	22	164
Coarse Flint	2	891	19502
Flint + Grog	10	245	4199
	32	244	3041
	74	2	55
		6085	95279
5. SAND-TEMPERED FABRICS	5	474	2135
	27	375	2377
	44	29	410
	67	24	139
	141	138	2086
		1055	7174
		8645	121996

further afield cannot be ruled out. Heavy mineral analysis of examples of the sandy and the glauconitic fabrics (samples of fabrics 141 and 4 respectively) reveals a high concentration of red garnet characteristic of Reading Beds, the nearest exposures occurring some 7km to the south (Wandibba archive).

Phase 2a. Bronze Age: Deverel-Rimbury

Sixty-nine sherds (670g) of fabric 12 were recovered from the Phase 3 enclosure ditch. This fabric, densely gritted with (often calcined) flint, is typical of local Deverel-Rimbury vessels (for distribution see Hawkes 1969). Two sherds, both probably from the same vessel, are decorated with a finger-impressed cordon (Fig 51.1) but no vessel forms survive in this fabric. The greater part of a bucket urn (152 sherds, not illustrated) in fabric 2 from feature 4786 also belongs to this phase. All this material is presumably residual from an occupation zone neither identified nor discovered.

Phase 2b. Late Bronze Age

There are 99 sherds belonging to this period, incuding eleven bases and ten rim sherds; five sherds of coarse sandy fabrics (two of fabric 18 from feature 771, and three of fabric 27 from feature 4727) were all intrusive, the rest of the pottery being variants of flint-gritted .vares (fabrics 2, 3, 4, 8, 9, 10, 13), fabric 2 comprising some 62% by number of the pottery of this period.

The forms represented are either wide-mouthed bowls (Fig 51.2) or wide-mouthed jars (Fig 51.3–4) with simple rims, although some examples are slightly thickened internally (Fig 51.5) or flattened (Fig 51.6). There is a considerable range of sizes represented by these vessels, with rim diameters ranging between 120–320mm, although numbers are insufficient to indicate any significant groupings by size. Bases are either simple (Fig 51.7) or slightly indented (Fig 51.8), and there are two perforated sherds (eg Fig 51.9). The pottery from the post-hole 6466 (Fig 51.4–9) is associated with one complete and one fragmentary cylindrical loomweight (Fig 70.2). There are no associations with metalwork or any radiocarbon dates.

Phase 3. Early Iron Age

A total of 2,384 sherds (25,873g) came from features associated with the enclosed phase of the site, including 116 rims and 15 bases. By no means all of this pottery is of Early Iron Age date, but fabrics which might be considered predominantly of this period include all of Groups 1 and 2, fabrics 20 and 25 from Group 3 and fabrics 4, 8, 9, 10, 11, 32, 72 and 74 from Group 4 (Table 6).

Forms most commonly associated with the finer fabrics are furrowed bowls, forms 1 and 2 (nine examples, Fig 52.10–18), cordoned bowls, form 3 (six examples, Fig 52.19–24) and a variety of other bowl forms including one possibly angular bowl, form 69 (Fig 52.25); seven wide-mouthed bowls, forms 5 and 6 (eg Fig 52.26–27) and eighteen round-bodied, form 7 (eg Fig 52.28–32), Table 6. Four furrowed and five cordoned bowls are haematite-coated, as are ten of the round-bodied bowls. Sixty sherds (c10%) of the Group 1 fabrics are haematite-coated, plus a total of eight other sherds from fabrics 3, 4, 5, 9, 10. Haematite-coated pottery accounts for rather less than 3% of the phase assemblage. Two round-bodied bowls are burnished. Only four fine ware vessels are decorated: two haematite-coated cordoned bowls (Fig 52.20,22), one uncoated cordoned bowl (Fig 52.23) and one haematite-coated round-bodied bowl (Fig 52.28).

Coarse ware vessels in organic and flinty fabrics are variants of bipartite, forms 10 and 11 (Fig 53.33–36), tripartite, forms 8 and 9 (Fig 53.37–46) and necked and shouldered jars, forms 12, 13, 15 and 16 (Fig 53.47–49), Table 6. Rims are usually plain but sometimes thickened (eg Fig 53.49). One tripartite (Fig 53.38) and one necked jar (Fig 53.47) are haematite-coated. There is a minimum of twenty-eight tripartite, fourteen bipartite and twenty-five other shouldered jars. Nine examples show signs of external tooling, six were burnished and four grass-wiped. Rims may be either finger-tipped (Fig 53.39) or fingernail-impressed (Fig 53.36), and finger-tipped (Fig 53.37) or slashed (Fig 53.40) decoration may occur on the shoulder or carination. One example of a tripartite jar (Fig 53.46) has a single perforation. Rim diameters range between 100–250mm for bipartites, 100–230mm for tripartites and 120–260mm, plus one example of 400mm, for the other jar forms. No significant groupings by size are discernible. The lack of consistent associations between vessels (Table 7)

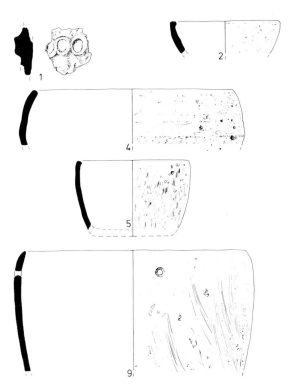

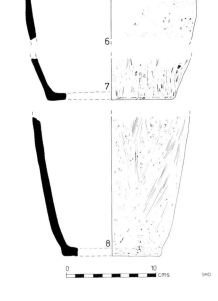

Fig 51. Winnall Down: Bronze Age pottery, scale 1:4.

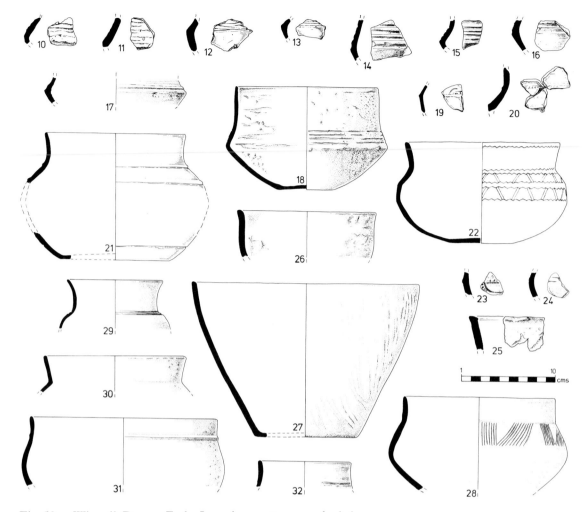

Fig 52. Winnall Down: Early Iron Age pottery, scale 1:4.

reflects the high proportion occurring residually in later contexts (47%). One shouldered jar (Fig 53.49), from feature 5FF layer 4749, is associated with a date of 2560±80BP (HAR 2653), and is stratified above five haematite-coated sherds from layer 4759. A tripartite jar (Fig 51.43) occurred in feature 574 layer 706 immediately below layer 575 with a date of 2540±90BP (HAR 2251). Fig 52.32 was from the same feature as HAR 2591, 2190±60BP.

Phase 4. Middle Iron Age

Phase 4 features produced 4,297 sherds (69,885g) including 327 rims and 91 base sherds. This phase is characterised by a comparatively restricted range of fabrics: fabric 33 from Group 2; fabric 29 from Group 3; fabrics 3, 22, 42 from Group 4; all of Group 5. Fabric 3 alone comprises 41% of the pottery of this phase.

The typical vessel is the 'saucepan pot', which accounts for more than 76% of all vessels definitely attributable to this phase (Table 8). Three examples are bipartite, form 17 (eg Fig 54.50–51), fifty-seven straight-sided, form 18 (eg Fig 54.52–57), seventy-two incurving, form 19 (Fig 54.58–66) and fifteen out-flaring, form 20 (Fig 54.67–68). Rims are usually plain and rounded, although 'proto-bead' rims are present on ten of the straight-sided, nineteen of the incurving and two of the outflaring types (eg Fig 54.63–65), there also being fifteen examples of internally thickened rims on incurving saucepans (eg Fig 54.66). Seventeen saucepans have incised grooves below the rim: six straight-sided, three incurving and one outflaring types have one band; one straight-sided and one outflaring types, two bands; and two straight-sided types have three bands. Irregular multiple grooving also occurs (eg Fig

54.61). In addition, seven bases attributable to saucepan pots have a single grooved line (eg Fig 54.69). Rim diameters (Fig 55) exhibit strongly preferred size ranges for these vessels, centering on 140–160mm for straight-sided types and 100–120mm for incurving types, although insufficient complete profiles were recovered to equate these dimensions with volume.

The only other forms properly belonging to this phase are the simple or carinated bowls, form 4 (thirty-one examples, Fig 54.70–74), and the narrow-mouthed jar, form 14 (fourteen examples, Fig 56.75–79). In addition, a number of shouldered forms 28 and 68 or bead-rim jars forms 21, 25 and 26 must belong to this phase (eg Fig 56.80–83) although they are separable from Late Iron Age or Roman examples only on the basis of fabric, and even then unreliably so (Fig 49). There are sixty-nine examples in prehistoric fabrics (predominantly fabrics 2 and 3), although the evidence from other sites would suggest that only a small proportion of these should belong to the Middle Iron Age, and the vast majority must belong to Phase 6 despite the evidence of the fabric. Since there is no reliable guide to the number of these vessels, they are not included in any of the analyses. The miniature thumb pot, form 28 (Fig 56.84), is of such simple form that parallels and accurate dating are impossible. Rim diameters for the bowls range from 100–200mm, and those of the narrow-mouthed jars (form 14) from 90–200mm. The diameters of the low-shouldered bead-rim jars from Phase 4 contexts centre between 100–160mm. Excluding the unreliable bead-rim jars, all vessels are found in association with each other save for the numerically small bipartite saucepans (Table 9).

Burnishing is a dominant element; all but one of the narrow-mouthed jars are burnished, as are the majority of the saucepans

Table 6. Pottery: form/fabric in Phase 3.

| | Bowls | | | | | Jars | | | |
Fabric	Furrowed	Cordoned	Angular	Wide-mouthed	Round-bodied	Tripartite	Bipartite	Other	Total
Group 1: 14	–	3	–	–	4	–	–	–	7
15	3	2	–	–	10	1	–	1	17
16	3	1	–	–	1	1	3	2	11
									Group 1 = 35
Group 2: 13	–	–	–	2	–	–	–	–	2
17	–	–	–	–	–	2	2	–	4
19	–	–	–	–	1	–	–	–	1
39	–	–	–	–	–	–	1	–	1
64	–	–	1	–	–	–	–	–	1
									Group 2 = 9
Group 3: 25	–	–	–	–	–	–	–	1	Group 3 = 1
Group 4: 3	1	–	–	2	–	2	2	6	13
4	1	–	–	1	–	3	–	3	8
8	–	–	–	–	–	1	1	1	3
9	1	–	–	–	–	–	–	1	2
10	–	–	–	–	–	5	–	1	6
11	–	–	–	1	1	6	2	4	14
22	–	–	–	1	–	–	–	1	2
32	–	–	–	–	–	–	1	1	2
33	–	–	–	–	–	4	–	–	4
									Group 4 = 54
Group 5: 27	–	–	–	–	–	1	1	–	2
44	–	–	–	–	1	–	–	–	1
67	–	–	–	–	–	–	–	1	1
141	–	–	–	–	–	2	1	–	3
									Group 5 = 7
LIA/RB 6	–	–	–	–	–	–	–	1	1
7	–	–	–	–	–	–	–	1	1
24	–	–	–	1	–	–	–	–	1
									LIA/RB = 3
TOTAL	9	6	1	8	18	28	14	25	109

(50% of the straight-sided, 64% of incurving and 93% of outflaring types). Almost half the bowls and 37% of the Phase 4 jars are also burnished. All of the Phase 4 fabrics contain burnished examples, and burnishing accounts for 31% of these sherds. Burnished bands below the rim appear as a decorative element on one example each of a bowl, wide-mouthed jar, saucepan and round-shouldered jar. One saucepan is heavily grass-tempered (Fig 54.58).

Decoration is not extensively used. The most common motifs are variants of an incised decorative form employing oblique hatching between horizontal lines or rows of dots (Fig 54.71), of which there are twenty examples, invariably on the upper part of the body: three on narrow-mouthed jars, three on bowls, nine on saucepans and five on other jars. Lattice designs, often poorly executed, occur on seven saucepans and one narrow-mouthed jar (*eg* Fig 56.81). One bowl (Fig 54.74) and one narrow-mouthed jar (Fig 56.77) have chevron designs above the shoulder, and one bowl has a design of large scrolls (Fig 54.72). Other partial decorative motifs are also illustrated (Fig 56.85 and 86).

There are five perforated bases: one belonging to a shouldered jar with four holes (Fig 56.80); one from a saucepan with a single central hole (Fig 54.68); and three other bases with three holes each. In addition, there is a perforated rim sherd from a straight-sided saucepan (Fig 54.56), and a narrow-mouthed jar with four perforations in the side of the body (Fig 56.79).

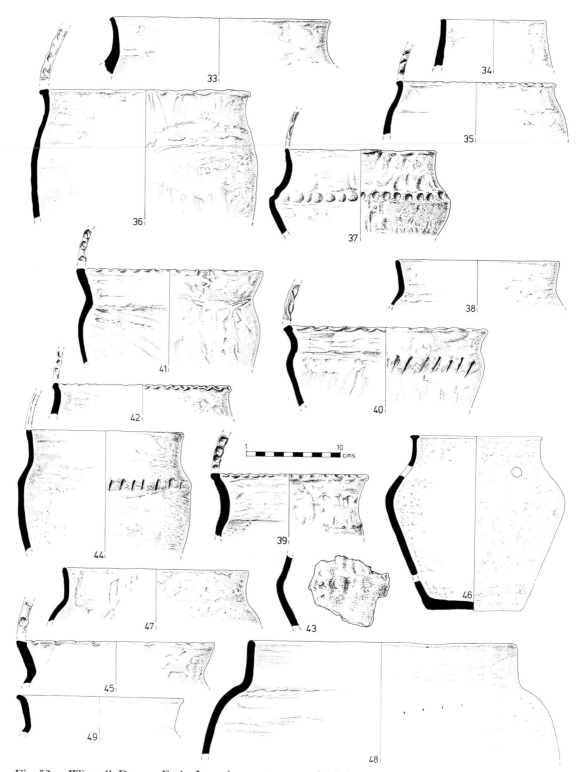

Fig 53.   Winnall Down: Early Iron Age pottery, scale 1:4.

Table 7.   Number of separate associations of Phase 3 vessels in Phase 3 contexts (maximum possible number of associations in brackets).

	Furrowed Bowl (7)						
Cordoned Bowl	1	Cordoned Bowl (2)					
Angular Bowl	–	–	Angular Bowl (1)				
Wide-Mouthed Bowl	–	–	–	Wide-Mouthed Bowl (1)			
Round-bodied Bowl	–	–	–	–	Round-bodied Bowl (7)		
Bipartite	–	–	–	–	1	Bipartite (5)	
Tripartite	–	–	–	1	3	1	Tripartite (14)
Shouldered Jar	–	–	1	–	1	–	–	Shouldered Jar (7)

Table 8. Pottery: form/fabric in Phase 4.

				Saucepan Types				
Fabrics		Simple bowl	Narrow mouth Jar	Bipartite	Straight-sided	Incurved	Outflaring	Total
GROUP 1								
	15	–	1	–	–	–	–	1
	16	2	–	–	–	–	–	2
GROUP 2								
	19	–	–	–	–	1	–	1
	28	1	–	–	–	–	–	1
GROUP 4								
	2	2	–	–	–	2	–	4
	3	13	10	2	52	51	14	142
	4	6	1	–	–	3	–	10
	9	2	–	1	–	–	–	3
	10	1	–	–	1	3	1	6
	11	2	–	–	1	2	–	5
	22	–	–	–	–	1	–	1
GROUP 5								
	27	–	–	–	2	–	–	2
	141	–	–	–	1	7	–	8
LIA/RB FABRICS								
	6	–	1	–	–	–	–	1
	30	–	–	–	–	1	–	1
	43	–	1	–	–	–	–	1
	73	1	–	–	–	–	–	1
	140	1	–	–	–	1	–	2
TOTAL		31	14	3	57	72	15	192

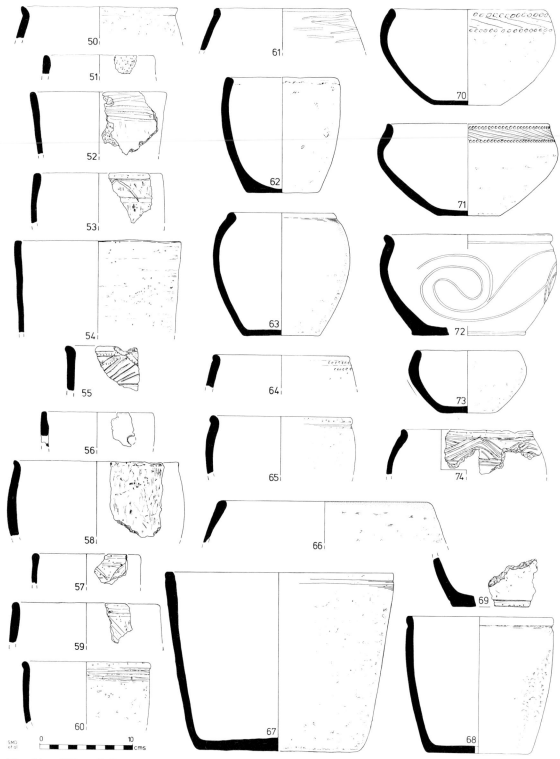

Fig 54. Winnall Down: Middle Iron Age pottery, scale 1:4.

Pit 5789, the fill of which appeared to be all of one phase, contained a narrow-mouthed jar (Fig 56.76) and a decorated bowl (Fig 54.74). Charcoal from the bottom of the pit yielded a date of 2190±60BP (HAR 2591). A straight-sided saucepan from feature 3738 layer 3938 (Fig 54.57) is associated with a radio-carbon date of 2140±80BP (HAR 2252) from charcoal in the top layer. A possible bipartite saucepan (Fig 54.51) was stratified below burial 500 which produced a date of 1990±70BP (HAR 2938) in feature 8564, and another saucepan (Fig 54.52) is associated with a date of 2150±80BP (HAR 2980) derived from skeleton 574 in grave 8630.

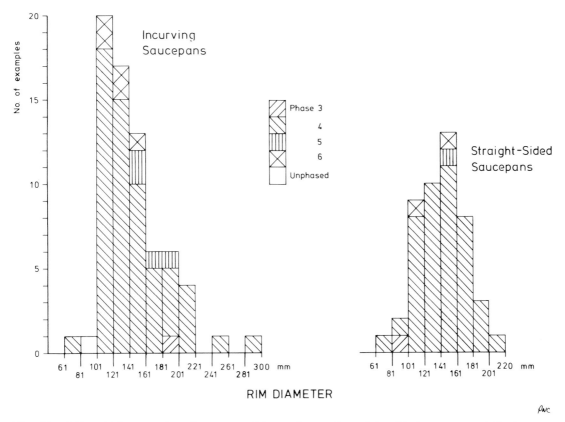

Fig 55. Winnall Down: rim diameters of incurving and straight-sided saucepans (all phases).

Table 9. Number of separate associations of Phase 4 vessels in Phase 4 contexts (maximum possible number of associations in brackets).

	Bowls	(7)					
Narrow-mouthed Jars	2	Narrow-mouthed Jars	(7)				
Bipartite Saucepans	–	–	Bipartite Saucepans	(1)			
Straight-sided Saucepans	3	4	–	Straight-sided Saucepans	(31)		
Incurved Saucepans	4	4	–	14	Incurved Saucepans	(28)	
Outflaring Saucepans	1	2	1	9	4	Outflaring Saucepans	(9)

Discussion

The Phase 2 thin-walled undecorated jars and bowls fall into the class of pottery described by Barrett (1976, 1978 and 1980) as post Deverel-Rimbury, for which a date between the eleventh and ninth centuries BC would be acceptable. This assemblage pre-dates material from the adjacent site of Easton Down (Fasham 1982), where an eighth or seventh century BC 'early decorated' group fills the gap between Phases 2 and 3 at Winnall Down, and demonstrates continuing activity in the area from the Late Bronze Age onwards.

The date for the beginning of Phase 3 is dependent on the stratification of the haematite-coated sherds below the radiocarbon date of 2560±80BP (HAR 2653). This date is comparable to results obtained at Longbridge Deverill (Hawkes 1961), where the earliest date from House 1 of 630±155BC (NPL 105) is associated with an assemblage containing haematite-coated, short-necked furrowed bowls. Suggestions that haematite-coating is more common in the later parts of the Early Iron Age (Cunliffe and Phillipson 1968, 235) may well be valid, considering the number of round-bodied bowls from Winnall Down that are haematite-coated. This form, together with the cordoned bowls, belongs to Harding's (1974) 'Early La Tene' phase, and implies a fifth century BC emphasis for the Phase 3 settlement.

By the fifth century BC haematite-coating would be expected to be in common use, and it is clear that chronology is not the only factor limiting its avail-

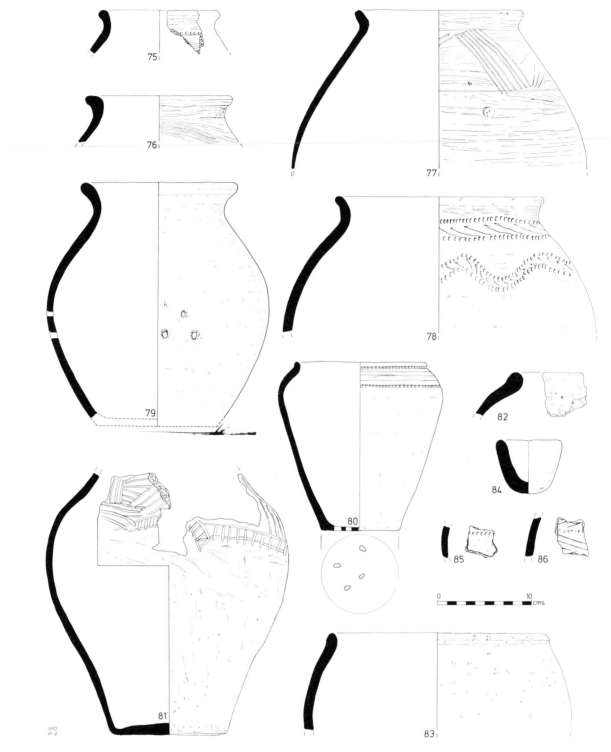

Fig 56. Winnall Down: Middle Iron Age pottery, scale 1:4.

ability on certain sites. Status may be a significant factor, although the present state of knowledge concerning site hierarchy prohibits any thorough consideration. Of the local Early Iron Age sites, excluding hillforts, Meon Hill (Liddell 1935) produced a substantial assemblage of cordoned bowls with as many as 25% of the sherds from some contexts being haematite-coated, but the completeness of the surviving record must be doubted. At Old Down Farm, Andover (Davies 1981) haematite-

coated pottery in Phases 3 and 4 of the Early Iron Age settlement accounted for less than 5% of the assemblage.

The suggestion that variations in marketing patterns are responsible for the scarcity of haematite-coated pottery at Winklebury (Smith 1977, 86) presupposes the existence of centralised production and an extensive trade network, for which there is at present little evidence in this period. Neither petrological examination of haematite-coated wares in Dorset (Partridge 1974) nor visual examination of fine-wares from sites in Hampshire has revealed any replication of fabrics indicative of commercial distribution. Nonetheless, the existence of some marketing system would provide a persuasive explanation for much of the data, and it can be argued that both Winnall Down and Old Down Farm are peripheral to the distribution of haematite cordoned bowls (Harding 1971, Fig 51).

Little need be said of the rest of the Phase 3 pottery; the coarse ware vessels, both plain and decorated, can be paralleled at most sites of this period. Organic tempered fabrics comprise 6% of the prehistoric assemblage at Winnall Down, and are known from many Iron Age sites in southern England, for example Ashville (Roche in Parrington 1978), Winklebury (Smith 1977, 90, fabric 15) and Old Down Farm (Davies 1981); chaff or grass tempering may be a small and often unrecognised, yet important, component of many Iron Age assemblages.

The conventional model (Cunliffe 1978, 45) would see the various regional Early Iron Age styles supplanted in the third century BC by saucepan pots. The earliest dates from Winnall Down for layers containing saucepan pottery are 2150±80BP (HAR 2980) and 2140±80BP (HAR 2252).

Subsequent excavation of the Winnall Down settlement complex prior to construction of the Easton Lane Interchange (Fasham and Whinney in prep) has revealed a previously unrepresented ceramic horizon comprising a distinctive group of largely undecorated saucepan pots. This material awaits detailed evaluation, but comparison with other sites in the Winchester region suggests that it is best considered as a chronological link between Phases 3 and 4, and that there is therefore a gap in the sequence at Winnall Down. Nevertheless, there is a considerable overlap between Phase 3 and 4 fabrics and forms (Fig 50).

Collis (1977b), in reviewing Professor Cunliffe's style-zones, has suggested that the St Catherine's Hill–Worthy Down style could be absorbed by the other groups. Stitched decoration occurs in southern England outside the distribution of the St Catherine's Hill–Worthy Down group.

Decoration on saucepan pots from central Hampshire lacks the variety of other regions, and the bowl with the scroll decoration (Fig 54.72) is not local (however defined) but has its affinities with examples from Sussex (eg Cunliffe 1978, 363).

The restricted range of Phase 4 forms and fabrics, the ubiquity of the burnished surface on these vessels and the evident preference for standardised sizing of the saucepan pots, apparent throughout southern England (Cunliffe 1978, 45), strongly suggests centralised production and distribution. Again,

comparison of fabrics from different sites has been unrewarding although, given the homegeneity of the clay, gravel and chalk formations of the region, it may well be that source determination by fabric alone will not be possible. Where inclusions diagnostic of particular geological formations are present, as in the west of England, petrological examination has demonstrated production and distribution of Middle Iron Age pottery on a regional basis (Peacock 1968).

The lack of secure stratification on the site makes it impossible to recognise chronological differentiation within the Phase 4 material, although the frequency with which all vessel types are associated with each other implies that all these forms were in use at the same time. In contrast to the nearby 'banjo' enclosure site in Micheldever Wood (Fasham in prep), saucepans are not regularly associated with recognisable Late Iron Age vessel forms, and it seems likely that there is a break in the occupation sequence at the end of Phase 4. A terminal date for the phase must therefore be sought prior to the introduction of the new ceramic types, probably in the late second or early first century BC.

The Roman Pottery

Fabrics

A total of thirty-seven fabrics could be assigned to the Roman period (Table 10), of which only six need be non-local: Fabrics 21 (samian) and 47 (amphora) are considered elsewhere in the report; fabric 36 (Terra Nigra); and three fabrics of uncertain origin, 31, 49, 70. Fabric 31, a soft white fabric with an abraded red colour coat, and fabric 70, a fine cream fabric with large quartz sands and sparse red iron oxides, both occur in late first century AD contexts at Clausentum. Fabric 49 is a wheel-thrown, black colour-coated fine ware.

On the basis of an examination of the pottery from feature 660, it has been suggested that as much as 30% of the greywares may be from Alice Holt (M Lyne, pers com), and most of these are first–early second century everted or bead-rim jar forms in fabric 6. Examples include Fig 57.95–96 (Lyne and Jefferies 1979, class 1.22), Fig 57.97 (class 3A), and Fig 57.92 (class 4.10).

Phase 5. Pre-Conquest

Phase 5 features yielded 589 sherds (12,371g), including 58 rims and 17 bases. Three vessel types were exclusive to this phase: one example each of a high-shouldered jar, form 47 (Fig 57.87); the rim of a possible pedestal-based urn, form 51 (Fig 57.88); and an externally-burnished, carinated bowl, form 45 with a multi-perforated base (Fig 57.89). Other vessels from the site of Late Iron Age type are also illustrated here (Fig 57.90–91). Associated with these forms were high and low-shouldered bead-rim jars, form 21, 25 and 26 (Fig 57.92–94) in both Roman and Prehistoric fabrics, and everted, form 22 (Fig 57.95–105), necked and cordoned, form 23 (Fig 58.106–108), chamfered rim jars, form 43 (Fig 58.109–111), and other miscellaneous small jar forms (eg Fig 58.112–114). A total of twenty-eight of these various jar forms

Table 10. Pottery: Late Iron Age/Roman fabrics.

GROUP	FABRICS	SHERDS No	SHERDS Wt in grams
6. MISCELLANEOUS GREY WARES			
Fine/Medium Sandy	6	2407	23555
	34	175	3292
Course Sandy	50	2	9
	59	36	342
	68	4	63
Coarse Sandy + Flint	45	505	6805
	46	228	3121
	52	7	77
	54	61	342
	81	1	4
Coarse Sandy + Grog	58	47	530
		3473	38140
7. ORANGE SANDY WARES			
Fine	24	204	1415
Fine/Medium	40	242	1491
	61	15	68
Medium	48	77	1960
Medium + Flint	37	33	1334
	53	8	72
Medium + Grog	60	135	4616
Medium + Grog + Flint	66	7	196
Medium + Shell	69	4	15
Coarse	7	47	530
	18	648	9521
	63	3	61
Coarse + Chalk	30	65	993
		1488	22272
8. REDUCED SANDY FABRICS			
	35	151	1719
	41	537	5310
	43	178	2020
	51	150	1674
	62	145	1311
	140	505	5073
		1666	17107
9. AMPHORAE	47 (Part of)	28	2013
		28	2013
10. OTHER STORAGE VESSEL TYPES	47 (Part of)	55	3042
		55	3042
11. TRADED WARES	21 *Samian*	74	749
	23	254	864
	31	32	226
	36 *Terra Nigra*	3	26
	49	21	139
	70	2	4
		386	2008
	TOTAL:	7096	84582

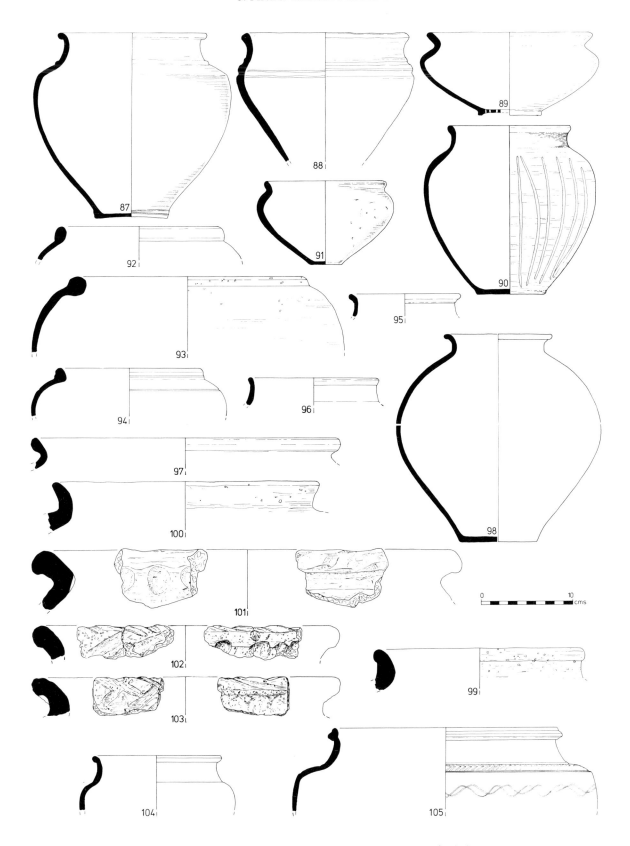

Fig 57. Winnall Down: Late Iron Age and Early Roman pottery, scale 1:4.

were recovered from Phase 5 contexts, although the majority of the types were found in Phase 6, and are included in the Phase 6 analysis (Table 11) and illustrations.

Phase 6. Early Roman

Phase 6 features contained 7,646 sherds (86,570g), including 638 rims and 227 bases. Table wares (Table 11) are defined as: bowls and dishes, forms 27, 24, 71, 39, 49, 55, 40 and 60 (*eg* Fig 58.115–117); beakers, forms 62, 52 and 56 (Fig 58.118–121); flagons, forms 48, 46 and 41 (Fig 58.122–124); platters, form 50 (Fig 58.125–126); lids, forms 38, 42, 58 and 59 (not illustrated), including the one mortarium from the site, form 61 (Fig 58.127). These comprise 27% of the recognisable vessel forms (85 examples). Correlation between individual vessel forms and fabrics is not strong (Table 11), although fabric 24, a fine sandy orange fabric, occurred only as a flagon and a mortarium. Few of the

'exotic' fabrics were associated with vessel forms: there is one flagon handle in fabric 34, and a fragment of a Terre Nigra footring platter, fabric 36.

Burnishing occurs on 5% of the bowls/dishes, 23% of the platters and 13% of the jars. In addition, eight jars have a burnished band below the rim (*eg* Fig 57.94), one a burnished band above the base, and one near complete vessel has a band around both base and rim (Fig 58.121). One greyware vessel, a butt-beaker (Fig 58.120), has a black slipped finish, and there is one red colour-coated bowl (Fig 58.116). Rouletting was present on only one vessel, a greyware beaker (Fig 58.119). There are two singly perforated sherds and a multi-perforated base from an unknown vessel form, fabric 6 (Fig 58.128).

The fragmentary nature of the material has made it difficult to assign the jars in particular to meaningful groups (Table 11). The

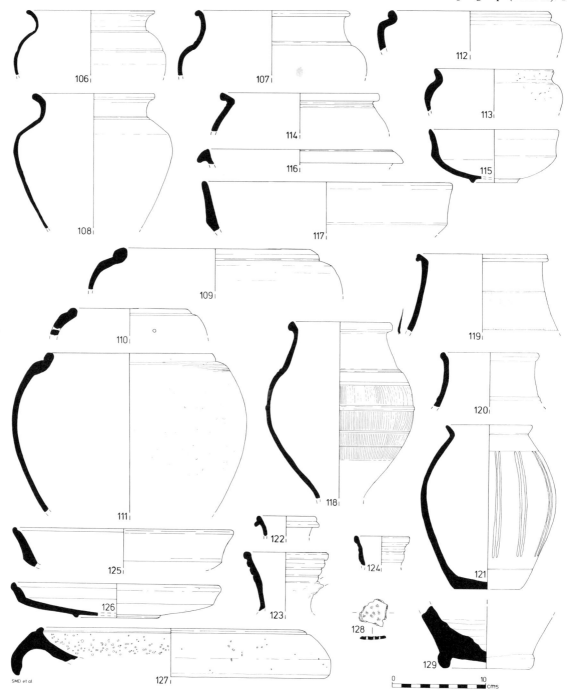

Fig 58. Winnall Down: Early Roman pottery, scale 1:4.

Table 11. Pottery: form/fabric in Phase 6.

Fabric	Bowl/Dish	Beaker	Flagon	Platter	Moratarium	Necked & Cordoned Jar	Bead Rim Jar	Chamfered Rim Jar	Everted Rim Jar	Total
GROUP 6 6	22	9	–	1	–	21	10	10	65	138
34	1	–	–	–	–	–	3	–	10	14
45	1	–	–	–	–	–	8	2	2	13
46	–	–	–	–	–	–	11	–	1	12
54	–	–	–	–	–	1	–	–	–	1
59	–	–	–	–	–	1	1	–	1	3
GROUP 7 18	–	–	–	–	–	–	27	–	2	29
24	–	–	4	–	1	–	–	–	–	5
37	–	–	–	–	–	–	1	–	–	1
40	1	1	–	–	–	3	–	–	2	7
48	–	1	–	–	–	–	3	–	–	4
60	–	–	–	–	–	–	9	–	–	9
63	–	–	–	–	–	–	1	–	–	1
66	–	–	–	–	–	–	–	1	–	1
GROUP 8 35	3	–	–	–	–	–	1	–	2	6
41	8	–	–	5	–	4	3	1	17	38
43	1	–	–	–	–	1	3	2	2	9
51	2	–	–	1	–	–	2	–	1	6
62	6	–	–	1	–	–	1	1	4	13
140	5	1	–	4	–	1	14	10	10	45
GROUP 11 23	–	1	2	–	–	–	–	–	–	3
49	–	–	–	–	–	–	–	–	1	1
PREHISTORIC 2	–	–	–	–	–	–	17	–	2	19
3	–	–	–	–	–	–	6	–	–	6
4	–	1	–	–	–	–	3	–	2	6
8	–	–	–	–	–	–	1	–	–	1
9	1	–	–	1	–	–	–	1	–	3
11	–	–	–	–	–	–	–	1	–	1
14	–	–	–	–	–	–	–	–	2	2
25	–	–	–	–	–	–	2	–	–	2
TOTAL	51	14	6	13	1	32	127	29	126	399

distribution of the rim diameters of the 127 probable Roman bead-rim jars, forms 21, 25, 26, 35, 44, 53 and 70 (Fig 59) and the 126 everted rim jars (not illustrated), suggests that more than one true type is represented. Only for the easily recognisable and closely definable forms, such as the 'Southern Atrebatic' type of jar with the chamfered rim, can there be any certainty of accurate identification of type, and a preference for vessel rim diameters of between 120–140mm is noticeable (Fig 60). Although excavation showed a sequence within Phase 6 (Fig 27), these distinctions are not reflected by the pottery.

Amphorae (based on information provided by Dr D P S Peacock)

From a total of 83 sherds assigned to fabric 47, 28 were identified as amphorae, the remainder belonging to thick-walled storage vessels of probable local origin. Five sherds, including the one rim, could not be ascribed to a type; the remaining 23 sherds (body sherds unless otherwise stated) are classified as follows:

Dressel 20: fifteen sherds. Southern Spanish in origin, commonly associated with marine products *c* 10BC – early second century AD, usually first century AD.

Dressel 1: three sherds certain, two others possible. 130 BC–1 BC/AD.

Richborough 527: two sherds. Mediterranean origin. Middle–late first century AD.

Dressel 30: two sherds certain, one a handle, the other an atypical base (Fig 58.129), plus one possible sherd. Southern Gaul, probably mid–second century AD.

The distribution and location of the amphorae across the site (archive) shows no particular concentration.

The Samian by V A Jones (Fig 61)

There were 64 sherds of samian. Three were intrusive in the upper layers of Phase 4 features, three were unphased, a Neronian or Early Flavian sherd and an intrusive Flavian/Trajanic sherd were in Phase 5 contexts and the remainder were in Phase 6. There were 25 first century sherds, eight Antonine, and the remainder were Flavian/Trajanic to Hadrianic/Antonine. Five sherds were from the kilns at Les Martres-de-Veyre, 33 sherds from southern Gaul and 26 from central Gaul (full details in archive). A sherd of an 18R or a 15/17R from southern Gaul still had kiln grit adhering to it.

The following sherds were decorated:

1. Form 29. Not assignable to a single potter. *c* AD55–70? South Gaul. Phase 6 ditch 9450.

2. Form 29. The lower zone contains a winding scroll with a 'candelabra' in the lower concavity. The 'candelabra' sits on an astragalus which is not the usual foot. The bifid leaf with a central bud (Hermet 1934, Pl 14.36) is found on a bowl from Richborough stamped by Bassus-Coelus (Cunliffe 1968, Pl LXXIX.4). The five fingered motif is on a bowl stamped by Quintio i in the Museum of London. The style of decoration is Group II, Cluzel 15, which Haalebos (1979, Taf 5.1) associates with stamps of Celadus and a mould signature of Sonicio. All the details are from Cluzel. *c* AD 50–70 South Gaul. Phase 6 ditch 1135.

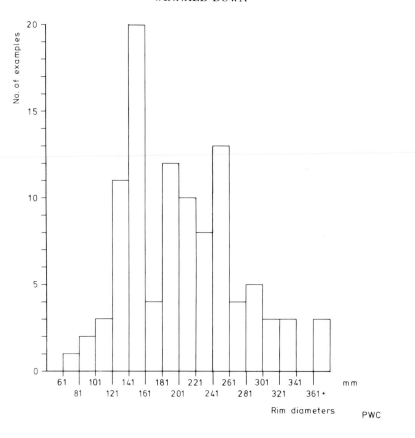

Fig 59. Winnall Down: rim diameters of bead rim jars.

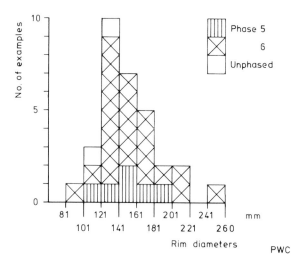

Fig 60. Winnall Down: rim diameters of 'southern Atrebatic' chamfered rim jars.

3. Form 29. Probably made by the eccentric mouldmaker for Bassus-Coelus. The upper zone contains a winding scroll terminating in nine-fingered fronds and rosettes and with bifid bindings at the junctions. In the background are roulettes. In the lower zone is a straight wreath of leaves (Knorr 1919, Taf 13 detail 31 and more clearly in J) and, below this, half medallions (Taf 13, detail 24) containing seven-fingered fronds and roulettes (Taf 13, detail 14). The pendant (Knorr 1919 Taf 13, detail 33 and seen on its side in L) is also found on a basal wreath on a bowl stamped by Severus i from Wroxeter. This mouldmaker was also used by Meddilus and Seno. *c* AD 65–80. South Gaul. Three sherds from Phase 6 ditches 660 and 6732.

4. Form 37. The wreath was used by M Crestio and Paullus (May 1930, Pl XXII. 130; Hermet 1934, Pl 88.7). The Colchester ovolo looks like Paullus. For the leaf see Vanderhoeven (1978

Heft 7, Taf 82, 669) with the ovolo of M Crestio. *c* AD 80–100 South Gaul. Phase 6 ditch 6718.

5. Form 37.   Two fragments from a panelled bowl, one sherd illustrated. The ovolo was used by the Cevialis ii – Cinnamus ii group (Rogers 1974, B 144). The warrior set sideways, is D103 (Dechelette 1904) and was used by several Antonine potters and appears on a form 37 from Alcester stamped by Cinnamus. The astragalus is Rogers R8 (Rogers 1974). *c.* AD 140–170. Central Gaul. Phase 6 ditches 471 and 2761.

6. Form 30.   Bowl with panelled decoration. Within the medallion is a winged cherub, P 264 (Dechelette 1904). In the upper left hand panel the letter 'I' is present and is the last letter of the stamp Albuci (Stanfield and Simpson 1958, Pls 120–123 for examples). Above the 'I' is the bird D1011 (Dechelette 1904) which appears on the form 37 from Irchester stamped by Albucius. The ring (Rogers 1974, E58) is found on bowls stamped by Albucius

(Stanfield and Simpson 1958 Pl 120.2). *c* AD 150–180. Central Gaul. Top layer of Phase 4 pit 8594.

The Stamps by B M Dickinson

7. Iucundus ii 5a (form not identified). (OF·IVC)VN. La Gravfesenque. This stamp was reserved mainly for form 29. It has been noted at Flavian foundations including Corbridge and Newstead. *c* AD 70–85. Phase 6 scoop 7215.

8. Viducus ii. Uncertain 1 33 VIOVCO(CI). 'Les Martres-de-Veyre'. VIOVCO2F may have been the original reading. The stamp never registers very clearly, as if the die were worn. Viducus's wares occur at Birrens where they presumably belong to the Hadrianic occupation, since they are also known at Malton and in the London Second Fire. *c* AD 105–125. Phase 6 ditch 660.

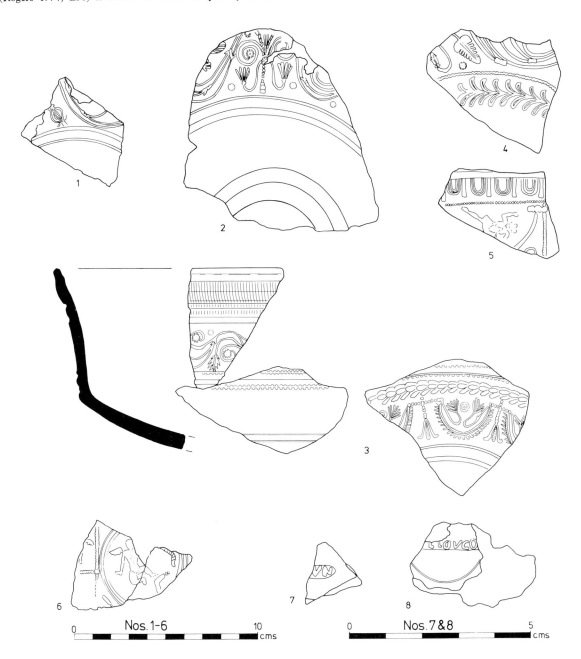

Fig 61.   Winnall Down: Samian 1–6, scale 1:2; 7 and 8, scale 1:1.

Discussion

The appearance of Late Iron Age vessel forms, the presence of Terra Nigra and Gallo-Belgic type table wares and bead-rim jars in fabrics associated with earlier assemblages point to a pre-conquest beginning for the re-occupation of the site. Although there is little evidence for domestic structures in the Roman period, the quantity of pottery, the presence of fine wares and the high proportion of table wares suggest that the Winnall Down area contained an occupation site, and it may be significant that only nine Roman sherds were recovered from Easton Down (Fasham 1982), just 1 km to the north, where there were no Roman features. The majority of the forms can be paralleled in the first period assemblage at Fishbourne (Cunliffe 1971, 175–216) and numerous other sites, and need be no later than the early part of the second century AD. A continuation into the middle part of that century is suggested by the Dressel 30 amphorae and the mortarium, the form finding parallels in the mid-second century assemblage at Verulamium (Frere 1972, 339, type 1031).

Medieval

Eighty-seven sherds of medieval pottery were recovered, sixty intrusive in earlier contexts, seventeen from medieval features and ten unphased. All the sherds were small and badly abraded, and represent a field scatter of unknown date.

The Briquetage by E L Morris (full details in archive)

Macroscopic Identification

Seventy-three (426.5g) sherds of ?briquetage were found in Phase 4 and 31 sherds (314g) in Phase 6. It was clearly distinguishable from the pottery and was oxidised to an orange colour (Munsell 2.5YR 6/6 – 6/8, 5/6 and 5YR 6/6) on the external surface with occasional examples having an oxidised skin on the interior. The core and internal areas were usually dark grey to light grey-brown (2.5 YR N3/ to 10YR 6/2 – 6/3). The organic tempering was burnt out on the oxidised surfaces but was still often visible in fresh fractures of the protected, reduced, core. The fabric was very porous due to the organic temper and the loosely structured, layered, nature of the clay matrix and the low temperature, or short duration, of firing which resulted in the incomplete oxidisation. Quartz sand formed 5–15% of the fabric. Highly organic-tempered pieces were smooth on the surface and had a small amount of fine quartz, while examples low in organic tempering were harsh to the touch and contained a higher quartz content. Flint was not visible macroscopically but the sandier sherds had rare fragments of chalk.

Vessel Forms

The sherds were from containers which had slightly sagging, rather rounded bases and either vertical or infolded rims. Three base sherds, all from the same vessel, were recognised and two rims were present. The base diameter was 100–120mm and the rim diameters were estimated at 160–280mm and 120–140mm. The containers were all hand-made with smoothed internal surfaces and, frequently, vertically-smoothed external surfaces. The average range of thickness of the body sherds was 80–100mm. The vessel form was not reconstructable but the larger sherds occasionally displayed a slight waist curve suggesting a cylindrical vessel of quite large diameter. Such a form would be comparable to the briquetage containers from the Iron Age salt-working site in Friar Street, Droitwich (Hunt forthcoming) where the vessels were in the shape of truncated cones some 200–260mm tall.

Microscopic analysis

Three body sherds, two organic and one sandy, were thin-sectioned and examined under the petrological microscope. The macroscopic fabric division was confirmed. For comparative purposes a sample of daub from the site was also thin-sectioned. There were insufficient numbers of different vessels represented to examine clay source variability by heavy mineral analysis and comparative material examination. There was no flint in either the organic or sandy fabrics but one piece of chalk was in the former and about 10% of the latter fabric was chalky. The daub contained 45–50% chalk (full details in archive and in Morris 1983). Most of the other inclusions in both the sandy and organic fabrics differed from those in the daub and from the inclusions in the pottery. It is most unlikely that the flint- and almost chalk-free briquetage fabrics were locally derived.

Discussion

The major question posed by the two different briquetage fabrics is were they from different and widely-separated sources, or were they variations from the same source which appear to be slightly different due to alternative preparation methods of wedging and tempering? This question is important if salt from more than one production site was used on Winnall Down. The majority of the briquetage came from just two containers, sherds of each being exclusive to Phases 4 and 6, and thus they cannot provide adequate data for stratistical testing of the heavy mineral context. The organic fabric briquetage dominates in both Phases, 74% by weight in Phase 4 and 91% in Phase 6. It is unlikely that the Phase 6 material is residual and its presence is likely to be due to the continued use of this method of drying and transporting salt during the early Roman period. At the Richett's Lane site in Droitwich (HWCM 600), vast quantities of container briquetage were discovered in late first/second century AD occupation levels (Sawle forthcoming). The source for the Winnall Down briquetage is likely to be in the Southampton Water area, where at least three salt-production centres are known, or from the six known centres in the Portsmouth-Langstone Harbour area (Bradley 1975, Fig 9).

Stone Objects

Introduction by D P S Peacock

A considerable number of stone fragments was recovered, some of which appeared to be fragments of querns. Table 12 summarises the frequency of rock fragments which could not be identified as artifacts. Of these, a majority will have been imported from some distance away but slate is particularly noteworthy because it presumably originated in Devon, although the purpose to which it was put is unclear. Many of the shapeless fragments of greensand, carrstone, sarsen and chert are probably small pieces of querns, the origins of which will be discussed below. The sources of many of the other rocks are fairly local; Marcasite, chalk and Melbourne rock (hard chalk) might originate on the downland, while the remaining materials may derive from pebbles in local river valleys, with the exception of those from Purbeck.

Table 12. Stone fragments not identified as artifacts. NP = Not Phased.

	Phase						
Stone	NP	2	3	4	5	6	Total
Greensand	6	–	8	8	1	9	32
Marcasite	16	1	17	6	–	12	52
Carrstone	4	–	3	4	–	2	13
Slate	10	–	3	10	2	14	39
Chalk	1	–	–	–	–	–	1
Unidentified Sandstone	2	–	1	3	–	–	6
Selborne Malmstone	1	–	–	1	–	1	3
Pebble (mostly flint)	2	–	9	11	2	14	38
Melbourne rock	–	–	1	–	–	–	1
Metamorphic Quartzite	1	–	–	–	–	–	1
Sarsen chert	–	–	–	2	–	–	2
Sarsen	1	–	2	–	–	–	3
Purbeck shale	–	–	–	–	–	1	1
Jasper	–	–	–	1	–	1	2
Calcite-dogtooth spar	–	–	–	–	–	1	1
Tufa	–	–	–	1	1	3	5
Unidentified	–	–	–	–	–	1	1
TOTALS	44	1	44	47	6	59	201

Table 13 summarises the distribution of querns in different types by phase. The diameters of the rotary querns are shown in Fig 62, which shows that rotaries are smaller in Phase 6 than in Phase 4. The most important rock type is the greensand from the Hythe beds of Sussex, probably the area between Midhurst and Petworth, although quarries have yet to be located. Sarsen is of more local downland origin, while the carrstone fragments may originate in the Folkestone beds of the Hampshire/Surrey/Sussex border. At present, little can be usefully said of the origin of the remaining rock types with the exception of chert, which could also derive from the cherty facies of the Hythe beds.

Most of the querns used on Winnall Down were thus imported from *c* 20 miles to the east, where presumably a large quarry and production centre awaits discovery, for the same rock type is commonly found in both Iron Age and Roman sites within a 50 mile radius of the suggested point of origin.

The Querns – Some observations by H M Jecock (full details in archive)

In 1937 Curwen published his seminal study on the Iron Age rotary querns of southern England, distinguishing two forms which he thought were contemporary – his 'Sussex' and 'Wessex' types. Although his stated intention was merely to provide 'a tentative (typological) scheme as a basis of study' (Curwen 1937, 133), no subsequent work has yet appeared despite the fact that, in recent years, much additional evidence has become available through excavation. To this can now be added the material from Winnall Down which, since it does not seem to fit comfortably into either of Curwen's categories, has highlighted the need for such a reappraisal.

The attributes used by Curwen to draw up his typology were chiefly the presence of a hopper and the method of handle attachment, but to a lesser

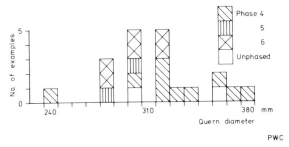

Fig 62. Winnall Down: diameters of rotary querns.

Table 13. Querns by form and phase. NP = Not Phased.

	NP	2	3	4	5	6	Total
Greensand							
Saddle	4	–	1	7	–	–	12
Rotary (all types)	2	–	–	8	3	7	20
Fragments	8	1	11	26	4	23	73
Sarsen							
Saddle	–	–	1	–	–	–	1
Fragments	1	2	6	6	–	–	15
Carrstone							
Rotary	–	–	–	1	–	–	1
Fragments	1	–	1	7	–	1	10
Unidentified sandstone							
Saddle	–	–	–	1	–	–	1
Rotary	–	–	–	1	–	–	1
Fragments	–	–	1	1	–	–	2
Limestone (?Purbeck)							
Rotory	–	–	–	1	–	–	1
Fragments	–	–	–	1	–	–	1
Meta-quartzite			1				
Saddle	–	–	–	–	–	1	1
Chert							
Fragments	–	–	–	1	–	–	1
TOTALS	16	3	21	61	7	32	140

extent also general morphology. A provisional survey of the extant material within the area of Wessex (Jecock 1981) has tended to confirm that distinctions can be made on this basis, but in addition to the Sussex and Wessex types, a third form can be identified, and it is this form that predominates during Phase 4 at Winnall Down. It differs from the others in possessing both a handle slot and a basin-shaped hopper cut into the top of the stone, attributes which were originally thought by Curwen to be mutually exclusive. Also, in nearly every instance this hopper would seem to be confined to the immediate area of the central feed-pipe, rising up to meet a flat rather than curved top surface of the upper stone (*eg* Fig 63.7; also special finds 154 and

438 in the archive).

Other examples of this form of quern come from the Hampshire sites of Balksbury (Smith forthcoming) and Winklebury (Smith 1977, 113, Fig 40.8 and 9). The distribution can be extended eastwards into Surrey, again at two hillfort sites, Holmbury and Hascombe (Thompson 1979, 292–3). It should be noted that within the broad typological grouping here defined there can exist considerable variety in precise characteristics of profile and form: this is evidenced by one quern from Winnall Down (Fig 63.8), and is a point that had been made for quern types in other parts of the country (*eg* Philips 1950, 77). The significance of this would seem uncertain,

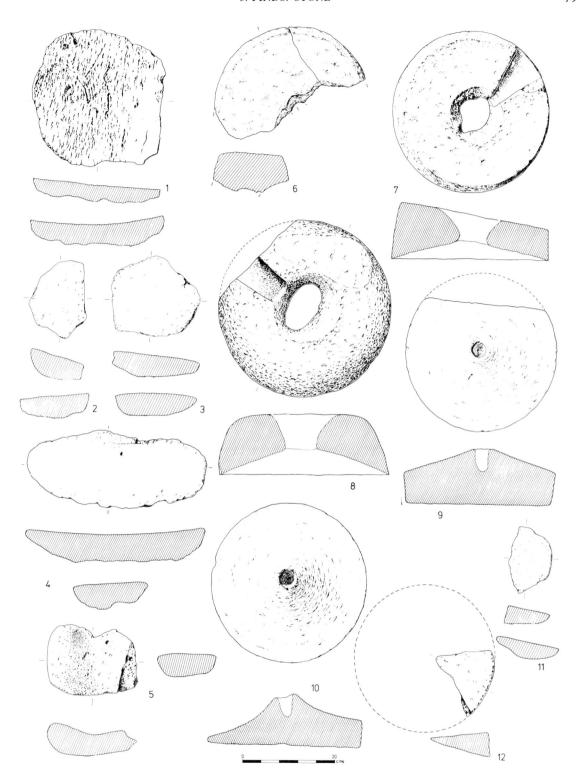

Fig 63.   Winnall Down: querns, scale 1:8.

but it may possibly be due to chronological factors and/or be related to the basis of production.

From the wide distribution of this third type, therefore, it will become clear that to persist with the logic of Curwen's nomenclature is inappropriate, if not also undesirable, from the arguments rehearsed above. Consequently, it is proposed to call this new type, type A, and to rename the old Sussex and

Wessex types B and C respectively. If this scheme is accepted generally, in future every quern can be so described to type, ideally accompanied by a petrological identification so that it can be seen whether individual types are coterminous with a variety of different rock sources (after the fashion of the form-fabric approach currently employed in pottery studies). Wider interpretations may then be possible.

It is necessary to consider the chronology of each type of quern. Rotary querns were not found at Winnall Down before Phase 4, contemporary with the appearance of the saucepan pottery styles whose period of currency Cunliffe (1978) and others (*eg* Collis 1977) have dated to after 300 BC. Indeed such a date for the inception of use of the rotary quern is in accordance with the evidence available from other southern English Iron Age sites (Jecock 1981, 12). Consequently, it is proposed on current evidence to suggest 300 BC as the *terminus post quem* for the innovation of rotary milling.

A consideration of the associations of individual querns would indicate that types A and C very probably coexisted during the third and second centuries BC, and survived perhaps into the first. This assertion would appear to receive support from a provisional distribution map (Jecock 1981, Fig 4) which shows the two types to be mutually exclusive in southern counties, along a line roughly coinciding with the modern Hampshire-Wiltshire border.

The evidence for type B is less conclusive, but all datable examples (known to the writer) are of the first centuries BC/AD, apart from one instance at Gussage All Saints and one possible example of the type at Winnall Down (Fig 63.6). But the distribution of this type is far more widespread and overlaps that of both the other types. Thus it is suggested that type B marks a typological development, perhaps originating sometime around 100 BC or slightly earlier, and provides the antecedent for querns after the Roman conquest which were generally thinner and more compact, but otherwise underwent no radical alteration. Such an interpretation is supported by the evidence from Winnall Down where type A querns are completely absent in favour of type B during Phases 5 and 6. But the number of dated examples upon which these judgements are based is not many, and it remains to be seen whether they will be borne out by the results of future excavations.

The following quern stones have been selected for illustration to show the range of types and rocks by phase (Fig 63). There are only a few Phase 6 rotary stones capable of illustration.

1.   Greensand saddle quern, subrectangular in shape and almost complete. 290 by 260mm and maximum thickness of 52mm. Phase 3 enclosure ditch 5, segment C, layer 718.

2.   Sarsen saddle quern, elongated form but not complete. Maximum width 160mm, maximum thickness 40mm. Phase 3 pit 3670.

3.   Unidentified sandstone saddle quern, partially complete, possibly sub-rectangular in form. Phase 4 pit 8585.

4.   Greensand saddle quern, elongated form, complete. 150mm long, 43mm wide, 53mm thick. Phase 4 pit 2940.

5.   Greensand saddle quern, fragment of elongated type. Maximum width 144mm, approximate thickness 58mm. Phase 4 pit 2902.

6.   Limestone (? Purbeck) upper rotary stone, incomplete. Diameter 330mm, thickness 80mm. Phase 4 pit 1631.

7.   Greensand upper rotary stone, complete. Note differential wear pattern caused by only partial rotation of stone. Diameter 340mm, thickness 115mm. Phase 4 pit 313.

8.   Greensand upper rotary stone, amost complete with differential wear. Diameter 370mm, thickness 130mm. Phase 4 pit 2416.

9.   Greensand lower rotary stone, almost complete. Note differential wear. Diameter 315mm, thickness 95mm. Phase 4 pit 9105.

10.   Greensand lower rotary stone, complete. Massive differential wear. Diameter 320mm, thickness 70mm. Phase 4 pit 9344.

11.   Meta-quartzite saddle quern. Fragment of elongated type. Maximum width 139mm, thickness 39mm. Possibly residual in Phase 6 enclosure ditch 493, segment B.

12.   Greensand upper rotary stone. Fragment. Diameter 300mm, maximum thickness 49mm. Phase 6 enclosure ditch 678 segment C.

Other objects of stone

The other, non quern, stone artifacts are summarized in Table 14.

Chalk

Spindle whorls. It was possible to obtain measurements of all but two of the spindle whorls. If the large Phase 3 whorl (No 1) is omitted, it would seem that the circular whorls were smaller in Phase 3 than in Phase 4. In Phase 3 the diameter was 35mm and thickness 10mm, while in Phase 4 the principal diameter was around 43mm and the thickness 9–18mm. There were two oval whorls.

The following are illustrated (Fig 64):

1.   Large irregular possible spindle whorl. About 65mm diameter, 26mm thick. Phase 3 enclosure ditch 5, segment A, layer 552.

2.   Flat, circular spindle whorl, with off-centred hole. Diameter 35mm, thickness 10mm. Phase 3 enclosure ditch 5, segment A, layer 573.

3.   Slightly conical, circular spindle whorl, slightly off-centred hole. Diameter 43mm, thickness 9–18mm. Phase 4 pit 7257.

4.   Fragmentary flat, circular spindle whorl, off-centred hole. Diameter 33mm, thickness 9mm. Phase 4 pit 7257.

5.   Irregular, almost circular, possible spindle whorl, off-centred hole. Diameter approx 45mm, thickness 16mm. Phase 4 pit 7399.

6.   Oval spindle whorl, almost central perforation. 37 by 32mm, 13mm thick. Phase 4 pit 3901.

7.   Almost complete, flat oval spindle whorl, 45 by 37mm, 12mm thick. Phase 5 ditch 3817 segment D, layer 3824.

A chalk spindle whorl was also found in Phase 3 enclosure ditch 5, segment A, layer 552; a further two were in Phase 4 pit 7257; one in Phase 4 pit 8601; and one in the unphased post-hole 3678.

8.   Conical bead of 11mm diameter with 4mm perforation. Phase 3 quarry pit 7624.

9.   Circular bead of 10mm diameter with 3–3.5mm perforation. Phase 3 quarry pit 9233.

Table 14. Stone artifacts (excluding querns).

		Phase					
		Not Phased	3	4	5	6	Total
Chalk	Loomweights	2	1	2	–	–	5
	Spindle whorls	1	3	7	1	–	12
	'Worked'	–	1	3	1	–	5
	Beads	1	2	–	–	1	4
	Mould	–	–	2	–	–	2
Greensand	Decorated weights	–	–	1	–	–	1
Sandstone	Whetstone	–	–	1	–	–	1
Shale	Bracelet	–	–	1	–	–	1
Carrstone	Grain rubber	–	–	–	–	1	1
Metamorphic quartzite	'Worked'	–	–	–	–	1	1
Purbeck Limestone	Roofing slate	–	–	–	–	1	1
Stone	Bead	–	1	–	–	–	1
Totals		4	8	17	2	4	35

10. Circular bead of 10–11mm diameter with perforation of 3–4mm. Phase 6 scoop 3245.

11. Collection of ten irregular small beads, all perforated. Presumably part of a necklace or bracelet. Unfortunately, unphased in scoop 6770.

12. *Chalk mould* by J Bayley (Fig 65). A large, chalk bar-mould with two parallel channels of trapezoidal cross section. Both splay out at one end as though to make a reservoir, but this would assume it was part of a two-piece mould for which there is no other evidence. There is no trace of metal in the channels, but all the surfaces (channels and raised areas each side) are blackened. Maximum surviving length 170mm. Lower chalk. Phase 4 pit 6595.

Worked chalk. There were also five pieces of apparently worked chalk; Phase 3 pit 8124 contained a piece of chalk with a partially-drilled hole; a similar piece, but with a completely drilled hole, was in the Phase 4 pit 7257. A small piece with three small, possibly natural, holes was found in Phase 4 pit 5609. Also in a Phase 4 pit, 7086, was a large slab with scratch marks on the surface.

13. Trapezoidal block of chalk with smooth sides and upper surface. Upper edges chamfered. Keyhole-shaped perforation created by drilling two almost adjacent holes through top surface. Maximum extant length 163mm, width 82mm to 122mm (maximum surviving), thickness 66mm. Phase 5 pit 10007.

The chalk loomweights are described in the general section on loomweights (90).

Miscellaneous stone objects

14. *Weight* by T C Champion (Fig 66). Height 96mm, maximum diameter 127mm. Sandstone from the Hythe Beds of the Wealden Lower Greensand. Rather less than one half of the whole weight survives; the fracture shows a narrow central perforation, 6mm in diameter, penetrating 45mm from the top, with traces of rust indicating the presence originally of the shaft of an iron hook or handle. The surviving portion weighs 1136g; the whole weight would originally have been c 2.4–2.5kg. The base is well smoothed, and the upper surface is decorated with a pattern of shallow excised lines.

It is difficult to discuss precise parallels for the decoration, since both the substance and the shape of the decorated surface are unusual, most Iron Age art occurring on more or less flat metal surfaces. Decoration on such a coarse-grained sandstone does not allow a similar precision of design or use of three-dimensional plastic motifs, and decoration of such a curved surface poses special problems. Apart from the very much larger decorated stones in Ireland, such as Turoe, the only other comparable objects are the Barnwood cone (Fox 1958, Fig 71), with a unique style of geometric ornament, and a series of decorated querns from north Wales and Ireland on which the decoration comprises mainly the repetition of simple motifs (Griffiths 1951). The closest parallels for this weight may, indeed, be found on pottery.

Although less than half of the original decoration survives, it appears to have been a unified design over the whole surface rather than a series of individual elements. The motifs used are curved-sided triangles elongated into spirals. Variations on this theme are common throughout British Iron Age art, but usually in more complex forms on bronzework. On pottery, similar motifs can be seen on sherds from Hunsbury (Fox 1958, Pl 77c).

The only published parallels for this weight are those from Winklebury, Hants (Smith 1977, Fig 40.4 and 7), which are of identical shape with similar iron hooks, though undecorated and rather heavier. Others were found at Winklebury, and further examples are known from Danebury (Cunliffe 1978, 273) and Portway Industrial Estate, Andoer (unpublished excavations). If they are rightly interpreted as weights for weighing something out rather than weighing something down, they represent an important stage in the development of Iron Age economy, so far only documented in southern central England, with increased emphasis on the role of exchange. Phase 4 pit 7372.

15. Fragment of whetstone, 36–58mm wide, 12mm thick. Sandstone. Phase 4 pit 122.

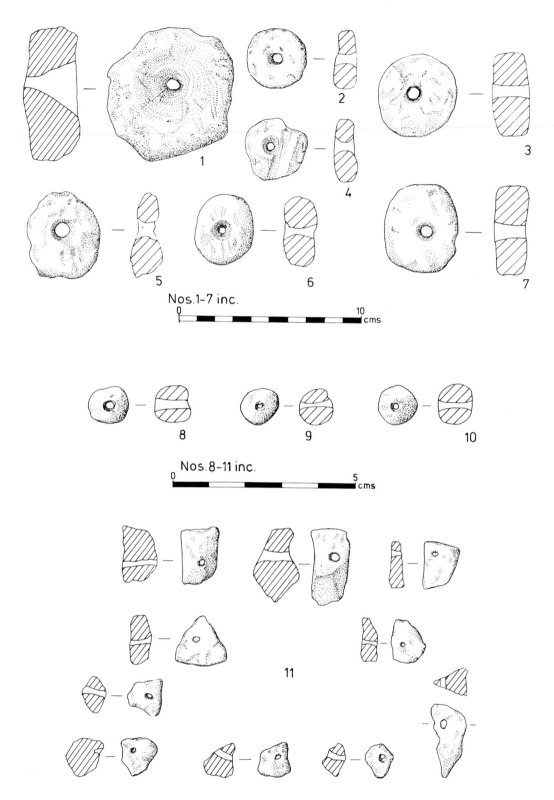

Fig 64.   Winnall Down: chalk objects 1–7, scale 1:2; 8–11, scale 1:1.

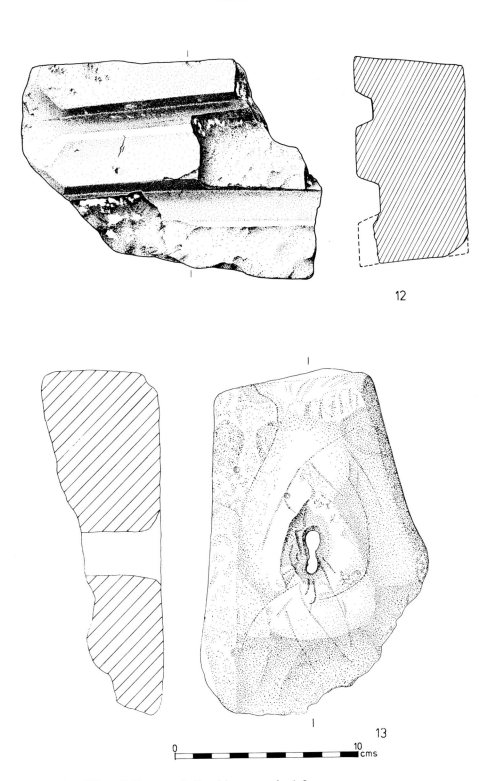

Fig 65. Winnall Down: chalk objects, scale 1:2.

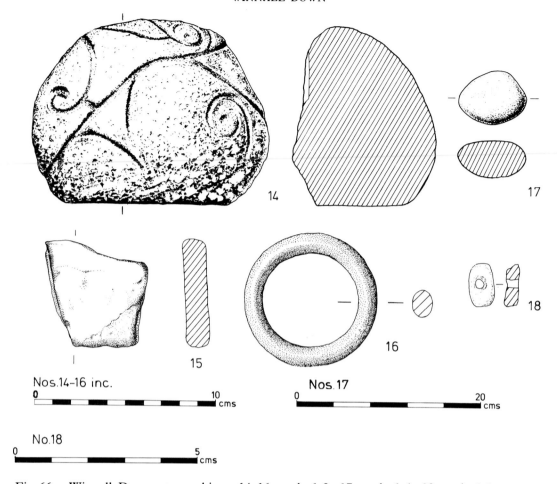

Fig 66.   Winnall Down: stone objects 14–16, scale 1:2; 17, scale 1:4, 18, scale 1:1.

16.   Complete shale bracelet, 72mm diameter and c 15mm thick. Phase 4. Left forearm of burial 174 in pit 4475.

17.   Grain rubber of carrstone. Phase 6 feature 7513.

18.   Oblong bead of unidentified stone with central perforation, 10mm by 5mm by 2mm. Phase 3 pit 2431.

Not illustrated are a Purbeck limestone roofing slate from the Phase 6 ditch 4607 segment B and a piece of worked metamorphic quartzite from Phase 6 ditch 660 segment K.

Flint by R P Winham

The 2,816 flint artifacts are summarized by phase in Table 15, which shows that only 1% of the collection were finished tools, 3.5% cores or core fragments, and 8% were retouched or utilized flakes. The 2,228 flakes represent 79% of the assemblage. As Table 15 shows, there is either a considerable volume of residual material, or flint working continued in some form or another until the early Roman period.

It was decided that useful analysis could only be done on a large and reasonably well-stratified group of this flint. The material from the Phase 3 deposits of enclosure ditch 5 satisfied these two requirements. There was little residual Neolithic or Bronze Age flint in the ditch. An analysis of Early Iron Age

material would supplement recent work in Hampshire (Fasham and Ross 1978, Fasham 1982).

The flint collection from this context consists of 132 waste fragments, chips and nodules; 298 flakes (5 broken); 23 retouched flakes (1 utilized as a borer); 6 utilized flakes; 14 cores; 10 core fragments; 2 core rejuvenation flakes; and 6 scrapers, incuding one used as a borer.

Tools form 7% of the total assemblage, largely in the form of retouched flakes. Scrapers alone, the only specific tool type recorded, account for 1.2%.

Measurements of length, breadth, breadth:length ratio and the angle between the striking platform and the bulbar plane were made, where possible, on a sample of 148 flakes (Fig 67).

Of the 148 flakes, one is primary (wholly cortical), 126 are secondary (partially cortical) and 21 are tertiary (non cortical). The ratio of tertiary:secondary is 1:6. This ratio drops to 1:1.8 if only retouched and utilized flakes and scrapers are considered.

The metrical analyses of flakes indicate that lengths between 31–50mm and breadths between 31–40m were most frequent. The breadth:length ratios, however, show no dominant category, with a spread from flakes with a ratio of 2.5–3.5 to flakes where the breadth exceeded the length. Approximately half fall into this latter category of broad flakes.

The angle between the striking platform and the bulbar plane is shown to be predominantly between 116–130°.

Table 15. Distribution of flint artifacts by phase.

	2	3	4	5	6	7	Not Phased	TOTALS
Flakes	7	707	527	36	456	8	437	2178
Retouched flakes	1	49	46	3	27	–	37	163
Utilized flakes	–	19	21	1	10	–	12	63
Cores and core fragments	1	29	25	–	28	–	15	98
Chips	4	34	25	2	30	2	37	134
Blades	–	2	–	–	–	–	–	2
Fragments/Nodules	1	20	13	2	26	–	63	125
Core/Platform rejuvenating flakes	–	8	5	–	2	–	9	24
Scrapers	–	8	1	–	5	–	4	18
Borers	–	1	2	–	2	–	–	5
Points	–	–	2	–	–	–	1	3
Hammerstones	–	1	–	–	1	–	–	2
Hand axe	–	1	–	–	–	–	–	1
TOTALS	14	879	667	44	587	10	615	2816

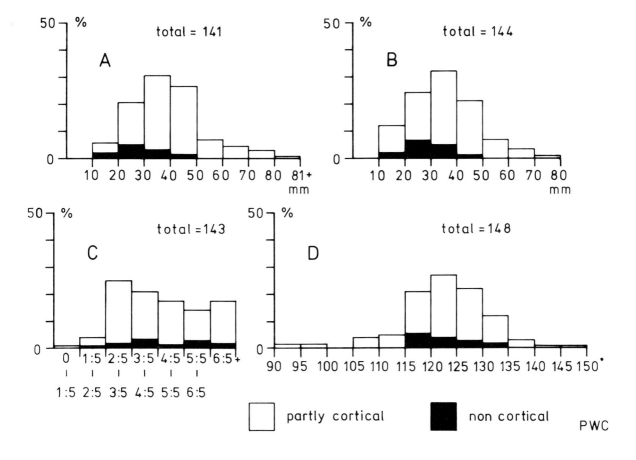

Fig 67. Winnall Down: metrical analysis of flint flakes. A – length of flake; B – breadth of flake; C – breadth to length ratio; D – angle between striking platform and the bulbar plane.

Although this assemblage is rather small, the trend was clearly for large, secondary flakes, with a tendency for them to be broad rather than long. The small percentage of tertiary flakes, the almost total lack of primary flakes and the small proportion of 'tools' compared with 'retouched flakes' suggest the lack of formalized flint working procedure with little detailed retouching. Any convenient flake, it seems, was picked out to retouch, rather than knapping to produce flakes of a specific type for retouching to form tools. This may indicate that flakes were utilized for the job in hand and then thrown away, rather than kept for further use.

The fourteen cores from this assemblage are divided into six class A2, two class B2, two class B3 and four class C cores (for definition see Clarke *et al* 1960). Of these only one class C core has no remnant cortex, and it is only among this class that more than a very limited utilization of the cores is suggested. The small number of cores precludes detailed analysis, but the impression is of a crude approach to core utilization, many having just one or two flakes removed, but with occasional attempts at regular flaking. The cores are very coarse nodules or irregular fragments.

This Early Iron Age assemblage can be compared only with Late Neolithic and Early Bronze Age sites in Wessex. The percentage of tools, when retouched and utilized flakes are included, is much higher than that encountered in the Micheldever Wood barrow flint industry (Fasham and Ross 1978, 51–52) or that suggested by Wainwright (1972, 66). This is possibly accounted for by the 'throw away' nature of the 'tools', and the lack of refined knapping producing more waste and flakes.

The percentage of tools proper, here all scrapers, is conversely small, but comparable with phases 1 and 2 on the Micheldever Wood barrow (Fasham and Ross 1978).

The ratio of tertiary:secondary flakes is much higher than at any phase in the Micheldever Wood industry, as might be expected among a poorly-developed or degenerate flint industry. This result would seem to continue the trend of the decline in production of non-cortical flakes documented from the Middle Neolithic, 52% at Windmill Hill, to the Middle Bronze Age, 20% in phase 4 of the Micheldever Wood barrow, by Fasham and Ross (1978 Table 9), the figure for Winnall Down Phase 3 being 14%.

The metrical analyses indicate that a longer and a broader flake size is present on Winnall Down than on Late Neolithic and Early Bronze Age sites such as Durrington Walls (Wainwright and Longworth 1971), Micheldever Wood barrow phase 4 (Fasham and Ross 1978) and Oakley Down (White and Reed 1970). On none of these sites does the 41–50mm long group reach more than 18%, while here the figure is 26.2%. The breadth measurements are more in line with those recorded from the above sites, especially Durrington Walls, but all have a slightly greater percentage below the 30mm-wide class.

The breadth:length ratios show a different pattern to those from the above sites. There is no one class dominating the flakes. The largest class is 2.5–3.5 with 24.3%, but higher-ratio classes do not fall below 15%. Of the above sites only the Micheldever Wood barrow in phase 4 has a high percentage (20%) in the class 2.5–3.5, but has a clearer preference for the 3.5–4.5 class. But the difference is perhaps not that significant, considering the small numbers of flakes analysed from Winnall Down, and it is likely that these two industries are comparable in this respect.

Half the flakes on the Micheldever Wood barrow had angles of 115–120° between the striking platform and the bulbar plane. On Winnall Down the angle was generally more obtuse, with over 50% of the flakes having angles between 121° and 130°.

The Winnall Down assemblage suggests that flint working was a crude industry in the Early Iron Age. Comparisons indicate that this industry could be seen to continue the trend of deteriorating flint working from the Late Neolithic to the Early Bronze Age, but a lack of comparative data from other sites of the Early Iron Age, and further Bronze Age sites, makes any broad conclusions tentative.

The following flints from Phase 3 are illustrated (Fig 68):

1. End scraper. Ditch 5 segment CC, layer 4568.
2. Scraper/borer? Ditch 5 segment CC, layer 4585.
3. Unfinished scraper. Ditch 5 segment CC, layer 4586.
4. Flake retouched for borer or point. Ditch 5, segment DD, layer 8028.
5. Axe. Residual in Phase 3 entrance post-hole 28.

Daub and burnt or baked clay
by P J Bates and R P Winham

Three hundred and twenty-two kilograms of daub or burnt or baked clay, excluding loomweights, were kept from the excavation. The loomweights are discussed below (p 90). The material came from 150 separate contexts, with quantities ranging from 1g to 109.8kg in a single context. The material from each context was examined and separated into fabrics; each fabric group was weighed; impressions noted and any significant dimensions were recorded (details in archive). Twelve different fabrics were identified on the basis of a visual examination, but only fabrics 1, 2, 6, 8, and 9 produced significant quantities of material, and the others may be variations of these. A breakdown of the material by phase and fabric is given in Table 16, and the material is dealt with, below, by phase.

The fabric distinctions are not as clear as with pottery; there is a range of firing or burning, from slightly burnt to severely burnt, with a range of different inclusions.

Fabric Descriptions

Fabric 1. Mixture of clay and ground-up chalk in varying proportions, but generally with clay predominating. Frequent chalk lumps and flints of up to 25mm diameter. Varies from very friable to hard. Very common, most of the 'daub' with wattle impressions is of this fabric.

Fabric 2. Clay, apparently with no or very little chalk, occasional small flints up to 5mm. Usually fired hard (sometimes washable), but may be over-fired/burnt and therefore friable. Very common, most 'baked clay objects' are of this fabric. Many indeterminate fragments.

Fabric 3. Clay with no or very little ground chalk but with fairly numerous chalk lumps and small flints of up to 5mm. Fired as fabric 2. Rare.

Fabric 4. Mixture of clay and a little ground chalk. Very few chalk or flint inclusions. Fired hard. Rare.

Fabric 5. Mixture of clay and a little ground chalk (as fabric 4) with numerous very small flint fragments up to 2–3mm. Fired hard. Rare.

Fabric 6. Clay containing small chalk lumps, small flints and often charcoal fragments. Generally, only lightly-fired and fairly friable. Fairly common. Often has smooth but irregular surface, suggesting waste material.

Fabric 7. Clay, possibly a little ground chalk, few small flints. Lightly fired. Rare; may be variation of fabric 2.

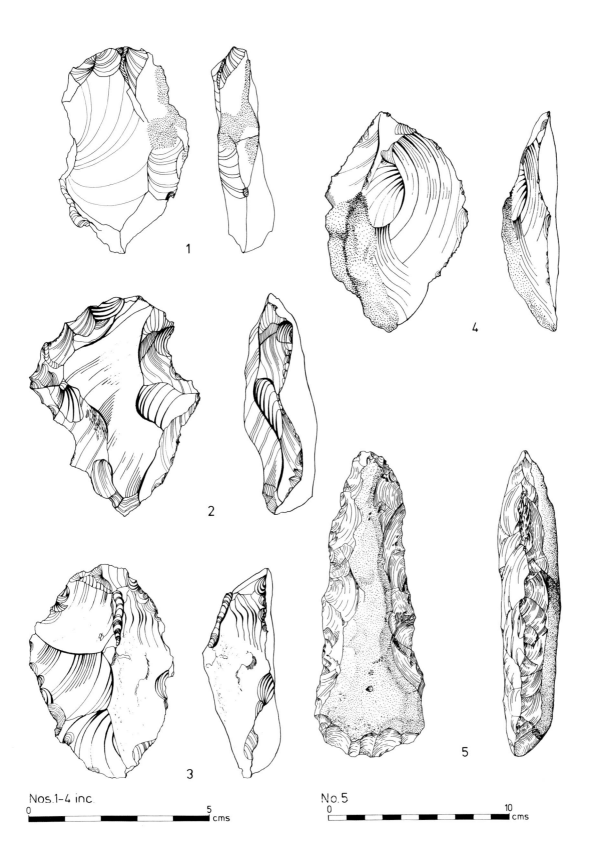

Fig 68.   Winnall Down: flint 1–4, scale 1:1; 5, scale 1:2.

Table 16. Daub and burnt/baked clay. x = % too small to calculate.

	FABRIC	1	2	3	4	5	6	Not Phased	Total Fabric Weight	% of all Daub and baked/ burnt clay
Wt in gms	1	27	948	29913	199417	3505	6592	3937	224339	
% of phase		87.0	95.4	90.7	80.2	14.4	78.8	69.1		75.8
Wt in gms	2	4	1	901	30901	952	1942	1432	36133	
% of phase		13.0	0.1	2.7	12.4	3.6	19.8	25.1		11.2
Wt in gms	3	–	–	25	–	–	–	50	75	
% of phase		–	–	0.07	–	–	–	0.9		.02
Wt in gms	4	–	–	46	34	41	18	22	161	
% of phase		–	–	0.14	0.01	0.2	0.2	0.4		.05
Wt in gms	5	–	–	35	12	–	–	–	47	
% of phase		–	–	0.1	x	–	–	–		.01
Wt in gms	6	–	5	–	13365	18942	27	–	32339	
% of phase		–	0.5	–	5.4	77.7	0.3	–		10.0
Wt in gms	7	–	–	–	7	72	7	–	86	
% of phase		–	–	–	x	0.3	0.1	–		0.3
Wt in gms	8	–	–	2060	1399	–	–	–	3459	
% of phase		–	–	6.2	0.56	–	–	–		1.0
Wt in gms	9	–	30	–	2428	–	7	257	2722	
% of phase		–	3.0	–	1.0	–	0.1	4.5		0.8
Wt in gms	10	–	10	–	–	35	–	–	45	
% of phase		–	1.0	–	–	0.15	–	–		.01
Wt in gms	11	–	–	–	17	–	–	–	17	
% of phase		–	–	–	x	–	–	–		.005
Wt in gms	12	–	–	–	–	–	52	–	52	
% of phase		–	–	–	–	–	0.6	–		.01
Wt in gms	-?-	–	–	–	1608	912	–	–	2520	
% of phase		–	–	–	1.0	3.8	–	–		.8
TOTAL		31	994	32980	249188	24459	8645	5698	321995	
% OF GRAND TOTAL		x	0.3	10.3	77.4	7.6	2.6	1.8		

Fabric 8. Mixture of clay and ground-up chalk, the latter predominating. Numerous chalk lumps and flints of up to 30mm (occasionally larger). Friable. Rare – ?cob.

Fabric 9. Clay usually mixed with some ground up chalk, and containing fairly numerous small flints and chalk lumps of up to 5mm. Fired fairly hard. Fairly common.

Fabric 10. Clay and chalk mixture with numerous small flint and chalk inclusions. Fired hard, almost pottery. Rare – probable variation of fabric 9.

Fabric 11. Clay and chalk mixture with high proportion of chalk. Few small chalk lumps of 2–3mm. 'Powdery' and friable. Rare – probable variation of fabric 8.

Fabric 12. Clay mixed with very finely ground chalk, very few small chalk lumps and flints. Fired fairly hard. Rare – probable variation of fabric 1.

Considered by Phase

Phases 1 and 2. The quantities involved are too small to analyse, except to note presence, and the comparatively large deposit of 948g of fabric 1 in the Late Bronze Age pit, 6686.

Phase 3. Generally, the material was fabric 1, but 887g out of 901g (98.4%) of fabric 2 occurred in the enclosure ditch 5 and there was a large deposit of fabric 8 material in pit 3670. Pits 2431 and 2630 in the north-central area of the site accounted for 95.3% of all

fabric 1 in this phase – suggesting a nearby structure or related activity, as the daub from 2431 was up to 125mm thick.

Phase 4. The majority of the material (77%) was from this phase and 81% of this material was from four pits: 4475 (44,277g), 5548 (20,139g), 6595 (109,897g) and 9344 (27,715g). Only from pits 4475 and 6595 was the daub substantially thick (over 40mm).In addition, pit 2416 produced daub 65–85mm thick.

Pits 4475 and 5548 were in the south-east corner of the site. They contained mainly fabric 1, but with a substantial quantity of fabric 6 (10,255g) in 4475. Pit 9344 was further to the south-east and contained largely fabric 2 (26,924g). Pit 6595 was to the south-west, near hut circle 4022, and contained only fabric 1. Pit 2416, within hut circle 1821, was in the north-central part of the site, and again contained only fabric 1.

The remaining material was distributed both in relation to the hut circles to the north and west and the pit complex to the south-east. Charcoal, identified as oak, was found *in situ* on some daub (fabric 8) from pit 7399.

Phase 5. The deposits in pit 5597 accounted for 81.1% of the material in this phase, and that from pit 9317 a further 14.3%. The former was central to the south-east quadrant of the site (within 5) and the deposit was mostly fabric 6. The latter was in the south-east and contained largely fabric 1, with some of fabrics 2 and 6.

Two pieces from pit 4475 were examined by J Bayley who reported that they were mainly acid soluble with very inhomogeneous textures. A piece of oak charcoal was attached to one of the samples.

Phase 6. The largest deposits in this phase came from pit 5676, (3686g), and pit 2846 (1758g), both containing both fabrics 1 and 2. Much of this material was fragmentary – but some daub had a smoothed outer surface and a wattle-impressed inner surface (Fig 67.1), and there were examples of finger-impressed daub (Fig 67.2 and 3).

Among the 'baked clay' objects were a number of fragments from pit 5548, weighing a total 13,105g, which were clearly from a very large structure – perhaps an oven. Nowhere can a total thickness be determined, but the maximum surviving thickness was 120mm.

Pit 4475, close to 5528, produced a quantity of decorated daub, with a ribbed and dot design running in the same direction as wattle impressions – and therefore presumably from a dwelling – although this might also be produced if the clay lined a basket, and there are fragments which curve substantially (Fig 69.4).

The following pieces are illustrated (Fig 69):

1. Daub with wattle impression and smoothed external surface. Fabric 1, 233g. Phase 4 pit 9344.

2. Daub/burnt clay with two smoothed surfaces and rounded edge. Finger impressions. Fabric 2, 725g. Phase 4 pit 9344.

3. Daub with one flat surface and impressions of four fingers of one hand. Fabric 1, 1797g. Phase 4 pit 3901.

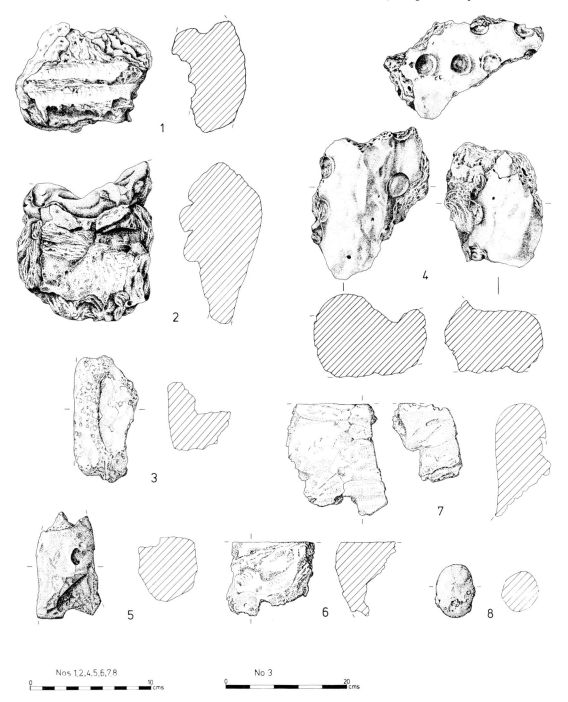

Fig 69. Winnall Down: daub and burnt/baked clay 1, 2, 4, 5, 6, 7 and 8, scale 1:3, 3, scale 1:6.

4. Series of daub fragments with corrugated surface and decorated with lines of dots impressed by end of stick. Decoration runs in same alignment as wattle impressions. Fabric 1, 4140g. Phase 4 pit 4475.

5. Baked clay object with flat and coned external surfaces, possibly a weight of some form. Fabric 2, 163g. Phase 6 scoop 9321.

6. Baked clay fragment with flat surface and curving edge. Burnt very severely, possibly a hearth surround or oven lining. Fabric 2, 172g. Phase 4 pit 5601.

7. Baked clay fragments with smoothed surfaces and curved edge. Function similar to No 6 above. Fabric 2, 300g. Phase 6 scoop 9317.

8. Egg-shaped baked clay object, possibly a sling missile (Wainwright 1979, Fig 76). Fabric 2, 40g. Phase 4 pit 8594.

Brick and Tile by R P Winham

Some brick and tile fragments were found in Phase 3 and 4 contexts but in all cases in upper, or potentially disturbed, layers. Thus, it is assumed that all brick and tile is of ultimate Iron Age or Roman origin (except for one glazed tile fragment of post-medieval origin).

There were no complete bricks or tiles among the 24,492g that were collected. Most were unidentifiable fragments, but some roofing tiles were present. Decorated or comb-impressed tiles came from the upper fill of the Phase 4 pit 684 which had been disturbed during, or was still partially open in, Phase 6, and from the Phase 6 scoop 1764 and the Phase 6 ditch 9136 segment A. A variety of fabrics were noted but not analysed.

Loomweights by P J Bates and R P Winham (Fig 70)

Chalk

Five fragments from four chalk loomweights were recovered. Three were cylinder-like lumps of chalk with a single perforation and came from the Phase 3 scoop 9553 and the Phase 4 pit 6595 (two examples). Two fragments from a probable triangular loomweight were in the unphased scoop 5879. The Phase 3 example was of lower chalk.

1. Complete smoothed chalk loomweight with single perforation at top. Phase 4 pit 6595.

Clay

The 137 finds of loomweight represented 83 separate examples. They were analysed by fabric, using the fabric divisions for the daub and baked clay objects.

Cylindrical. Two fragments of different cylindrical loomweights were found in the Phase 2 post-hole 6466. Both were of fabric 9.

2. Slightly irregular cylinder; 100mm high, 110mm diameter, central perforation 18–30mm. Weight 1,693g. Heavily burnt on one side. Phase 2 post-hole 6466.

Triangular. Six types of triangular loomweight were defined by a combination of fabric, thickness, and number and angle of perforations.

3. Type A. Crudely-shaped with very rounded corners and curved sides. Sometimes not of constant thickness. Three perforations, no evidence of wear. Fabric 8. Twenty-six fragments from a minimum of eleven loomweights. The illustrated example has an additional perforation through its apex. Estimated total weight c 200g. Phase 3 pit 2676.

4. Type B. None of this type was complete. It appears regular and well-finished with probably only two perforations. Deep grooves around at least one corner. Fabric 2. Fourteen fragments from a minimum of ten loomweights. Estimated total weight of illustrated example c 1,700g. Phase 4 pit 7399.

5. Type C. More coarsely fashioned than Type B. Thicker with three, and larger, perforations. No grooves. Fabric 2. Four fragments from four loomweights. Estimated total weight of illustrated example c 1,950g. Phase 4 pit 3901.

6. Type D. Regular and well finished, three perforations and no grooves. Fabric 1. Twenty-one fragments from nineteen loomweights. Estimated total weight of illustrated example c 2,885g. Phase 3 pit 2630.

7. Type E. Generally well finished with rounded corners. Three perforations, groove worn round at least one corner. Fabric 9. Thirty-nine fragments from a minimum of twelve loomweights. Estimated total weight of illustrated example c 1,850g. Phase 3 pit 2431.

8. Type F. Larger and thinner variant of Type B with three holes and groove round one corner. Fabric 2. One example has two parallel holes across one corner (not illustrated). Ten fragments from a minimum of eight loomweights. Estimated total weight of illustrated example c 1,650g. Phase 4 pit 3738.

One fragment of a triangular loomweight was found in a Phase 2 context, post-hole 6490. The 119 fragments, representing 66 loomweights, from Phases 3 and 4 are shown distributed by type in Fig 71, which also shows the weight of seventeen more or less complete examples from all phases. Eight small fragments came from Phases 5 and 6 and three from unphased contexts. All were probably residual.

Cylindrical loomweights were in use in Winnall Down in the Late Bronze Age and associated with one triangular weight. There were no typically Late Bronze Age pyramidical weights as found, for example, at Eldon's Seat (Cunliffe and Phillipson 1968); the lack of continuity between Phases 2 and 3 may account for this. In Phase 3, triangular loomweights of types A, D and E were used almost exclusively. Of the six records of types B, C and F only one type F was securely stratified at the bottom of a feature, the remaining five coming from the upper fill of Phase 3 features and therefore not necessarily belonging to Phase 3.

Types B, C and F might, therefore, be seen as Middle Iron Age types while Types D and E in Phase 4 contexts could be residual although, in two cases, there were large fragments of Type D loomweights (pits 1631 and 4475).

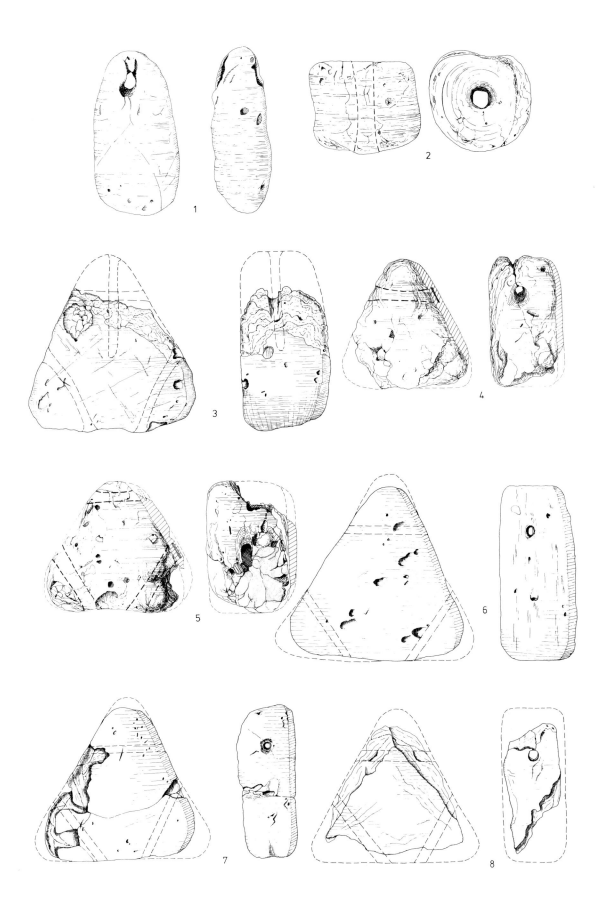

Fig 70. Winnall Down: loomweights, scale 1:4.

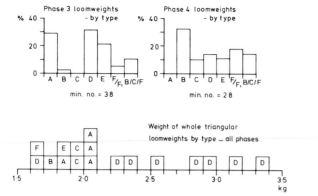

Fig 71. Winnall Down: loomweights – types by phase.

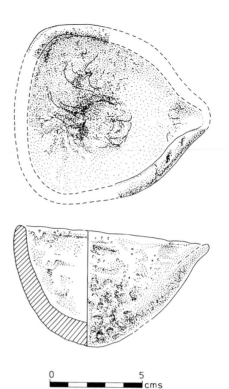

Fig 72. Winnall Down: crucible, scale 1:2.

The concentrations of nine Type A weights in Phase 3 pit 2676 and of six Type D weights in Phase 3 pit 2630 probably represent dumps from single looms. The thickness, length of side and weight of five of the latter group were measurable. Thickness ranged from 70–110mm, weight from 1,650–3,325g and length of side was constant at about 190mm. Otherwise, there were insufficient complete examples but the overall variations recorded were: thickness, minimum 40mm (Type A) maximum 114mm (Type A); length of side, minimum 150mm (Type B) maximum 210mm (Types A and D); estimated total weight, minimum 1,650g (Types D and F) maximum 3,325g (Type D); diameter of perforations, minimum 5mm (Type F) maximum 15mm (Types C and D). There were in addition three fragments of uncertain form.

Some patterning was discernible with different types of triangular loomweights being used in different phases, which might reflect technological developments. There was no rigid standardization of clay loomweights, nor indeed of chalk versions, but their function probably demanded a variety of size and weight, as much as variations in these two fields were not purely related to the local maker.

Metal Working Debris (based on reports and data from J Bayley)

The few artifacts associated with metal-working and other possibly associated items are listed in Table 17. The chalk mould from Phase 4 is described above.

Crucibles (Fig 72)

Fragments of a crucible, reconstructed in drawing. Reconstructable parts include a rounded base and two rim sections including a pouring lip to form a triangular crucible, as at Gussage All Saints (Sprat-

ling 1979, Fig 99). The crucible is extremely vitrified but to a varying extent, one side being far more deeply affected than the other. There are two corroded blobs of metal in the vitrified surface, a small one just below the rim inside and a larger one on the outside near the bottom. The larger blob was analysed with the Milliprobe (XRF spectrometer); only copper and tin were detected, suggesting the metal melted in the crucible was bronze. Phase 3 pit 1053.

There are two other crucible fragments; a small fragment from the Phase 6 ditch 660 and a larger piece from Phase 6 deposits in enclosure ditch 5. The latter shows signs of heating in both inner and outer surfaces – the outer surface having a thin vesicular layer with traces of fuel ash 'glazing', while the inner surface appears a purplish-red colour. This is often seen in crucibles that have been heated fairly strongly. It is 18mm thick and there is no evidence to suggest what was heated in it. No bronze scrap was discovered during the excavation.

Over-fired clay

The eight pieces of over-fired clay had all been subjected to unusually high temperatures. They may have been associated with metal-working, but equally with any other process which involved high temperatures. One piece from the Phase 4 pit 4475 has a funnel-shaped channel in an irregular surface. It is unlikely to be a reservoir for a casting mould, or even part of a mould, as it is too irregular. It was probably part of a larger baked clay structure.

Table 17. Metal-working debris and occurences of iron-bearing stone.

| | Phase | | | | | | | |
	2	3	4	5	6	7	Not Phased	Total
Crucible	–	1	–	–	2	–	–	3
Moulds	–	–	1	–	–	–	–	1
Hearth slag	–	–	1	–	2	–	–	3
Slag	–	3	4	–	2	–	1	10
Forged bloomery iron	–	–	1	–	–	–	–	1
Overfired clay	–	–	5	1	1	–	1	8
Marcasite	1	16	7	–	11	–	17	52
Natural Ironstone	–	3	4	–	4	–	–	11
Total	1	23	23	1	22	–	19	89

Slag

There are three pieces of slag from the bottom of bowl hearths and ten other finds of slag.

Bloomery Iron by Professor R F Tylecote

One iron lump is an irregular, rusty and magnetic piece weighing 180g. A section was cut which revealed slag stringers seen end-on. These were associated with groups of carbides. The background was ferrite of very large, green size and had a hardness of 71–76 HUI. There were no Neumann lamellae and no nitride needles. It is a very pure piece of iron and must have less than 0.01%P. It is a typical piece of forged bloomery iron made from one of a very low phosphorous content. Phase 4 pit 7257.

Marcasite and natural ironstone formations

The 63 pieces of ferruginous stone have been tabulated to indicate the general chronological spread of their presence on the site.
Metalworking did occur at Winnall Down in Phases 3, 4 and 6 but it was on a small scale and presumably for domestic consumption.

Glass

Twenty-two fragments of glass were recorded from deposits other than topsoil: one intrusive piece in Phase 3 quarry pit 8101; one in the shallow Phase 4 pit 4460; thirteen in Phase 6 contexts; and seven

were in unphased deposits. There were no distinguishing features to any of the small fragments. Those from Phase 6 could be Roman but equally could be intrusive, as the pieces from Phases 3 and 4 (J Bayley pers com).

Antler and Bone Objects by R P Winham identifications by J P Coy and J M Maltby

Red deer antler (Figs 73 and 74)

1. Part of a shed antler with main shaft and two tines sawn off; pieced together from ten burnt fragments. A drilled hole, 19mm diameter, occurs at the intersections. When viewed with the main shaft to the left and brow tine to the right, the uppermost surface survives only in fragments and puncture marks and two circular depressions occur just below the uppermost tine. Where the depressions, both 12mm diameter and 6mm deep, occur, the surface has been smoothed. Although a fragment is missing, this surface of the brow tine does not appear to have been worked. On the opposite side, several punctures and cut marks appear around the drilled hole with a few puncture marks on the main shaft.

There are no signs on the fragments remaining that the main shaft was smoothed off. The brow tine has had the surface smoothed, and just beyond two small drilled holes, 2mm across and 3–5mm deep, occurs a depression shaped like a stylised figure with head and arms as stumps, formed by a four-pointed star-shaped depression (2mm deep and 13 x 13mm maximum dimensions). One of the star 'points' merges into a circular depression through a channel 4mm wide, 2mm deep. In this analogy, the circular depression is the body. It is 12mm diameter and 4mm deep (similar to those on the other side of the antler). Beyond this depression is an irregular puncture, 3mm in diameter by 2mm deep, and a few more puncture marks.

Two of the fragments, forming one of the depressions on the main shaft, are burnt on the inside, indicating the object was broken before or during the process of burning. Phase 3 pit 7330.

2. Antler sawn off at base and part way along the main shaft and brow tine. A drilled hole, *c* 15mm diameter, occurs at the intersections, with an irregular section on one side where the

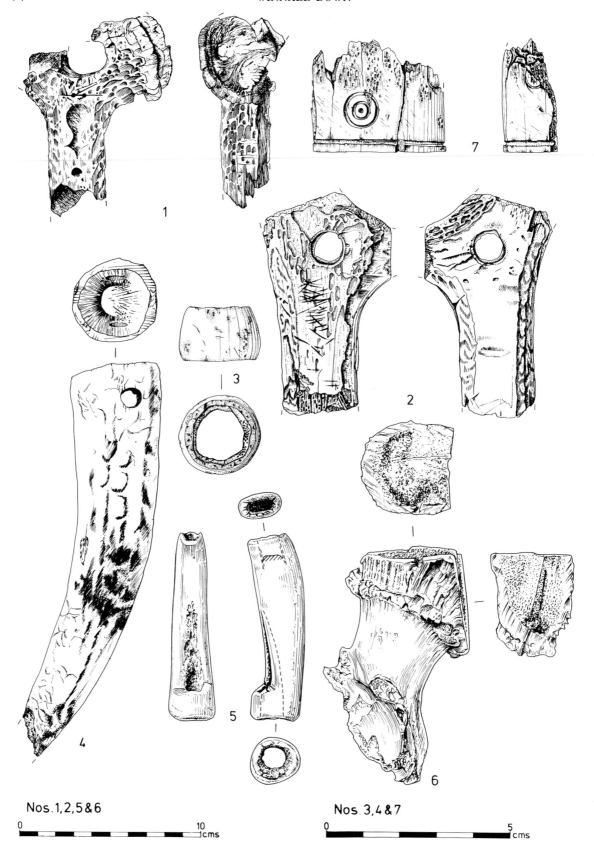

Nos. 1, 2, 5 & 6

0   10
|_____| cms

Nos. 3, 4 & 7

0   5
|_____| cms

Fig 73.   Winnall Down: antler 1, 2, 5 and 6, scale 1:2; 3, 4 and 7, scale 1:1.

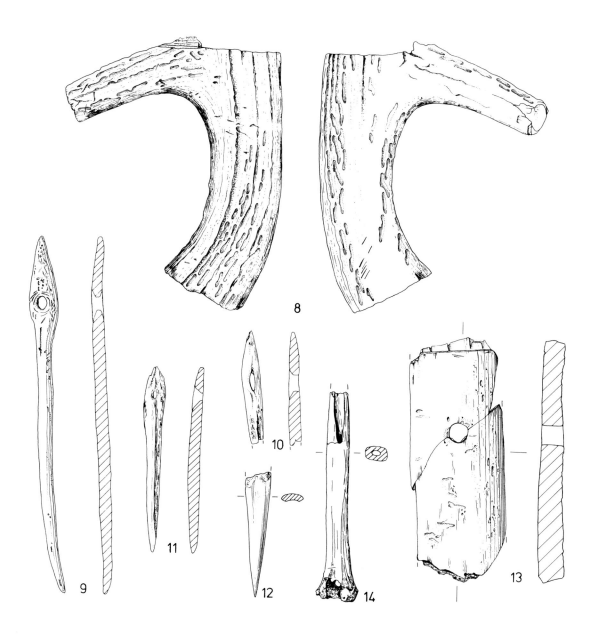

Fig 74. Winnall Down: antler and worked bone 8 and 14, scale 1:2; 9–13, scale 1:1.

antler has been whittled flat. On the opposite side, many cut and scratch marks are visible, and there are indications of further whittling near the sawn end of the main shaft. The piece possibly served as a work surface which would not blunt tools, although other functions have been postulated, such as a handle or hammer. Phase 5, pit 5401.

3. Ring made from section of tine, sawn off at both ends and smoothed all over. Worked on the inside but not smoothed by wear. Phase 3 post-hole 527.

4. Tip of tine, sawn off and perforated right through. On one side, around the drilled hole, the surface has been smoothed off, perhaps to make drilling easier. The tip shows a modern break. Perhaps a pendant, although similar items are used in Kenya as containers for substances like snuff (S Wandibba pers com). The smoothing on the tip may have been done by the deer itself. Phase 3 pit 7330.

5. Much-eroded antler tine, sawn both ends and cut and hollowed. Possibly a handle. Phase 3 pit 1053.

6. Sawn off antler base. Phase 6 ditch 660.

Table 18. Objects of worked antler and bone by phase.

| | Phase | | | | | | |
	2	3	4	5	6	7	Unphased
Antler							
Sawn	–	1	2	1	1	–	–
Decorated	–	1	–	–	–	–	–
Ring	–	1	–	–	–	–	–
Pendant	–	1	–	–	–	–	–
Comb	–	–	1	–	–	–	–
Bone							
Sawn, polished etc	–	1	7	–	1	1	1
Comb	–	–	1	–	–	–	–
Point	–	1	–	–	–	–	–
Gouge	–	1	–	–	–	–	–
Needles	–	–	2	1	–	–	–

7. Sawn off main shaft fragment, badly eroded, probably originally circular. The central core of the antler remains. The surface has been removed and worked all over and has incised decoration in the form of a line 1mm wide running around the shaft and a 'dot with two concentric circles' design; one whole, one partial, remaining. Almost certainly the end of the handle of a 'weaving comb' (Hodder and Hedges 1977, 17–28). An exact parallel for the common dot and circle motif comes from Gussage All Saints (Wainwright 1979, 118, Fig 92.5000). Phase 4 pit 1095.

8. The upper main shaft with a piece of a middle tine, sawn off at the ends. No other signs of working. Phase 4 pit 9109.

Bone (Fig 74)

9. Needle from wall fragment of a long bone of a large mammal. Shows extensive working, and has been polished all over. Length 103mm. The drilled hole occurs 17mm from blunt end, where the width is 7mm. Phase 4 pit 328.

10. Needle, from a long bone (species unknown), that has cavity running down the centre, punctured by a hole which may be natural. It has been polished and presumably used as a needle until broken, although needles are not usually made from such a bone. Length 49mm, perforation 9 x 3mm. Phase 4 pit 5414.

11. Needle, from wall fragment of long bone of large mammal, perhaps cattle canon bone. Length 50mm. The drilled hole occurs 6mm from blunt end, where the width is 5mm. Phase 5 pit 5597.

12. Tip of point or pin. Phase 3 pit 10109. Length 65mm.

13. A fragment of a large mammal rib with a drilled hole in the middle and incised lines, one across the rib and others indicating the 'teeth', suggesting a comb made from the whole rib. Phase 4 pit 5414.

14. Gouge, of sheep or goat tibia in two fragments. One end is shaved down, exposing the central cavity. There is a hole through the other end. The surface is shaved and polished. See Wheeler (1943, 303–306) for discussion of similar gouges and Crowfoot (1945, 157–158) for the suggestion that these are beaters for weaving. Length 112mm. Phase 3 pit 2431.

Cow tibia with smoothed surface, broken at one end and with punch marks, from Phase 4 pit 9668; and a cow radius with punch marks on both sides, from Phase 4 pit 5548 (neither piece illustrated).

There were nine bone fragments which had been polished, drilled, sawn or cut. They are not illustrated, but are described below:

Sawn horse metapodial from Phase 3 pit 4156.

Sheep metatarsus split lengthwise and polished, with two drilled holes, 3mm diameter, set opposite each other at one end, from Phase 4 pit 7399.

Long bone fragment from large mammal, burnt and polished. Phase 4 pit 1473.

Fragment of small mammal, burnt and polished, from Phase 4 pit 4475.

Sheep metatarsus, polished, with hole, 4mm diameter, cut through near one end, and the other end sawn or broken off and smoothed. Possibly also drilled through top. Phase 4 pit 2553.

Split cow metatarsus, with 4mm diameter hole drilled near one end, expanding the natural hole. Phase 4 layer 3810 in enclosure ditch 5.

Horse scapula with possible bored hole, from Phase 6 ditch 1300.

Broken off cow metacarpus (adult) with hole drilled through. Phase 7 ditch 1378.

Horse metatarsus, proximal end, cut, grooved and broken. Unphased, pit 7676.

All but six of the worked pieces of antler and bone are from Phases 3 and 4 (Table 18). There is a limited range of finished objects and only a restricted amount as working debitage. There are more finished and personalized objects in Phase 3 than in Phase 4. Bone working appears to be restricted to Phases 3 and 4 and its distribution indicates that it occurred in the south-east quadrant of the site.

Chapter 4
The Environmental Evidence

The Animal Bones by J M Maltby

Phase 2. Bronze Age

Only 21 fragments belonging to this phase were examined and just five were identifiable (one cattle fragment, four sheep/goat fragments). The remaining material consisted of seven unidentified large mammal fragments, a fragment from a sheep-sized mammal and eight fragments from unidentified mammals.

Phase 3. Early Iron Age

Animal bones were recovered from all 31 sections of enclosure ditch 5, 21 of the pits, 111 small pits and scoops in the quarry to the north of the enclosure, ten postholes, 21 other scoops and a hearth. Excluding articulated partial skeletons of cattle and sheep, 3,308 fragments were examined including 204 bones of small mammals and amphibians. The majority of the bone was found in the pits, ditch and quarry. Cattle and sheep/goat fragments were dominant in all context types, although bones identified specifically as goat were rare. Pig and horse were the only other species represented in any numbers (Table 19).

The Enclosure Ditch 5

The density of bone recovered from the ditch sections was low. Including the partial skeletons of cattle, the density of fragments ranged from 1.56 fragments/m^3 (5II) to 33.57 fragments/m^3 (5D). Overall, 10.56 fragments/m^3 were recovered from all sections of the ditch. The densest concentrations were located mainly in sections to the west and north-west of the ditch's circuit (Fig 84) reflecting, in particular, the distribution of cattle bones, although the same trend was found in the fragment densities of the other domestic species on a smaller scale. Cattle, horse and unidentified large mammal fragments were all relatively better represented in the ditch than in most of the pits, where sheep/goat, pig and unidentified sheep-sized mammal fragments formed a much greater proportion of the assemblages. Four sections of the ditch contained articulated bones of cattle: 5AA, 5F, 5MM and 5N. In addition, cattle vertebrae and unidentified large mammal vertebrae were well represented in the ditch in general. Considering the relatively high proportion of eroded fragments (42.7%), the proportion of

cattle longbones with surviving articulations was high (68.4% of the scapulae, humeri, radii, femora, tibiae and metapodia fragments). Poor preservation did, however, have a much more serious effect on the sheep/goat sample. Only 16.1% of the longbone fragments had any surviving articulations and the sample was dominated by fragments with good survival qualities, particularly loose teeth. The horse sample was similar in many respects to that of cattle and contained a relatively high proportion of complete limb bones (although sometimes displaying butchery marks). The small pig sample was dominated by loose teeth and mandible fragments, whereas most bones of the axial skeleton were poorly preserved. Dog was represented by only six fragments. A red deer antler fragment was found inn 5HH.

The Pits

In general, the density of bones in pits was higher than in the ditch, although three small pits (262, 5934, 7924) contained no bone at all. In the others, the total fragment density ranged from 3.97 fragments/m^3 (8483) to 596.49 fragments/m^3 in the very small pit 1053, which is probably atypical. However, nine other pits had bone densities of over 60 fragments/m^3 (Fig 84). Overall, including two partial sheep skeletons but excluding bones of rodents and amphibians, 54.21 fragments/m^3 were recovered from the 26 pits. The evidence for patterned variation in the densities of bones in these pits is flimsy. The cluster of four pits to the north of the enclosure contained high densities of bone, whereas pits with dense concentrations of fragments were found less frequently elsewhere. Sheep/goat fragments were found in greater numbers than cattle in all pits except 2411, 3111 and 8485. Sheep-sized fragments were also found more commonly than large mammal fragments (Table 19).

Two pits (2431, 3111) contained unusual faunal assemblages which merit special mention. Pit 2431 contained a very high proportion of sheep/goat fragments (137) in relation to cattle (6), and a high proportion of unidentified sheep-sized fragments (116) in comparison to those of large mammal (18). A large number of the sheep/goat and sheep-sized

Table 19. The distribution of animal bone fragments from types of Early Iron Age features.

	Ditch	Pits	Quarry	Postholes	Scoops	Total
Cattle	297	142	245	3	12	699
Horse	51	50	60	–	4	165
Sheep/Goat*	105	314	148	6	16	589
Pig	31	61	28	1	2	123
Dog	6	2	15	1	–	24
Red Deer (*Cervus elaphus*)	1	3	1	–	–	5
Large mammal	212	134	286	7	22	661
Large artiodactyl	11	6	4	1	–	22
Sheep-sized mammal	67	386	202	16	17	688
Unidentified mammal	23	38	51	6	4	122
Short-tailed Vole (*Microtus agrestis*)	1	20	–	–	–	21
Water Vole (*Arvicola terrestris*)	–	1	–	–	–	1
Small mammal	1	7	–	–	–	8
Dom.duck/mallard (*Anas platyrhynchos*)	3	–	–	–	–	3
Thrush sp	–	–	1	–	–	1
Lark sp	–	–	1	–	–	1
Unidentified bird	–	–	1	–	–	1
Frog (*Rana* sp)	–	7	–	–	–	7
Toad (*Bufo* sp)	–	96	–	9	–	105
Unid. amphibian	–	62	–	–	–	62

* 105 fragments identified as sheep, three identified as goat. The table excludes bones from articulated partial skeletons.

bones belonged to very young animals, their bones being porous, fragile and small. A minimum of five individuals was represented and tooth-eruption evidence indicates that they had lived at most only for a few days. The bones in this pit were exceptionally well preserved. Only 13.4% of the 298 fragments were eroded and 76.7% of the sheep/goat longbones had surviving articulations.

The bones in pit 3111 were also well preserved. Only 22.2% of the 171 fragments were eroded and an extremely high proportion of cattle longbones had articulations surviving (95.4%). The pit contained a remarkable concentration of cattle (52 fragments) and horse (22 fragments). The cattle sample contained a high proportion of complete, or almost complete, vertebrae and longbones. On the other hand, no phalanges, tarsals or carpals were found. Butchery marks were observed on eleven cattle bones and these indicated that the carcases had been disarticulated and stripped of meat before disposal. A similar pattern was discovered in the horse assemblage. In contrast, no limb bones of sheep/goat were found. All 24 sheep fragments belonged to the skull, mandibles and their teeth. The 14 fragments identified as pig included nine porous bones, which

may have belonged to the same individual. The other pig fragments consisted of skull or mandible fragments.

The animal bones were generally less well preserved in the other pits (32.9% were eroded), but the survival of the bone was still significantly better than in other context types. In addition to the fragments listed in Table 19, two partial, articulated skeletons of sheep were found in 2558. The first of these consisted of the limb bones of both back legs of an immature animal; the second was represented by lumbar vertebrae, os coxae, a tibia and an astragalus of a lamb that had lived for no more than a few weeks. In the pits in general, good preservation allowed for a much more evenly-distributed representation of sheep/goat elements, and fragile elements such as the ulna, scapula and femur were better represented in these than in other deposits. The cattle sample, apart from pit 3111, contained relatively fewer vertebrae, tarsals and phalanges than in the ditch. The pig assemblage, although better preserved in the pits, again consisted predominantly of skull and mandible fragments and loose teeth. Several of the pits produced substantial numbers of amphibian bones and a few rodent bones (Table 19).

The Quarry Areas
A total of 1,043 fragments was recovered (Table 19) but most were in a poor state of preservation. Cattle fragments outnumbered those of sheep/goat but the poor preservation conditions had a serious effect upon all the principle species. Loose teeth were found in abundance, 57.6% of the fragments were eroded, and the percentage of longbones with surviving articulations was low both for cattle (52.2%) and particularly for sheep/goat (17.1%). Fifteen fragments of dog were identified and the species was thus slightly better represented than in other deposit types. The various categories of unidentified material formed a comparatively high proportion of the total sample.

Post-holes and Scoops
Only a few fragments were recovered from post-holes. Little can be said about them other than that sheep/goat and sheep-sized fragments were better represented than cattle and large mammal fragments. The material from the scoops came from a variety of small features scattered throughout the settlement. The bones were poorly preserved and the proportion of the unidentified material in the small total sample was high.

Intra-Site Variability
Intra-site analysis demonstrated that species representation depended largely upon the type of context excavated. The overall percentage of the principal stock animal fragments varied, as shown in Table 20. Bones of cattle and horse were better represented in ditch 5, the quarry pits and pit 3111 than elsewhere. This is a good example of how much intra-site variability can affect the overall representation of a species in a faunal sample. The overall fragment percentages for Phase 3 deposits were dependent simply upon the amount excavated from the differ-

ent types of context. Had all the ditch been excavated, for example, and the densities and types of bone from the excavated sections been typical of the rest of the ditch, the estimated overall percentage figures would be changed to 53.1% cattle, 10.5% horse, 29.4% sheep/goat and 7.1% pig, representing a 8.7% increase in cattle and a 8.0% reduction in the number of sheep/goat fragments. Similar estimations could be made with other feature types, but the exercise is purely academic without an understanding of the derivation of the types of bone elements recovered in the different deposits.

It can be argued that a combination of differential preservation, butchery, and disposal practices produced most of the observed faunal variability. Detailed study of the bones demonstrated how much differential preservation can affect the nature of a bone sample. Estimations of the percentage of eroded bones and the proportion of cattle and sheep/goat limb bones with surviving articulations showed that bones in the pits were preserved best of all, followed by those from the ditch, quarry, post-holes and scoops. Preservation conditions had a direct bearing upon the composition of the assemblages of the different species. The percentages of loose teeth of cattle and sheep/goat increased in deposits with poorly preserved bone (Fig 75). It appears, however, that preservation conditions affected cattle and horse bones less than those of sheep/goat. In the ditch, loose teeth formed a dominant part of the sheep/goat assemblage. Only the shaft fragments of the radius, tibia and metapodia were found in any numbers, apart from teeth. The more fragile parts of the sheep/goat skeleton did not survive. In the quarry, the bias towards loose teeth was even more marked. In the pits the sheep/goat bone elements were much more evenly represented (Fig 75). Although the cattle assemblage was also influenced by factors of

Table 20. The variation of principal stock animal fragments against select features and feature types in the Early Iron Age.

	Cattle	Horse	Sheep/Goat	Pig	Total Fragments
Ditch 5	61.4	10.5	21.7	6.4	484
Pit 2431	3.8	0.0	85.6	10.6	160
Pit 3111	46.4	19.6	21.4	12.5	112
Other Pits	28.5	9.5	51.9	10.2	295
Quarry	50.9	12.5	30.8	5.8	481
Post-holes	30.0	0.0	60.0	10.0	10
Scoops	35.3	11.8	47.1	5.9	34
Total	44.4	10.5	37.4	7.8	1576

Fig 75. Winnall Down: the distribution of cattle and sheep/goat bone elements in a range of Early and Middle Iron Age contexts.

differential preservation, it was only in the quarry that there was a significant bias towards loose teeth. The superior preservation of large mammal bones in these deposits was aided by the presence of a much greater proportion of bones of mature animals. Both the sheep/goat and pig samples contained a large number of immature animals and thus possessed many more porous, unfused and fragile bones.

There is also evidence for the differential disposal of the carcases of cattle and sheep. Several examples of articulated cattle vertebrae and a relatively high proportion of cattle longbones butchered for meat were found in the ditch. Pit 3111 contained a similar assemblage in a well-preserved deposit. Few of the other pits, however, had significantly high densities of cattle bones in comparison with those of sheep/goat. It would appear that the concentrations of vertebrae and limb bones in certain deposits represent evidence for the disposal of parts of cattle carcases that had been stripped of meat but were not required for marrow processing. The ditch, when being infilled, would have been an ideal depository for butchery waste of this size. The distribution of sheep/goat bones was different. Very low densities were recovered from the ditch. The question of whether this was simply the result of poor preservation in the ditch fills, or a combination of that and other factors, remains.

The evidence from pit 3111 may be of some significance here. No limb bones of sheep were associated with the large number of cattle and horse limb bones and vertebrae that were present. If the bones from this pit were derived mainly from one particular butchery event in which meat was stripped from cattle and horse bones, the lack of sheep limb bones may indicate that, on that occasion, sheep carcases did not pass through that stage of the butchery process. The presence of only skull and teeth fragments of sheep/goat seems to suggest that only the heads of possibly three animals were dumped in the pit. It can be suggested that the meat from sheep tended to be kept on the bone, whereas it was stripped off the bones of the larger mammals. If so, we would expect more sheep bones to be associated with cooking waste, and cattle bones to be under-represented in such contexts. The greater abundance of sheep/goat bones in most pits may therefore be a reflection of the fact that more cooking waste was incorporated into those deposits.

It is possible too that the lack of cattle and horse phalanges and tarsals in pit 3111 may have some significance. Their absence from this pit cannot be explained by poor preservation or recovery bias alone. It is possible that these bones were disarticulated from the major limb bones during the initial stages of skinning and carcase dismemberment. Thus, the concentrations of limb bones, vertebrae and skull fragments may represent a secondary process, in which these bones had meat stripped from them. Alternatively, we may be witnessing a deliberate policy of infilling in the pit, in which the large bones were selected for dumping.

Although differential preservation of cattle and sheep/goat bones was undoubtedly an important factor in the intra-site variability, it does seem that we can also observe a disparity in the treatment of carcases of these species that resulted in a different pattern of disposal of many of their bones.

Cattle
Twenty-three mandibles bore evidence of dentition, of which 17 had fully-erupted cheek toothrows and belonged to adult animals probably all over five years of age. The less reliable epiphyseal fusion evidence also suggests that mature individuals were well represented. Metrical analysis was limited, but the small size of the cattle represented is typical of the cattle bones recovered from contemporary sites elsewhere in England (Maltby 1981a). The methods of butchery also appear to be typical. Sixty-eight bones bore evidence of knife cuts made during skinning, disarticulation or filletting. Only five specimens bore chopmarks. The most common cutmarks were found on the distal humerus and proximal radius and ulna and were associated with the disarticulation of the elbow joint. Disarticulation cuts were also found on several distal scapulae, the mandibular ramus, the os coxae, the astragalus and the proximal metatarsus. Cutmarks associated with meat stripping were found on some of the lumbar vertebrae, scapulae and occasionally on the major limb bones. A relatively high number of major longbones, however, were complete, or almost intact, inferring that processing of marrow was not of high priority.

Horse
The treatment of horse carcases appears to have been very similar to cattle. Thirteen bones bore evidence of knife cuts, the most common being found on the distal humerus and os coxae. They were associated with the disarticulation of the elbow and hip joints respectively. A relatively high number of horse limb bones were complete, suggesting that marrow extraction was not of great priority. Nearly all the horse bones represented belonged to adult animals.

Sheep/Goat
The almost complete absence of goat is typical of most Iron Age sites in Britain (Maltby 1981a). The ageing evidence will be analysed in detail in the discussion of the Phase 4 material. Eight of the 22 mandibles with surviving dentition had fully erupted toothrows. Thirteen belonged to much younger animals, mostly under a year old. It is perhaps significant, however, that none of these young, fragile mandibles were found in the ditch or quarry. The poor preservation of sheep/goat bones in those contexts may thus have biased the ageing data. On the other hand, four of the very young mandibles came from one pit (2431), among a concentration of bones of young lambs. The limited metrical data showed that the sheep were of the small, slender-

limbed type common on British Iron Age sites (Maltby 1981a). The small size of the carcases and, to some extent, the preservation conditions, resulted in few butchery marks being observed. Only nine fragments of sheep/goat had knife cuts recorded on them.

Pig

Pig bones were poorly represented in all contexts other than some of the pits. Many of their bones belonged to immature animals, but the paucity of quantifiable data made detailed ageing or metrical analysis impossible.

Phase 4. Middle Iron Age

Excluding partial and complete skeletons of the major domestic species, 6,572 fragments were recovered from all deposits. This total includes 884 bones of small mammals and 133 fragments of

amphibians. Most of the bones came from 83 of the pits, with small collections being recovered from the ditch, the hut gullies and some of the scoops, quarries and post-holes (Table 21).

The Pits

The density of bone fragments in the pits varied enormously. Including partial skeletons, the density of fragments from pits containing bone ranged from 0.62 fragments/m^3 (8095) to 227.27 fragments/m^3 (3673). The mean density from 81 pits where volumes could be estimated was 54.99 fragments/m^3. Pits with fragment densities of over 60 fragments/m^3 were found most commonly towards the centre of the site (Fig 83). Twelve of these had densities of over 90 fragments/m^3. Densities tended to decline towards the south, east and particularly the north, the further away from the hut groups they were. The pits scattered in the western half of the settlement included several that contained high densities of

Table 21. The distribution of animal bone fragments from types of Middle Iron Age features.

	Pits	Ditch	Hut Gullies	Scoops	PH	Total
Cattle	644	84	69	37	4	838
Horse	186	20	21	16	1	244
Sheep/Goat*	1155	28	75	38	11	1307
Pig	214	11	18	10	6	259
Dog	66	3	2	3	–	74
Red Deer (Cervus elephus)	10	–	1	2	1	14
Hare (Lepus sp)	2	–	–	–	–	2
Large mammal	701	75	101	56	10	943
Large artiodactyl	25	3	4	1	–	3
Sheep-sized mammal	1422	17	87	44	20	1590
Unidentified mammal	174	9	26	14	8	231
Short-tailed Vole (Microtus agrestis)	212	2	–	–	–	214
Water Vole (Arvicola terrestris)	501	–	–	1	–	502
Woodmouse (Apodemus sp)	18	–	–	–	–	18
House Mouse (Mus musculus)	1	–	–	–	–	1
Common Shrew (Sorex araneus)	6	–	–	–	–	6
Pigmy Shrew (Sorex minutus)	2	–	–	–	–	2
Small mammal	141	–	–	–	–	141
Mallard (Anas platyrhynchos)	3	–	–	–	–	3
Grey Lag Goose (Anser anser)	1	–	–	–	–	1
Grey Heron (Ardea cinerea)	3	–	–	–	–	3
Thrush sp (Turdus sp)	8	–	–	–	–	8
Duck sp (Anas sp)	1	–	–	–	–	1
Unidentified bird	1	–	1	–	–	2
Frog (Rana sp)	27	–	–	–	–	27
Toad (Bufo sp)	58	–	–	–	–	58
Unidentified amphibian	47	–	–	–	1	48
Unidentified fish	–	–	1	–	–	1
Unidentified species	1	–	–	–	–	1

PH = post-holes. *190 fragments identified as sheep, one as goat. Totals exclude articulated bones of domestic mammals and hare but include complete or partial skeletons of small mammals, birds and amphibians.

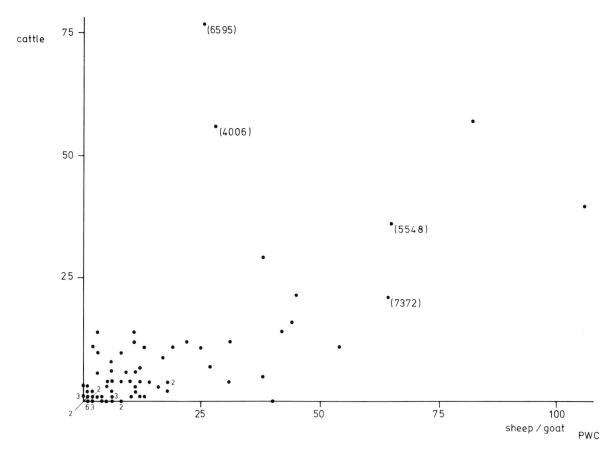

Fig 76. Winnall Down: numbers of cattle and sheep/goat fragments in Middle Iron Age pits.

bone. The fragments of the major species – sheep/goat and cattle – were distributed in the same general pattern (Fig 85). Most of the pits contained more sheep/goat fragments than cattle, although pits 4006 and 6595 were notable exceptions (Fig 76). These pits also contained a high proportion of horse bones. Preservation of bones in the pits was quite good. Including partial and complete skeletons, the percentage of eroded fragments was only 14.6% of the total. In addition, however, 5.8% of the fragments bore evidence of canid and rodent gnawing. Excluding the bones from skeletons, 41.5% of the sheep/goat and 63.0% of the cattle limb bones (scapula, humerus, radius, femur, tibia, metapodia) possessed surviving articulations.

Eighteen of the pits contained partial or complete skeletons of animals, and 47 sets of associated bones were found. These can be divided into three categories: i) the burial of a complete, or substantial parts of a, carcass with little or no evidence of skinning or butchering; ii) the bones of neonatal or foetal skeletons; iii) the dumping of parts of the carcase after skinning and dismemberment.

i)   There were five examples of this type. The complete burials of a pig and a dog in pit 6595 have already been described. Another fairly complete skeleton of an adult, probably female, dog was

discovered in pit 1490. No butchery marks were found and it can be inferred that the animal was buried whole. In pit 7257, the hind limbs, pelvis, sacrum, lumbar vertebrae and some of the thoracic vertebrae and ribs of a sub-adult sheep were recovered. It is possible that a set of the left humerus, radius and ulna belonged to the same animal. No butchery marks were observed and, although the limb bones were scattered, it is clear from the plan of the layer that the ribs and vertebrae at least were dumped as a complete unit. Finally, pit 10161 contained the substantial remains of two skeletons. The first was that of a horse and included the skull, most of the vertebrae and ribs, and complete right forelimb, the left scapula and humerus, the pelvis and the right femur. The animal was male and about six years old, judging by the wear on the incisors. In the top layer of pit 10161, most of the bones of an adult hare (*Lepus* sp) were recovered. Unfortunately the skull was crushed and it was not possible to determine whether the species was the mountain (*Lepus timidus*) or the brown hare (*Lepus capensis*).

ii)   Bones from newborn or possibly foetal dog skeletons were found in four pits. A single animal was represented in pits 4006 and 8564. Pits 6038 and 7257 contained the remains of a minimum of two and four animals, respectively.

iii) The majority of the associated bones belonged to parts of carcases that had been dumped after skinning or butchery. Seven sets of hindfeet were recovered. Two belonged to cattle: the first (in 7257) was complete from the tarsals downwards; the second (in 895) consisted of only the chopped meta-tarsus and three tarsals. Four tarsals and the metatarsals of a horse were found in pit 4006, the third tarsal bearing knife cuts on its anterior surface. The sheep hindfeet came from pits 8601 and 8630. The former context included the bones of the left foot, the latter contained the bones of both feet, and knife cuts were found near the proximal articulations of the metatarsi. Bones from the hindfeet of two dogs were found in pits 1055 and 7372. Only two partial sets of bones from the forefeet were found. The first (in 3738) belonged to a horse, the second (in 8630) belonged to a sheep.

Nine sets of vertebrae were found. Four belonged to sheep/goat in pits 636 (three cervical), 1941 (15 thoracic and lumbar, and one of the lumbar vertebrae bearing a knife cut on the ventral surface of the lateral process), 5601 (all cervical and two thoracic vertebrae) and 8630 (five thoracic vertebrae). A lumbar and eight thoracic vertebrae of a pig were recovered from pit 4475. Two partial vertebral columns of horse were found in 4006. The first consisted of the butchered sacrum and the last two lumbar vertebrae; the second consisted of the pelvis, the lumbar vertebrae and several thoracic vertebrae and ribs. It is possible that a pair of femora in the same layer also belonged to this animal. Two dog thoracic vertebrae and eight caudal vertebrae were found in pits 7257 and 7372 respectively.

Three sets of skull and mandibles were found in pits 7257 (dog), 8601 (horse) and 8630 (sheep). The sheep skull had cut marks on the occipital condyles where it had been detached from the vertebrae. Two sets of sheep tibiae, calcanea and astragali were found in pit 1941. Both sets bore knife cuts on the astragalus and one had cuts on the distal tibia and calcaneus as well. These were made during the removal of the hindfeet. Finally, seven sets of the upper forelimb were found. Sets of butchered radii and ulnae of a horse and a sheep were found in pits 1491 and 1941 respectively. Pit 4006 contained five sets of bones. Four belonged to cattle and one to horse. It is possible that the preponderance of other limb bones of large mammals in this pit also belonged to the dismembered remains of relatively few individuals, whose bones had been stripped of meat but not broken open for marrow.

In addition to the major domestic species, ten fragments of red deer antler were recovered. Substantial numbers of small mammal and amphibian bones were found in some of the pits. Five species of bird were represented in small numbers (Table 21). Of the unidentifiable fragments, those of sheep-sized mammals outnumbered those of large mammals.

The Ditch
252 fragments dated to this phase were located in seven sections of the enclosure ditch. The density of fragments ranged from 6.25 fragments/m^3 in 5R to 352 fragments/m^3 in 5KK, although only this and another small sample from 5CC produced a substantial density of bones. As in Phase 3, cattle fragments outnumbered those of sheep/goat. Preservation, however, was poor and 70.8% of the fragments were eroded. The bones of horse and unidentified large mammal were also comparatively better represented than in most pits (Table 21).

The Hut Gullies
404 fragments were recovered from eleven gullies. Densities of fragments were generally low (Fig 85). Preservation was poor and a large percentage of eroded fragments (64.4%) and loose teeth was recovered. Despite their poor survival, sheep/goat fragments outnumbered those of cattle (Table 21).

The Scoops, Quarries and Post-holes
Twenty-two scoops and quarry features produced 222 fragments of which 140 came from one extensive area of quarries to the north of the settlement (7741). Once again, the bones were badly preserved and 64.1% of the fragments were eroded. Sixty-two fragments were found in twenty post-holes. 55.7% of the fragments were eroded.

Intra-Site Variability
The bones of sheep/goat dominated the assemblage. This, however, was a direct reflection of the fact that most of the material came from pits. The percentages of identified fragments of the principal domestic species (excluding articulated bones) are displayed in Table 22. Overall, the percentages of the principal stock animals in the pits were similar to those obtained from the pits of the previous phase. Comparisons of the percentages of the different bone elements (Fig 75) showed that, in general, the bones recovered from pits in Phases 3 and 4 had basic similarities. Apart from the greater abundance of loose teeth in the Phase 4 pits, the sheep/goat assemblages bore close comparison. Some pits had exceptionally well-preserved samples, which resulted in the recovery of higher percentages of fragile bones such as the scapula, ulna and femur. Preservation was quite good in general and this resulted in a fairly even distribution of the different bone elements. This applied to the cattle sample as well, and the assemblages from most pits had similarities to those from pits of Phase 3 date (Fig 75).

There were interesting variations from this general pattern, however. Two pits (4006 and 6595) contained high proportions of cattle and horse in comparison with sheep/goat (Fig 76). Pit 4006 contained a large number of mandibles, scapulae and complete, or almost complete, longbones in addition to the articulated sets of bones from the foreleg described above. Butchery marks associated with the stripping

Table 22. The variation of principal stock animal fragments against types of features in the Middle Iron Age.

	Cattle	Horse	Sheep/Goat	Pig	Total Fragments
Pits	29.2	8.5	52.5	9.7	2199
Ditch	58.7	14.0	19.6	7.7	143
Hut Gullies	37.7	11.5	41.0	9.8	183
Scoops	36.6	15.8	37.6	9.9	101
Postholes	18.2	4.5	50.0	27.3	22
Total	31.6	9.2	49.4	9.8	2648

and dismemberment of the carcases were found in abundance. The cattle sample from 6595 was similar in many ways but contained a higher percentage of mandible and skull fragments (Fig 73). The density and concentration of such bones in these pits suggest that they were filled predominantly with the butchery waste of large mammals. Although there are significant differences between these samples and those from the earlier pit 3111, it seems likely that these pits provide evidence for similar processing of meat.

The isolation of these pits from the main group of pits may be significant. Such butchery may have been more common at the outskirts of the settlement. A similar example of such disposal was found at Old Down Farm (Maltby 1981b). At Winnall Down, pits on the outskirts of the settlement tended to produce relatively higher percentages of cattle and horse than in most pits located near the centre of the settlement, although the amounts of bone recovered in many cases were small. It was also found that pits which contained partial or complete skeletons tended to contain higher percentages of cattle and horse bones. It is possible that, in certain circumstances, substantial parts of unwanted carcases were dumped together with other large waste bones.

The greatest densities of sheep/goat and pig fragments were located in the pits nearest the huts, and presumably nearest the cooking areas. The amount of canid gnawing found on bones in these assemblages suggests that much of the bone was not dumped directly into the pits, but may have lain around in a midden or on the ground (and thus accessible to dogs) before secondary disposal amongst the pit fills. The fall-off of bone densities in pits away from the huts may therefore be a reflection of increasing distance from cooking and meat preparation areas.

Despite the variability within each phase, comparisons of the types and proportions of bones recovered from the pits in Phases 3 and 4 would suggest that there was little change in disposal practices between the two phases. It could also be implied that the relative proportions of the major domestic species eaten remained essentially unchanged, if one compares the pit contents only. The data from other Phase 4 deposits was limited in abundance and quality. The poor preservation in the hut gullies, for example, resulted in the recovery of a very high proportion of loose teeth of cattle and sheep/goat (Fig 75) and this was typical of the other types of context as well.

Cattle
Cattle mandibles in all phases were recorded and analysed using the method of Grant (1975). The method involves the recording of eruption and wear stages on the molars and the assigning of a numerical value to the mandibles. The older the mandible, the greater the wear on the teeth and the greater the numerical value. The Phase 4 deposits produced the largest sample, with 36 specimens (Fig 77). Most of the mandibles had numerical values of over 30, and all those with values of 38 and above had completed their tooth eruption sequence (fourth permanent premolar in wear). Absolute ageing of the tooth eruption sequence in prehistoric cattle is still problematic but it is likely that this stage was not reached until at least five years of age, and most of the cattle represented must have been at least this age and substantially older in many cases.

There was a smaller group of mandibles with numerical values of 8–13, with their first molar in early stages of wear, possibly belonging to animals about a year old. There were also five specimens from neonatal mortalities. Few mandibles were found with numerical values of 15–30, suggesting that animals between 2–5 years of age were not slaughtered very often. If the sample is typical of the animals raised by the inhabitants, this suggests that the fattening of cattle quickly for meat production was not commonly practised. The adult cattle could have been used as dairy or traction animals. Unfortunately, there was very little sexing data available to establish the proportions of bulls, steers and cows present. Some of the cattle may simply have been slaughtered for their meat after a slow period of growth. The mortality pattern of cattle at Winnall

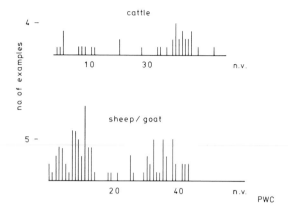

Fig 77. Winnall Down: ageing analysis of cattle and sheep/goat mandibles from Middle Iron Age contexts.

Down has parallels with the samples from Balksbury (Maltby 1981a), the later phases at Gussage All Saints (Harcourt 1979, 151), Eldon's Seat, Dorset (Cunliffe and Phillipson 1968, 229), and possibly Old Down Farm (Maltby 1981b), although the sample there was small. The problem with the interpretation of the Winnall Down sample is that there is no means of determining whether the mandibles thrown in the pits represent an accurate cross-section of the mortality pattern of the cattle husbanded by the inhabitants. Certain age groups may be under-represented either because of differential disposal practices or through the redistribution of stock between settlements.

The results of the metrical analysis will be considered in the discussion of the Phase 6 material. A total of 98 cattle bones had knife cuts observed on them, whilst fourteen possessed chop marks. The most common records of knife cuts were on the scapula (16), humerus (15), radius (12) and mandible (12). The types and methods of butchery were similar to those described for the previous phase and those from contemporary deposits at Old Down Farm (Maltby 1981b).

Horse

Eleven of the twelve ageable mandibles had fully erupted tooth rows. No neonatal mortalities were recovered. Similar mortality patterns have been found on several Iron Age sites (Maltby 1981a). It is possible that Harcourt's (1979, 160) theory, that horses at Gussage All Saints were not reared but rounded up and trained from about three years of age, may have some validity here, although other explanations can be put forward (Maltby 1981a). Horses were probably used as transport and pack animals. Their importance as meat producers must not be overlooked and 26 horse bones bore knife cuts, most frequently on the humerus (7), radius/ulna (6) and the os coxae (4). Most of these cuts were associated with the disarticulation of the cubital and hip joints. There is clear evidence from the types of butchery and similar distribution of their bones that

cattle and horse carcases were treated in similar ways.

Sheep/Goat

The only evidence for goat was a single horncore and it is safe to assume that almost all the ovicaprine sample belonged to sheep. Detailed analysis of the mandibular molars was carried out using the same method as on the cattle mandibles (Grant 1975). The results showed two major groupings (Fig 77). The first contained mandibles with numerical values of 0–14 and included mandibles of neonatal mortalities and those with, at most, only the deciduous premolars and first molar in wear. Most of these mandibles must have belonged to animals that died under a year old, although absolute ageing is again problematic. Certainly these mandibles belonged to sheep that had not attained the optimum age and weight for culling for meat, although butchery marks on several bones attest to their utilisation for that purpose.

The second major group had numerical values of over 30 and possessed fully erupted tooth rows. Modern tooth eruption rates would age these mandibles at two years and upwards. Most of the sheep represented in this group were probably significantly older than this, since the tooth eruption rate was probably slower, and a substantial number of mandibles had heavy wear on some of their molars (nv =35+). Interpretation of this mortality pattern depends upon whether it was representative of the kill-off strategies of the inhabitants. Preservation was extremely good in most pits and bias towards the sturdier, older mandibles was probably less than usual. On the other hand, disposal practices could have favoured the dumping of young mandibles in these pits. For example, a proportion of the older mandibles may have been removed elsewhere after primary butchery, although there was no clear evidence in this phase for the different treatment of old and young carcases. Redistribution of stock between settlements must also be considered. It is interesting to note, however, that three major excavations of Middle Iron Age deposits in Hampshire (Winnall Down; Balksbury, Maltby 1981a; and Old Down Farm, Maltby 1981b) have produced similar sheep mortality profiles. A wider range of samples is still needed from other types of settlement in the region, but the present evidence suggests that, even if significant redistribution of stock was taking place, it did not manifest itself in significant variations in the relative numbers of sheep of different ages being eaten at these settlements.

If the mortality patterns are representative, they could have been created by a subsistence exploitation of sheep, in which a relatively high number of neonatal mortalities through natural causes would be expected. In addition, the kill-off of older lambs would facilitate the availability of pasture for the selected individuals required for breeding, dairy and wool production. The relative importance of these latter commodities is difficult to assess without knowledge of the sex of the adult sheep. Unfortunately, little sexing evidence was forthcoming from the samples. Both milk and wool would have been useful products but, given the seemingly high rates of immature mortalities, their production would have been of secondary consideration to the necessity of maintaining a viable breeding population. The importance of manure from large flocks of sheep for arable production also should not be overlooked.

Sixty-four sheep/goat bones had knife cuts observed on them. The types and frequency of butchery of the major bones were very similar to those described at Old Down Farm (Maltby 1981b). Most common were cuts associated with the disarticulation of the hip and cubital joints and the hind feet.

Pig

Of the 23 mandibles with evidence of ageing, all but three had reached the stage where the second molar had come into wear, but only six had reached the stage where the third molar was in an early stage of wear. If late eighteenth-century estimates (Silver 1969, 298–9) are of any relevance, most of the mortalities must have been of second and third year animals. In this sample, no mandibles of neonatal mortalities were found, although a few other bones were recovered that belonged to such animals. Most pigs, therefore, were slaughtered for their meat at a young age, but the intensity of this process does not appear to have been great.

Eighteen pig bones were recorded as butchered; sixteen of these had knife cuts and two had chop marks. Most knife cuts were observed on scapulae (5). These had been made both during the disarticulation of the scapula from the humerus, and during the removal of meat from the blade of the bone. Cut marks were found occasionally on other bones, and the limited evidence suggests that the carcases of sheep and pigs were treated in the same way.

Dog

Dogs were quite well represented in this phase. The presence of several skeletons of newborn animals is evidence that dogs were kept at the settlement, and could be taken to imply that their numbers were controlled, although natural mortalities cannot be ruled out. Similar occurrences of neonatal mortalities have been found on several contemporary sites (Maltby 1981a, 1981b). The presence of butchery marks on dog bones (there were six examples) is also typical of other Iron Age sites in southern England. Most of the cut marks were caused during dismemberment and dog meat must have been regarded as an occasional supplement to the diet.

Phase 5. Late Iron Age – Romano-British

Only 313 fragments of animal bone were recovered from Phase 5 deposits. The majority came from pits and scoops and a few were found in various gullies (Table 23). Fragments of cattle and sheep/goat, as usual, dominated the identifiable assemblage, although no bones were specifically identified as goat. Horse and pig bones were found in smaller quantities, whereas dog and red deer were represented by one bone each. Ninety-six fragments were found in the large irregular pit 10007, and the relatively high numbers of cattle (27) and horse (15) fragments found in this pit had a significant bearing on the overall fragment totals for these species (Table 23). In all pits 34.1% of the bones were eroded. As usual, preservation of bone from the shallow scoops was poor and 58.0% of the fragments were eroded. No partial or complete skeletons were recovered and the sample is too small for further detailed analysis to be fruitful.

Table 23. The distribution of animal bone fragments from types of features in Phase 5.

	Pits	Scoops	Gullies	Total
Cattle	39	23	7	69
Horse	17	9	–	26
Sheep/Goat*	22	36	12	70
Pig	5	9	1	15
Dog	–	1	–	1
Red Deer (*Cervus elaphus*)	1	–	–	1
Large mammal	28	40	8	76
Large artiodactyl	1	–	1	2
Sheep-sized mammal	20	21	5	46
Unidentified mammal	2	4	1	7

* Nine fragments identified as sheep, none as goat.

Phase 6. Romano-British

A total of 4,242 fragments were dated to this phase, excluding partial skeletons of domestic animals. The total includes 83 bones of small mammals including 76 bones from two skeletons of house mouse (*Mus musculus*). Most of the bones were recovered from gullies and scoops (Table 24).

Ditches and Gullies

Apart from two partial skeletons of horses and one of pig, 2,865 fragments were recovered from these features. The densest concentration of fragments was found in the gullies of enclosures C and D (Fig 88), particularly in features 660 and 678 (119.18 fragments/m^3 and 89.21 fragments/m^3 respectively). The two sets of articulated horse bones were found in these pits. Fourteen vertebrae were found in 660K and a foreleg from the radius/ulna downwards was recovered from 678A. No butchery marks were found on either set of bones. The density of bone fragments in the gullies of enclosures A and B was low and this general pattern was found in the cattle and sheep/goat assemblages as well (Fig 88). Cattle and sheep/goat fragments dominated the assemblage, with cattle being slightly better represented in most deposits. As in the ditches and gullies of previous phases, fragments of horse and unidentified large mammal were relatively well represented. Pig was quite poorly represented, although eight vertebrae and three ribs of one animal were found in 6718B. Preservation conditions again favoured the survival of large mammal bones. Of the fragments, 62.2% were eroded and 60% of the cattle limb bones, but only 31% of the sheep/goat limb bones, possessed surviving articulations. The bones were better preserved, however, than in many of the earlier ditch and gully deposits. Dog was quite well represented, but red deer was rare. Domestic fowl bones appeared in the assemblages for the first time (Table 24).

The Pits

Twenty-five pits produced animal bone but the total assemblage (470 fragments excluding ten cattle vertebrae in pit 2846, five pig phalanges in pit 5676 and most of a dog skeleton in pit 1688) was quite small. Only the pits with the partial skeletons produced over 50 fragments of bone and, although several other pits produced high densities of fragments (Fig 88), the number of bones recovered in many of the shallow pits was small. 63.6% of cattle limb bones and 44% of sheep/goat limb bones had surviving articulations. The assemblage as a whole was therefore better preserved than the one from the gullies but not as well preserved as the bones from the Phase 4 pits. Although the sample was small, sheep/goat and unidentified sheep-size mammal fragments again outnumbered those of cattle and unidentified large mammal respectively in the pits (Table 24). Pig, horse and dog bones were found in relatively small numbers. Enough of the major bones of the dog skeleton in pit 1688 was recovered to be certain that the whole skeleton had been buried in the pit, which

was possibly dug specifically for this act. No butchery marks were found on the skeleton. The animal was quite small, having an estimated shoulder height of 407mm, using Harcourt's (1974) factors of conversion from the length of its radius.

The Scoops and Hollows

A total of 804 fragments were examined excluding the house mouse skeletons that were the only faunal contents of feature 6737. Not surprisingly, the bones from these deposits were poorly preserved (62.8% were eroded). Once again it seems that sheep/goat bones survived less well than cattle. Only 14.9% of the sheep/goat limb bones had surviving articulations, compared to 48.3% for cattle. Consequently, it is surprising that sheep/goat bones were found more commonly than those of cattle. The same applied to the sheep-sized mammal fragments compared with those of large mammal (Table 24). These deposits did produce the only fish bone identified to species from the excavations, and this belonged to a conger eel (*Conger conger*). Horse, pig and dog were, as usual, represented in small numbers.

The Post-holes and Other Features

Only 27 fragments were recovered from such contexts (Table 24).

Intra-Site variability

Excluding partial skeletons, exactly the same number of cattle and sheep/goat fragments were recovered from the Phase 6 deposits (Table 25). As in the previous phases, however, the relative percentages of fragments of the principal stock animals varied according to the type of feature from which they were excavated. Sheep/goat were better represented in the pits, scoops and hollows, whereas cattle fragments were the most common in the ditches and gullies. Preservation factors again played an important part in this variability. The percentages of the different bone elements of cattle and sheep/goat varied in the different feature types, although the small cattle sample from the pits was similar to the one from the gullies. Poor preservation conditions in the scoops and hollows produced a much higher proportion of loose teeth, with corresponding decreases in the percentages of several of the other cattle bone elements. The sheep/goat assemblages were dominated by loose teeth throughout, contributing more than 40% of the samples from both the gullies and the scoops. Mandible fragments and shaft fragments of the radius, tibia and metapodia were the other common elements in a poorly preserved collection.

Comparisons with samples obtained from the other major phases show that the cattle assemblages from the Phase 6 gullies and pits were similar in their contents to those from the pits in the previous phases, although they contained relatively more carpals and tarsals (Figs 75 and 78). The poorly-preserved sample from the Phase 6 scoops bore its greatest resemblance to the assemblage from the

Table 24. The distribution of animal bone fragments from types of Early Romano-British features.

	Ditches/ Gullies	Pits	Scoops/ Hollows	Post-holes/ Others	Total
Cattle	618	52	154	7	831
Horse	184	19	23	1	227
Sheep/Goat*	541	107	179	4	831
Pig	96	13	18	2	129
Dog	50	16	11	3	80
Red Deer (*Cervus elaphus*)	2	–	1	–	3
Large mammal	910	96	173	6	1185
Large artiodactyl	17	3	2	–	22
Sheep-sized mammal	342	132	188	3	665
Unidentified mammal	96	31	52	1	180
House Mouse (*Mus musculus*)	–	–	76**	–	76**
Short-tailed Vole (*Microtus agrestis*)	1	–	–	–	1
Water Vole (*Arvicola terrestris*)	2	–	–	–	2
Mole (*Talpa europaea*)	1	1	–	–	2
Small mammal	1	–	–	–	1
Domestic Fowl	2	–	–	–	2
Raven (*Corvus corax*)	1	–	–	–	1
Bittern (*Botaurus stellaris*)	–	–	1	–	1
Rook/Crow (*Corvus frugilegus/ corone corone*)	1	–	–	–	1
Conger Eel (*Conger conger*)	–	–	1	–	1
Unid. amphibian	–	–	1	–	1

* 70 fragments identified as sheep, none as goat.
** Bones from two skeletons. All other partial skeletons are omitted.

Table 25. The variation of principal stock animal fragments against types of features in the Romano-British period.

	Cattle	Horse	Sheep/Goat	Pig	Total Fragments
Ditches/Gullies	43.0	12.8	37.6	6.7	1439
Pits	27.2	10.0	56.0	6.8	191
Scoops/Hollows	41.2	6.2	47.9	4.8	374
Postholes	(50.0)	(7.1)	(28.6)	(14.3)	14
Total	41.2	11.3	41.2	6.4	2018

Phase 3 quarry pits (Figs 75 and 78) and, to a lesser extent, the assemblages from the Phase 4 hut gullies. Apart perhaps from the partial skeletons, no evidence for a concentration of bones derived principally from the butchery of large mammal carcases was found in the Phase 6 deposits, although it is likely that this practice continued. The sheep/goat sample from the Phase 6 pits was not as well-preserved as those from the pits of Phase 3 and Phase 4 date. This resulted in the recovery of higher percentages of loose teeth, mandible, radius and tibia fragments.

The Phase 6 sample from the gullies bore some resemblance to the Phase 3 ditch assemblages, although the latter contained a higher proportion of loose teeth and mandible fragments (Figs 75 and 78).

Because of the nature of the samples and because of the frequent changes to the enclosure system, it is impossible to draw many conclusions about the intra-site patterning of the faunal material. The gullies of enclosures C and D contained the densest concentrations of bone fragments, which may sug-

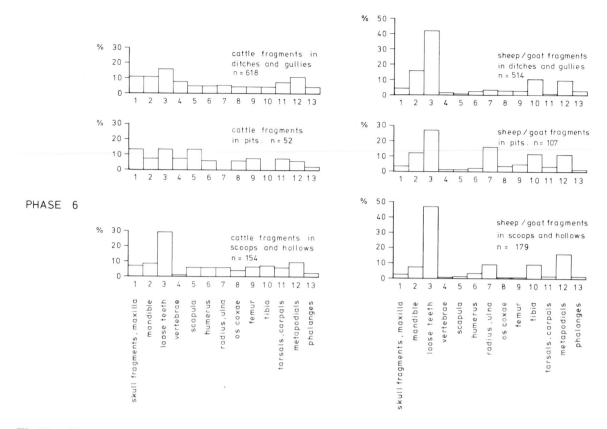

Fig 78.   Winnall down: percentages of bone elements of cattle and sheep/goat in Romano-British deposits.

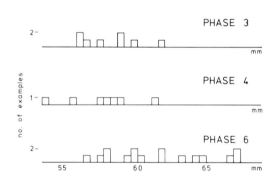

Fig 79.   Winnall Down: measurements of cattle astragali from Phases 3, 4 and 6.

gest that cooking and/or butchery areas were located nearby, at least when these gullies were infilled.

It is also difficult to be certain whether there were any significant changes in the relative proportions of domestic animals eaten. It seems very likely that sheep/goat fragments were under-represented in Phase 6 deposits because they were affected more by the poor survival conditions than cattle bones and, overall, the sheep/goat assemblage was less well preserved than the one from Phase 4. The increase in the percentage of cattle fragments in Phase 6 does not, therefore, necessarily imply that cattle had become more important. Indeed, if one accepts that

the major factor in the changes in the bones represented in these samples was that of differential preservation, it is possible to suggest that there was in fact little change in species representation between Phases 4 and 6.

Cattle

Eighteen mandibles had evidence of toothwear. Of these, 13 had fully erupted tooth rows, three had the third molar coming into wear and two had only their first molar in an early stage of wear. No neonatal mortalities were found, although poor preservation conditions may have destroyed them. Otherwise, the sample is very similar to those of the previous phases, with the emphasis upon the culling of adult cattle.

Although there was no evidence for any change in the exploitation of cattle eaten at the settlement, there was a notable development in the sizes of the animals represented. Although metrical analysis was limited in this and the earlier phases, there is evidence that more larger cattle were present in the Phase 6 deposits. Measurements of the lengths of the astragali (Fig 79) show the presence of some larger specimens than in the earlier phases. Other measurements showed that, although in many cases the size range was similar, more of the Phase 6 cattle bones fell into the upper end of the range, producing a consistently higher mean measurement. It is possible that more steers and bulls (which generally have larger bones than cows) were represented in the

Phase 6 deposits, but there is no firm evidence for this and it is more likely that we are observing a real increase in the average size of cattle represented.

Similar increases in cattle size are well documented on other Romano-British sites (Maltby 1981a), although the rapidity of such changes is open to doubt. The Romano-British material from Winnall Down belongs to the first and second centuries AD, which may imply that the Roman invasion had a direct influence on cattle in the area, either through the introduction of new stock or by the development of better husbandry techniques. Certainly, in other parts of Europe, Roman influence on cattle size appears to have been significant (Boessneck and von den Driesch 1978, Bökönyi 1974). Unfortunately, hardly any measurable material was recovered from Late Iron Age deposits and it is possible that changes in cattle size began in that period and developed more gradually.

Forty-two cattle bones bore knife cuts and eleven had chop marks. The increase in the relative number of chop marks compared to the earlier phases may indicate a development in butchery techniques or technology, but it must be remembered that the weathering on many of the bones may have obliterated evidence of fine knife cuts and these may be under-represented. The decrease in the frequency of knife cuts observed in the Phase 6 sample is probably also the result of the poorer preservation conditions. Similarly, although there were fewer complete limb bones, much of the fragmentation could be accounted for by erosion and gnawing, rather than marrow extraction.

Horse

Most of the horse bones recovered continued to belong to mature animals. Unfortunately too few measurements could be taken to establish whether there were any significant changes in the size of the animals. Estimates of shoulder heights of four animals using the conversion factors of Kiesewalter (1888) ranged from 1182–1378mm (c 10.3–12 hands). These were similar in range to estimates from 18 specimens from Phase 4 deposits (1107–1130mm), which in turn were typical of the small ponies represented in other contemporary settlements in southern England (Maltby 1981a).

Only two bones bore evidence of knife cuts but this need not imply that horsemeat had become less popular. Weathering of the bones probably destroyed the evidence for such fine knife cuts on some bones, as it did on the cattle sample, although the fall off of observations of horse butchery was much steeper. Horse bones did, however, continue to be found alongside the bones of the other major domestic species, in numbers comparable to those of the previous phases and there seems no reason to doubt that horses continued to be exploited for meat, although they were probably more important as transport and pack animals.

Sheep/Goat

No goat bones were identified in these assemblages. Sixty-four mandibles bore evidence of tooth eruption. Using Grant's (1975) method of analysis, it was clear that a higher percentage of mandibles had fully erupted tooth rows (nv =30+) than in the Phase 4 deposits. There was still a peak of mandibles with the first molar in an early stage of wear and relatively few with numerical values of 15–30. No neonatal mortalities were represented (Fig 80). Once again, however, comparisons with earlier material must take into account variations in preservation conditions. The majority of the mandibles in this phase came from gullies, which were less amenable to the preservation of young mandibles, and it is interesting to note that seven of the eleven ageable mandibles recovered from pits belonged to this youngest age group. Although this evidence is inconclusive, it does suggest that the sample of mandibles was more biased towards older mandibles than the sample from the Phase 4 deposits. Once again, therefore, it is conceivable that there was no significant change in the ages of animals eaten by the inhabitants, and possibly no change in their exploitation.

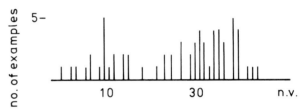

Fig 80.   Winnall Down: ageing analysis of sheep/goat mandibles from Romano-British deposits. Method follows that of Grant (1975) nv = 30+.

Metrical analysis of sheep bones was limited throughout the deposits by their poor survival and by the presence of so many immature animals. Nevertheless, there is some evidence of an increase in the overall size of sheep represented in this phase. Taking as an example the maximum distal width of the tibia (the measurement with the largest sample), twelve specimens of Phase 4 date had a range of 21.2–23.7mm and a mean of 22.3mm. The eight Phase 6 specimens had a range of 21.9–25.6mm and a mean of 23.9mm. These samples are small but the results are supported by metrical analysis of other bones as well.

Whether this apparent change in sheep size coincided with the Roman invasion or began in the Late Iron Age remains to be seen. There is good evidence for an increase in the average size of sheep in most areas of Roman Britain from Iron Age levels (Maltby 1981a). The actual factors that produced these changes are still open to speculation. Only fourteen sheep/goat bones bore evidence of knife cuts and three chop marks. Once again poor preservation conditions probably destroyed further evidence.

Pig

Pig was poorly represented in this phase. Thirteen mandibles produced ageing data. Of these, six did not have their second molar in wear. A higher proportion of young mandibles was therefore found than in earlier phases but the sample size was inadequate to be certain whether this variation had any significance. None of the mandibles had gone beyond the stage of early wear on the third molar. Six pig bones bore knife cuts and two had chop marks. Metrical evidence was extremely limited, but there was no evidence for the presence of wild pig (*Sus scrofa*) in any of the phases.

Dog

Dog continued to be quite well represented, although no neonatal mortalities were encountered in the assemblage. Only one knife cut was observed on a dog bone.

Domestic Fowl

The appearance of two domestic fowl bones is interesting, since the species was absent from the pre-Roman assemblages. The absence or rarity of all poultry appears to be a feature of Iron Age sites in southern England and it is only in the Romano-British period that domestic fowl appear to have been kept (or at least eaten) in any numbers.

Shell

There were 87 instances of oyster shell, examples ranging from a fragment to several almost complete shells. Three came from Phase 3 features, two of which might have been intrusive, though the third was well stratified in quarry pit 7746. There were seven examples in Phase 4 features. Four were intrusive but there were well stratified occurrences in scoop 6280 and pits 7086 and 7257. The majority of the oyster shells (74 instances) came from Phase 6: 47 in ditches, 23 in scoops, three in post-holes and one in a pit. There were also three unphased occurrences.

Mussell shells were recorded five times: one in a Phase 5 scoop, two in Phase 6 ditches and once each in a Phase 6 pit and a Phase 6 scoop.

Clearly, oysters were not being brought to the site in large quantities before the Roman period, but there were isolated examples in Middle Iron Age contexts.

The Plant Economy by M A Monk

Soil samples, in 6000cc units, were selected on archaeological criteria from a range of contexts in each phase; they included pits, post-holes, ditches and building gullies. The MARC3 flotation machine was used to recover the charred plant remains (Lapinskas 1974). Of the flots submitted for analysis, 77% of the samples produced charred material (110 of a total of 143), mainly seeds of 'weeds' and fragments of cereals.

Of the contexts sampled, 39 produced plant remains of which 23 were from Phase 4. The majority of these samples were from layers in pits: 24 pits were sampled in total, 18 of them from Phase 4. In addition, samples were obtained from four building gullies (all Phase 4), five post-holes (one each in Phases 3 and 6, the others unphased), four scoops (one each in Phases 2 and 6 and two unphased), a length of Phase 4 gully/ditch, and a segment of the Phase 3 enclosure ditch 5.

A presence and dominance analysis (Hubbard 1975, Renfrew 1972) was carried out for the main cereal taxa (Tables 26 and 27). Also calculated were the grain/chaff and grain/weed seed ratios (archive and Monk and Fasham 1980).

Phase 2 Late Bronze Age and Phase 3 Early Iron Age

Phase 2 of the occupation sequence produced one sample from the shallow scoop 4786, containing one grain of barley. Phase 3 was represented by three contexts producing plant remains. From pit 5797 one grain of barley was identified. Barley (in this case *Hordeum vulgare/hexastichum*, hulled six row barley) was also present in post-hole 3744. Post-hole 3744 produced a grain/weed seed ratio of 1:7.0. The slight evidence from post-hole 3744 suggests that the plant remains derived from waste from crop processing that had been charred by use as tinder in firing ovens, hearths or kilns (Monk forthcoming).

Phase 4. Middle Iron Age

The 93 samples from this phase producing plant remains were taken from a variety of contexts, but mainly from layers in pits.

The building gullies

The samples from these contexts (406, 491, 1820 and 1847) contained very little material, mainly cereal fragments, in contrast to the pits in the eastern part of the site where the weed seed element generally predominated. But because the samples taken were few and the number of items from them were small, it is difficult to put much emphasis on this evidence. It is, however, entirely possible that a real variation existed, the material from the gullies having arisen from casual loss and charring of cereals being prepared for dietary use (post storage and pre-milling). In this connection *Triticum* sp (wheat) grains were more commonly present in samples from this general area of the site, bread being more usually, though not necessarily, made out of wheat flour.

Table 26. Plant remains: percentage presence analysis for cereals and grasses in the samples from Phase 4 (Middle Iron Age). Total number of samples, 85.

	%
Hordeum vulgare/hexastichum	33
Hordeum sp	65
Triticum dicoccum	5
Triticum spelta	47
Triticum sp	49
Avena sp	9
Bromus sp	56
Gramineae (large)	21
Gramineae (small)	41

Percentage dominance analysis for all taxa in samples from Phase 4 (Middle Iron Age).

	%
Hordeum vulgare/hexastichum	–
Hordeum sp	16
Triticum spelta	2
Triticum sp	7
Avena sp	–
Bromus sp	12
Gramineae (large)	–
Gramineae (small)	7
Leguminosae	22
Chenopodiaceae	10
Galium sp	5
Rumex sp	4
Tripleurospermum sp	4

Those taxa with a less than 2% dominance have been omitted.

The Pits

The pits associated with this phase showed a wide range in type and distribution, although most of those from which samples were taken were located in the eastern part of the site. There were beehive, cylindrical and miscellaneously-shaped pits. The majority of plant remains came from the beehive-shaped pits, although this was partly due to sample bias in favour of this group. Of these, the majority were located in the southeastern corner of the site (exceptions were 4006, 6595 and 5594).

The majority of identified plant remains were seeds of weeds, particularly legumes (*Leguminosae*), *Medicago* sp (the medicks), and *Trifolium* sp (the clovers) which, in percentage dominance terms, were more important than barley (particularly in pit 7312) the most dominant cereal (see Table 26). However, the percentage presence analysis showed the barleys to be the most important cultivar in evidence (63%), against the wheats (52%).

The function of the pits

The preponderance of the weed seeds recovered from almost all the pits is highlighted in the grain/weed seed ratios for the samples. However, there were one or two of the pits which on closer examination produced a quantity of grain material. In particular 5789 had a grain/weed seed ratio of 1:0.07 in its primary fills, a ratio characteristic of a storage product and quite unlike the fills of the other pits. In contrast, the upper fills of this pit produced very little charred material and all the recovered items were seeds of weeds. There was also a marked contrast in the upper and lower fills in terms of composition. The bottom layers 5827 and 5828, below the primary weathering of the pit (Limbrey 1975, 304), consisted of a deposit of carbon and ash-stained loam, while the upper infill layers consisted in the main of weathered chalk rubble and clean brown loam. The only significant piece of evidence that would counter the interpretation that this material was the product of primary storage in the pit is the relatively high incidence of straw fragments in the primary fills (basal fragments 5 and nodal 11). It is, however, possible that the grain was incompletely cleaned of large contaminants like straw before storage.

Two further pits, 5597 (Phase 5) and 7372, also gave low grain/weed seed ratios in their primary fills

Table 27. Plant remains: percentage presence for cereals and grasses in the samples from Phases 5 and 6 (Late Iron Age and Roman). Total number of samples, 15.

	%
Hordeum vulgare/hexastichum	29
Hordeum sp	57
Triticum spelta	21
Triticum sp	50
Bromus sp	43
Gramineae (large)	29
Gramineae (small)	29

Percentage dominance analysis for all taxa in samples from Phases 5 and 6 (Late Iron Age and Roman).

	%
Hordeum sp	29
Triticum sp	14
Bromus sp	7
Gramineae (large)	7
Leguminosae	29
Chenopodiaceae	7

Those species with less than 2% dominance have been omitted

(1:0.08 and 1:2.5, respectively). This also suggests that the charred material recovered from them was residue from a primary storage product (the ratios for their upper fills were 1:0.69 for 5597 and 1:10.4 for 7372). Although finds of charred remains have been found in what appeared to be primary contexts in pits from other sites, this represents the first occasion where the evidence has been studied closely by using and comparing grain/weed seeds ratios for both the primary and secondary fills. Helbaek (1952, 1957 and Clay 1924) thought the charred grains from pits at Itford Hill (Late Bronze Age) and Fifield Bavant (Iron Age) had become charred as a result of grain drying or parching activities in or close to the pit: he did not interpret this material in terms of storage. The only significant published parallel is that of charred grain found at Weston Wood, Albury, Surrey (Harding 1964) in the base of a storage pit associated with the remains of a possible storage jar.

The charred state of the plant remains in the base of these three pits from Winnall Down can perhaps be explained by the practise suggested by Reynolds (1974) of sterilising the pits after use by building fires in them to burn away dry fungus and rotted residue. Accepting this, re-use would require cleaning out the burnt material thoroughly (thereby removing the evidence), but in the case of pit 5789 at least this was not done, probably because the pit was not needed again. Abandonment of pits, post-sterilisation, might have been a common practice but, without more detailed archaeobotanical study of their primary fills, the evidence for a storage function will not be recovered.

Not only is there good evidence in the ethnographic record for the storage of grain and other food products in pits, but recent experiments by Reynolds (1974) and Bowen and Wood (1968) have demonstrated the viability of this practice on a wide range of subsoils in southern Britain. These experiments were undertaken in the knowledge that the Roman agricultural writers like Columella and Pliny also described such practices, but this report is one of the few published examples of a detailed archaeobotanical study to examine the issue.

A detailed discussion of grain storage practices will be presented elsewhere (Monk forthcoming), but one further point is relevant here concerning Pliny's reference to pit storage. Pliny writes 'The most paying method however of keeping grain is in holes called *siri* as done in Cappodocia and Thrace and in Spain and Africa; and before all things care is taken to make them in dry soils and then to floor them with chaff; moreover the corn is stored this way in the ear. If no air is allowed to penetrate it is certain no pests will breed in the grain' (Pliny, 304–8). The two points at issue here, apart from the mode of storage, are that pits should be dug in dry soil and that they should be floored with chaff. The first point would seem to be borne out by the location of Iron Age pits in Britain on free-draining soils like the chalk and gravels. The second point, concerning the chaff, could, given the possibility of sterilisation by fire, explain the usual high degree of chaff and weed seeds in the charred remains from the pits. Although this explanation does not concur with this writer's current interpretation of three of the pits from Winnall Down, it is nonetheless a possibility.

In addition, the storage of grain 'in the ear' would imply that the grain was being stored unthreshed and hence also uncleaned, a practice sometimes used for seed corn (Lucas 1958, 3). The resultant charred material, if in a primary position post-sterilisation, would be in an uncleaned state. It is not possible from the archaeobotanical evidence alone to substantiate or deny any of these hypotheses. The suggestion, on the present evidence, is that in the majority of cases, except pit 5789 and possibly pits 5597 (Phase 5) and 7372, the pits had been backfilled with a mixture of domestic refuse and waste from other sources. This is likely, therefore, to mean that the archaeobotanical remains in these pits are of mixed origin, though they may include post-storage residue charred in the sterilisation process.

A general appreciation of the plant economy of Winnall Down in the Middle Iron Age

Six row hulled barley (*Hordeum vulgare/hexastichum*) was the most predominant cereal in the samples from this phase (Table 26). The predominance of barley (percentage presence 63%) over wheat (percentage presence 52%) for the Middle Iron Age phase at this site is paralleled at Owlesbury four miles south of Winnall Down. The wheats were largely represented in the Winnall Down samples by the presence of grains, but there was also a high incidence of glume bases typical of *Triticum spelta* (Spelt) suggesting that this was the main wheat species present. In addition to wheat and barley, some few fragments of oats, *Avena* sp, were also recovered, though in the absence of flower bases their species could not be determined. At Owlesbury, oats also make their first appearance in samples dated to the Middle Iron Age.

In addition to the cereals there were a few fragments of cultivated legumes: two fragments of *Vicia faba* (the cultivated bean) in pits 4475 and 7372 and a tentative identification of pea (*Pisum sativum*) fragments from pits 5548, 5555 and 5604. Both species have been found on other Iron Age sites in southern Britain: both were present in the samples from the Glastonbury lake village, and Owlesbury produced beans from Middle Iron Age contexts, suggesting that their first appearance in Britain was around this time (Murphy 1977a). Because the cultivated legumes are less likely to be exposed to fire than the cereals, they tend to be under-represented in charred plant remains samples relative to their importance in the economy.

Distribution of the main cereal taxa across the site

The distributional study made of the remains across the site was of limited value because the samples were taken unequally across the site. But there was some suggestion that barley predominated over wheat in the eastern half of the site, particularly in the southeastern corner (seven of twelve contexts showed a barley dominance against one of wheat with four equal). The situation was reversed in the western part of the site where the circular buildings were located, and a dominance of wheat against barley in five of the eight contexts was recorded.

Weed seed contaminants and the ecological implication

The high representation of weed seeds relative to crops in the samples has been commented on above as an indication that the charred material was likely to have been the waste from crop processing. The most predominant taxa overall in the samples were the legumes *Medicago* sp and *Trifolium* sp, though members of the *Chenopodiaceae* (Goosefoot family) were also represented in some numbers. The *Medicago* sp/*Trifolium* groups consisted of a number of species whose preferred general habitats are grassy places and field margins from which they are likely to invade sown cereals, as was the case here.

Tripleurospermum cf *maritimum* sp *inodorum* (Scentless maizeweed), particularly common in pit 5548, *Lithospermum arvense* (Corn Gromwell) and *Galium* sp (cf *aparine*) (Goosegrass/Cleavers) are also common weeds of corn fields and, as such, their presence in the samples is not out of place. *Galium aparine* tends to be an early germinating weed and hence seems to be more often associated with autumn sown cereals like the wheats, in this case probably Spelt. Other noted contaminants in these samples were *Plantago* sp (the Plantains), a common weed of grassy places on base rich soils, *Polygonum aviculare*, *P convolvulus*, *Atriplex* sp and *Chenopodium album* – all species that abound on disturbed, nitrogen rich soils.

It may be significant that *Bromus* sp (the Brome grasses) was present in lower numbers in the Winnall Down samples than in the Micheldever Wood 'banjo' samples, in view of the fact that there seems to be a strong association between Iron Age sites with a dominance of Spelt and those that produce large numbers of *Bromus* sp seeds, as at Old Down Farm, Portway and the Micheldever Wood 'banjo' (Murphy 1977b), suggesting that *Bromus* is a common weed of Spelt.

It is difficult from this evidence alone to assess the degree of weed contamination tolerated in grain crops. The only evidence for a cleaned, stored product, from pit 5789 layers 5828 and 5827, seems to indicate that the Iron Age farmers at Winnall Down went to some trouble to clean their crops thoroughly. The range of weed contaminants was similar to those from the Micheldever Wood 'banjo' (Monk forthcoming), although the numbers involved were much higher, suggesting either a relatively greater degree of weed contamination in the samples from Winnall Down, or that the samples are the residue of better cleaning practices. Overall, the frequency of identifiable remains from Winnall Down was far higher, an average of 14 fragments per sample, than from the Micheldever Wood 'banjo', average of 1.11 fragments per sample. The explanation for this difference is not clear but it is likely to relate to a basic difference in site function, economic basis and waste disposal practices (Monk and Fasham 1980).

The high incidence of weed seeds from plants that are normally small in stature in the Winnall Down samples, eg *Medicago* sp/*Trifolium* sp, *Tripleurospermum* sp, *Stellaria* sp (Chickweed), *Cerastium* sp (Mouse-eared Chickweed) and the small seeded grasses, and the high frequency of straw node and basal fragments, 20 nodal and 13 basal fragments in pit 5548, indicate a harvesting technique involving cutting the straw close to the ground and/or uprooting the plant. According to the Classical sources the method of harvesting employed in the Iron Age was to harvest the ears alone. Although it is impossible to say whether the straw fragments in the samples were from barley or wheat, it is likely, given the high incidence of grains of the former, that barley straw was involved. In general, barley straw is shorter than wheat and because of this and its fibrous nature it is not as useful, and could have been cut low or easily uprooted from the thin chalk soils. It is possible then that the Classical references to harvesting by the ear refer only to wheat; the longer, sturdier wheat straw may then have been harvested separately for thatching, *etc*. Some indication that ear harvesting was confined to the wheats could be inferred from the Micheldever Wood 'banjo' samples where *Triticum spelta* was in the majority and the incidence of both short growing plants and straw fragments was low.

Phases 5 and 6. The Late Iron Age–Early Romano-British Period

The change in nature of the site between Phase 4 and Phases 5 and 6 may mean that there was a change in emphasis from arable to pastoral farming. Although the samples from the later phases were relatively few, several of them produced charred plant remains. Of the Phase 5 contexts, the most productive in remains was the beehive pit 5597 which has already been discussed above (p 113) in connection with the storage function of these pits. The most predominant cereal represented in this pit was barley (*Hordeum* sp) though one or two fragments of wheats (*Triticum* sp) were present. Although a range of weed seeds were also present in this context, including *Polygonum convolvulus* (black bindweed), *Galium* sp (goosegrass, cleavers), *Rumex* sp (Docks) and *Bromus* sp (Brome grasses), there was a higher incidence of cereal fragments, particularly in the lower fills of this pit. The other two contexts from this phase (1645 and 5401) were both pits of uncertain form and produced cereal fragments including barley and spelt.

The samples from Phase 6 were few and produced little evidence, although the shallow pits 2846 and 9057 produced some cereal fragments of wheat and barley. A sample from pit 1019 in the quarry area also produced grains of wheat and barley and a few charred weed seeds (*Atriplex* sp, *Rumex* sp, *etc*), while a further sample from a shallow scoop produced one indeterminate seed of a legume.

It is possible that many of these remains from later contexts are in fact residual from the intense occupation in the Middle Iron Age.

Unphased contexts

Five unphased contexts produced plant remains: post-holes 2261, 2926 and 4162, and scoops 1258 and 10421. Only one post-hole produced any number of items, including one grain of barley. Scoop 10421 also produced grains of wheat and barley and *Bromus* sp. If nothing else this material demonstrates the widespread distribution of cereal remains across the site.

Summary

The evidence of the plant remains indicates that Winnall Down, during its peak period of occupation in the Middle Iron Age, was an arable farming community dependent on the production of cereals, but particularly hulled six row barley, a crop well suited to the local dry chalk soils. The detailed study of the plant remains has not only provided evidence of harvesting technique and crop processing but has also indicated the use of the waste product from crop processing as tinder to fire kilns/ovens, *etc*, and the storage of the cleaned crop in pit silos as documented by the classical agricultural writers.

Pit 5548: a comparison between the charcoal and the carbonised seed evidence

It was suggested earlier (p 112) that the material in some of the pits had been charred as a result of being used as tinder to fire ovens, kilns or hearths. If this was the case then it can be argued, on the basis of modern fire craft, that the chaff waste, *etc*, would be used in conjunction with quantities of small wood (twigs, *etc*) and that the charred remains of both types could be dumped together in the same midden. The addition of larger pieces of wood in the case of an open fire may well confuse the issue, but fires that require constant, intense heat without developing into large conflagrations may be built up with small wood and chaff only.

To test the possible association of 'chaff' waste and twig charcoal of small shrubby plant species, the charcoal and seed remains from several contexts were compared. Pit 5548 produced a significant correlation, particularly for the contiguous layers 5590 and 5593. The majority of the charcoal in these layers consisted of twigs and small shrub material including *Corylus* (Hazel), *Pomoideæ* (a sub-family of the *Rosaceæ*) and *Prunus* sp. By comparison, the grain/weed seed ratio for these two layers was 1:17

and 1:10.2 respectively – significantly high ratios given the average for the pit as a whole at 1:5.5.

Unfortunately, this pit was atypical for the site as a whole, being rectangular in plan, straight-sided and with a ledge at the base of one side. The contents of the two layers in question produced weed seeds in greater quantities than most of the pits, and amongst them was the largest concentration of *Tripleurospermum* sp found on the whole site. All these characters would suggest something anomalous about this pit and would condition any general statements about the correlation between twig charcoal and chaff waste. It is, however, possible that the characteristic fill may relate to its function, which as yet is unclear, though it could be an Iron Age corn dryer or parching oven that had been backfilled with material accumulated during its use or during the use of a similar structure close by. Helbaek (1952, 231) interpreted Iron Age pits as corn dryers. Without independent structural evidence and comparanda from other sites, this interpretation is hardly more than speculation. Whatever the functional explanation of this pit, there does appear to be some benefit in comparing the evidence from the analyses of charcoal and seed remains, although the possible relationship between wood tinder and chaff tinder requires further investigation.

Wood charcoal by C Keepax

Forty-one samples, generally those with high charcoal concentrations, were selected from the available Winnall Down material and submitted for wood identification after removal of the charred seeds (above, p 112). The samples came from a variety of contexts: ditches, hut gullies, pits and post-holes. All of the charcoal discussed in this report was obtained by flotation. 'Flots' which had passed though the 1mm sieve were not identified, as identifications become difficult below this size and biased results are obtained (Keepax unpublished data). Some fragmentation had occured within the >1mm grade, resulting in unidentifiable material. The maximum size of fragments was usually about 5mm². Twenty fragments were picked out from each sample and the number from each taxa counted. Further fragments were identified, until most of the sample had been examined, or it was felt that a representative amount had been processed, usually 50, 100 or 150 fragments per sample. Where there were less than twenty fragments in a sample they were all counted (taxa lists in archive). The majority of the samples examined were from Phase 4, thus not allowing satisfactory inter-phase comparison. The additional time and cost were too expensive to justify further analysis. Figure 81 suggests that there are no obvious differences between the samples for each period that may not be accounted for by variation in the number of samples.

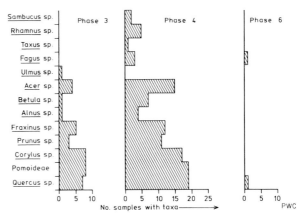

Fig 81.   Winnall Down: charcoal taxa from samples from different archaeological periods.

The following thirteen taxa were identified: *Quercus* sp (oak), Rosaceæ, sub-family Pomoideæ (*eg*, hawthorn), *Corylus avellana* L (hazel), *Acer* sp (*eg*, maple), *Fraxinus excelsior* L (ash), *Prunus* sp (*eg*, blackthorn), *Rhamnus catharticus* L (buckthorn), *Betula* sp (birch), *Alnus glutinosa* (L) Gaertn (alder), *Fagus sylvatica* L (beech), *Sambucus nigra* L (elder), *Taxus baccata* L (yew), *Ulmus* sp? (elm? – one sample only). All except birch, elm and yew have been identified from other sites along the line of the M3, particularly the Micheldever Wood 'banjo' enclosure (Keepax forthcoming). There do not appear to be any significant differences between the results from the 'banjo' enclosure and from Winnall Down.

Theoretically, the number of fragments of various taxa from any deposit is completely meaningless. The charcoal has been affected by many agencies during burial, excavation and separation, and it is likely that the amount of fragmentation occurring is highly variable. It was therefore surprising that some samples *eg*, 601 and 602, both from the Phase 3 pit 5797 layer 5798, showed repeatable results (Fig 82).

This suggested the possibility of characterising certain deposits by the charcoal within them. Histograms were therefore plotted of the number of fragments from each taxa within individual layers from the Phase 4 pit 5548. These were not subjected to statistical analysis, but a few points of interest did seem to emerge.

Many of the layers showed a variety of charcoal results, in which it was difficult to see general relationships (Fig 82B). A few layers, such as 5584 and 5568, seemed to show patterns not repeated elsewhere. They were also distinguished by noticeably high and low charcoal concentrations respectively. The separate identities of these particular layers therefore seemed to be underlined.

Two layers, 5590 and 5593, were distinguished by consisting almost entirely of twiggy material (Fig 82B). This seemed to suggest a similar (or closely contemporaneous) origin or, alternatively, that the

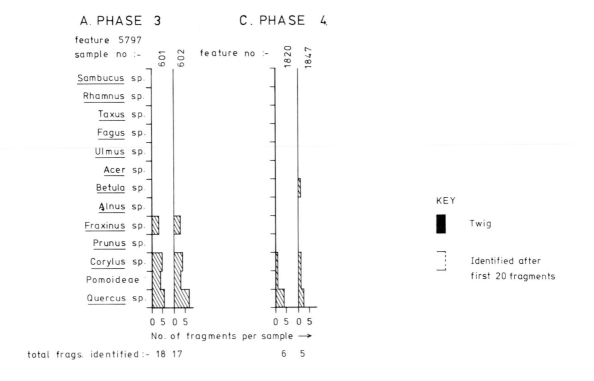

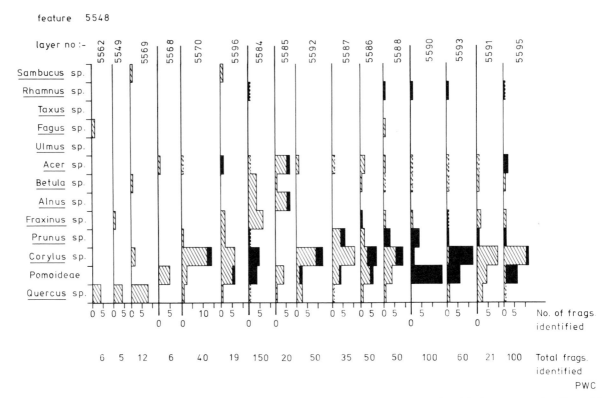

Fig 82. Winnall Down: charcoal. Number of fragments for each taxa identified per sample (first 20 fragments only). A, repeatable results from two different samples in pit 5797. B, fragments from each taxa within individual layers in pit 5548. C, charcoal from two shallow features, 1820 and 1847. Usually 20 fragments were picked out from each sample and the number from each taxa counted. Further fragments were then identified until most of the sample had been examined or it was felt that a representative amount had been processed (usually 50, 100 or 150 fragments per sample). Where less than 20 fragments occurred, all were identified.

difference between them observed in the field was not significant. Their separate nature compared to other layers was indicated.

The three upper layers, 5562, 5549, and 5569, produced very similar results which were distinguished from the rest of the feature in that oak predominated. They also contained less charcoal than the other layers (with the exception of 5568). This again seemed to suggest a similar origin, or that the differences between the three layers observed in the field were not significant. When the separate identity of these layers and their stratigraphical position is considered along with the paucity of material, it is tempting to suggest that this charcoal might be derived. For example, the feature may have been filled to the top of layer 5570 (see Fig 19) and then remained for some time as a depression which gradually filled up with material already containing charcoal from elsewhere. It is interesting to note that other shallow deposits from this site yielded similar quantities and types of charcoal (*eg*, 1820 and 1847, Fig 82C). This charcoal might also be seen as part of general 'background noise' and not of particular significance to the features concerned.

The above comments are extremely tentative in view of the small numbers of fragments counted and the relatively crude methods of comparison, and the given interpretation is only one possibility. It does, however, indicate an interesting field for further study.

The Human Skeletal Remains by J Bayley, P J Fasham and F V H Powell

The skeletons from Winnall Down represent 31/32 individuals (6 adults 25 children). There was one cremation and 78 instances of scattered bone. All these are shown by phase in Table 28.

In general, the bone preservation was good with most of the skeletons, including the infant skeletons, being complete. Ages of adults were calculated from dental attrition (Brothwell 1972) and estimated statures were calculated from the formulae of Trotter and Gleser (1958). The dental formulae are in the archive, apart from burial 629 which is included below (p 120). Where possible, sexing was based on observations made on the whole skeleton. Where this was not possible, the innominates were used with the skull characteristics and muscle markings as less reliable alternatives. Skull measurements and adult long bone measurements are in Tables 29 and 30 respectively. F V H Powell is responsible for the comments on the complete skeletons, J Bayley provided identification of the 'loose' human bones and P J Fasham has edited the two elements and added comments. Full details are in the archive.

Infants

The infants can of course be aged approximately. None appeared to have died as a consequence of premature birth.
a) Neo-natal. One complete individual and bones from seven other neo-natal infants were recorded.
b) Over birth-sized (6 ± 3 months). Bones from four individuals.
c) Less than *c* 1 year. Twenty individuals and twenty-four loose bones.
d) 1–3 years. Ribs and vertebrae of one individual.

Children

Burial 126. Fragmentary but more or less complete skeleton of 5–6 year old child. Phase 6 grave 685.

Burial 506. Very fragmentary skeleton of child less than 12 years old. Phase 4 grave 8294.

Burial 505 (Fig 21) is the skeleton of a child of 8 or 9 years, basing the age on the state of tooth eruption and the non-union of the ischium, pubis, and ilium of the innominates. The estimated stature is 1.178m or 3 feet 10½ inches. It is possible that this individual may be female, though the sexing of children's skeletons is very tenuous. Neck caries is present on one premolar. Though the skull is fragmentary, osteoporosis was observed on the internal surface of the occipital, along the venous sinus. Phase 4 grave 8184.

Adolescent

Burial 174 (Fig 22) is the skeleton probably of an adolescent male of less than 15 years. The estimated stature is 1.538m or 5 feet ¼ inches. The left fibula shows a significant degree of lateral bowing with the bone measuring 8mm away from the straight at mid-shaft. The left mandibular canine has an anomaly of bifurcated roots. Phase 4 pit 4475.

There were also several bones from an individual estimated to be 15–20 years from other layers in pit 4475. As these other bones include another pair of patella they must be from a second individual.

Adults

Burial 500 (Fig 22) is the skeleton of a male aged between 35 and 40 years. The estimated stature is 1.68m or 5 feet 6¼ inches. The muscle markings are moderate throughout the skeleton. No marked abnormalities were observed apart from two instances of ankylosis. The left wrist showed extensive ankylosis with osteoarthritic lipping on the distal ends of the ulna and radius, as well as the carpal bones. The carpals themselves showed healed fractures which indicate a severe trauma. The left elbow joint, particularly the proximal end of the ulna, had slight osteoarthritic lipping which may be related as a reaction to the trauma at the wrist. The type and degree of injury suggests a fall forward onto the left hand.

The second instance of pathological ankylosis was to the first metacarpal of the left foot. Bony growths are seen at the distal articulations and the area of the articulation itself has been extended downwards. The cause of this ankylosis is unknown but an injury may again be to blame. Phase 4 pit 8564.

Burial 629 (Fig 23) is the skeleton of a female of approximately 17 to 25 years and having an estimated stature of 1.558m or 5 feet 1¼ inches. The sexing was based on the skull characteristics, as the innominates failed to survive. Reconstruction, using UHU glue, of the skull and mandible had to be done before measurements could be taken.

Slight osteoarthritic lipping was observed at the proximal end of the right humerus and the glenoid fossa of the right scapula, with slight to moderate lipping at both femoral condyles and proximal

Table 28. Distribution of complete human skeletons and 'loose' human bones by Phase.

Complete or partially complete skeletons

	Phase					No Phase	Total
	3	4	5	6	7		
Male adult	–	1	–	–	–	1	
Female adult	–	2+?2	–	–	1	4+?1	
< 15 years	–	1	–	–	–	1	
1–12	–	2	–	1	–	3	
< 1	1	9	–	4	6	20	
Neo-natal	–	1	–	–	–	1	
Cremation	–	–	–	1	–	1	
	1	18	0	6	0	7	32

Odd bones

	3	4	5	6	7	No Phase	Total
Adult	21	14	–	5	–	1	41
Adolescent	–	1	–	–	–	–	1
1–3 years	–	–	–	–	–	1	1
c 1 year	–	–	–	1	–	–	1
Over birth-sized (b±3 months)	–	2	–	2	–	–	4
Birth-sized (neo-natal)	1	6	–	–	–	–	7
Infant	1	2	1	13	1	5	23
	23	25	1	21	1	7	78

ends of both tibiæ. The lumbar region of the vertebral column shows signs of injury or possible traumatic osteoarthritis. L2 shows marked lipping while the other lumbar vertebrae have slight lipping. L5 is wedge-shaped and compacted.

The major pathological area of this skeleton is of the teeth and alveolar region. There is a high degree of abscessing and ante-mortem tooth loss. Alveolar resorption is marked. The dental formula is (symbols used are the same as used by Brothwell 1972):

X X X X X $\cancel{3}$ $\cancel{2}$ $\cancel{1}$	1 2 3 4 5 6 7 8
X X X $\cancel{5}$ $\cancel{4}$ 3 $\cancel{2}$ $\cancel{1}$	1 2 $\cancel{3}$ 4 X X 7 8
A A C A	

There is much attrition of the lower incisors and canines. This wear may be attributed to some occupational habit, as in chewing leather for softening, or to constant chewing by the front teeth because of the molar loss. Perio-dontal disease may be the cause of the tooth loss. Phase 4 grave 10312.

Burial 574 (Fig 22) is the skeleton of a female with an estimated stature of 1.583m or 5 feet 2½ inches. The number of teeth and their condition did not allow for accurate ageing. It would be safe to say, however, that the individual was over 25 years.

Arthritic lipping was observed on several of the centra of the vertebral column. The skull was quite thick, having a parietal thickness of 8 mm, with much internal pitting observed on the frontal, parietals, and occipital. One maxillary molar and one mandibular molar had both neck caries and attrition to the dentine. Loose bones 3566 and 3566a may be associated. Phase 4 pit 8630.

Burial 650 (not illustrated) is the skeleton of a young female probably of 18 to 20 years. Most of the long bone epiphyses have united but the line of fusion, in most cases, is still visible. The epiphyses of the pelvis have not united. The estimated stature is 1.624m or 5 feet 4 inches. The state of preservation of the skeleton is poor with much shattering. A possible septal aperture may be present on the right humerus but certainty is impossible due to breakage. The skull was extremely fragmented and impossible to reconstruct. Only the left half of the maxilla was present. Most of the right maxillary teeth were found loose. The mandible is also fragmentary with only the left side being complete. It should be noted that the mandibular left canine has not erupted properly and was still in the crypt completely formed. The maxillary left canine also has not fully erupted and is twisted mesially. Un-phased grave 11034.

Burial 508 (Fig 21). Based on the pelvis and muscle markings, this skeleton is probably that of a female. However some pelvic

Table 29. Skull measurements.

Measurements	Skeleton 500	Skeleton 629	Skeleton 508	Skeleton 174
L	185	189	174	–
B	145	134	127	120
B'	101	92	91	92
H'	140	141	128	–
LB	98	108	105	–
S_1	135	132	115	–
S_2	130	139	118	116
S_3	119	119	105	–
S_1'	116	116	101	–
S_2'	118	122	104	101
S_3'	93	97	90	–
BiB	108	114	103	–
G'H	67	–	–	–
GL	93	–	–	–
GB	62	–	–	–
G_2	59	–	34	–
G_1'	40	–	–	–
J	116	–	–	–
$0_1'$	38	–	–	–
$0_2'$	33	–	–	–
FL	38	37	34	–
FB	29	29	30	–
NB	23	–	–	–
NH'	33	–	–	–
SC	8	–	–	–
DC	23	–	–	–
W_1	–	–	–	108
ZZ	–	–	42	43
RB	32	–	–	–
H_1	–	–	29	–
M_2H	27	–	24	27
CH	67	–	56	–
CyL	72	–	54	–
ML	–	–	–	–
M<	–	–	–	–
RL	–	–	–	–

characteristics suggest the possibility that it may be a male. The estimated stature is 1.543m or 5 feet ¾ inches, which further suggests a female individual. The line of fusion of the epiphysis of the lesser trochanter of the left femur is just visible, which would indicate that the individual was in her early 20's at the time of death. The attrition on the molars also suggests an age of 20 to 25 years.

A most striking anomaly of this skeleton is a complete metopic suture of the frontal bone. Another anomaly is the sacralisation of the 5th lumbar vertebra. Caries in the mandibular molars were all in the neck of the tooth. Phase 4 quarry pit 8265.

Burial 35 (Fig 23) was submitted to Harwell for a radiocarbon determination. It was unfortunately not examined before being sent. From the site drawings and the photographs it appears to be the skeleton of a mature, but not elderly, adult, probably female. Phase 4 grave 2022.

Cremation

Cremation 133. Long bone fragments predominate. A low temperature during burning is suggested by the colour of the bone (white on the surface but black internally), and the absence of any fissuring or heat cracks. Identification of age or sex was impossible.

Table 30. Measurements of adult bones.

Measurement	500		629		574		505		650		508		174	
	L	R	L	R	L	R	L	R	L	R	L	R	L	R
FeL_1	446	433	412	410	422	–	239	258	–	–	399	399	–	–
FeD_1	24	24	25	26	25	23	15	16	23	24	22	22	22	22
FeD_2	37	34	34	33	34	35	19	19	32	33	34	35	30	30
Platymeric Index	648	706	735	787	714	657	789	842	718	726	647	629	733	733
TiL_1	373	369	339	–	353	–	206	210	–	–	329	329	–	–
TiD_1	40	39	30	–	39	39	19	20	31	35	38	38	32	33
TiD_2	30	29	29	–	29	29	19	10	22	26	29	31	23	24
Platycnemic Index	750	763	743	–	743	763	1000	1000	709	745	605	815	718	727
HuL_1	311	316	291	302	–	–	185	190	–	311	273	227	269	276
HuD_1	24	25	25	26	22	24	–	13	20	20	22	22	21	22
HuD_2	16	18	16	16	17	17	–	10	16	16	16	15	15	16
Head Diam.	–	–	40	44	42	42	–	–	–	44	40	42	–	38
HaL_1	–	247	216	219	230	–	–	–	–	240	210	210	204	204
UIL_1	253	273	239	240	–	252	150	149	255	–	227	228	229	230
FiL_1	–	–	–	–	–	346	199	197	–	–	316	–	–	–
Clavicle L.	152	147	127	–	–	–	87	86	–	–	129	123	125	123
Glenoid Fossa Length	38	42	38	41	34	35	–	–	–	34	34	34	30	34
Glenoid Fossa Breadth	27	–	27	28	24	25	–	–	–	26	24	24	24	24

Discussion

The few skeletons and the skeletal fragments from Winnall Down are not, of course, assumed to be representative of the entire population. There are many factors which would affect the age and sex distribution of people casually buried in disused pits or even deliberately buried in graves. There were eight instances of a complete skeleton being buried in the same feature as another complete skeleton or with 'loose' bones. Six examples were in Phase 4, one in Phase 6 and one was unphased. There were also two examples in Phase 4 of several different 'loose' bones occuring in one feature. The full details are described in the relevant phase section. The ratio of infant (up to one year) to adult (excluding adolescents) was 7:2, cf Gussage All Saints where it was 5:2 (Keepax 1979).

There was only one formal burial, that of an infant in Phase 3, but only two of the twenty-three records of isolated skeletal fragments belonged to infants in the Early Iron Age. This compares with ten out of twenty-five and sixteen out of twenty-one in Phases 4 and 6. This may well be a reflection of changes in burial practice between Phases 3 and 4. There are examples of all age ranges up to 35–40 recorded years.

Two individuals show signs of ante-mortem accident. The ankylosis of burial 500 is thought to have been caused by a fall to the left, and 629 had signs of injury or traumatic osteoarthritis in the back. Burial 174 had a lateral bowing of the left fibula. Of the five adults examined two had osteoarthritis: 574 in the vertebrae and 629 in the arm and shoulder. In the general fragments, there were three instances of osteoarthritis.

Apart from skeleton 629 whose ten teeth, five lower and five upper, had been lost ante-mortem and where there were three abscesses and one curious tooth, there was one further instance each of ante-mortem tooth loss and abscess in 508, and caries was present in skeleton 574 and the young 174. The latter had a bifurcated canine root. One adult maxilla and three adult mandibles were among the 'loose' human bones, caries was noted in one of these mandibles and ante-mortem tooth loss in a second.

The one male was 168cm (5' 6¼") tall and the females over 17 years old were between 154cm (5' ¾") and 162cm (5' 4"). These heights are comparable with those at Gussage All Saints (Keepax 1979).

Among the adult population there seems to have been a fairly high incidence of injury, two out of the five examined, and osteoarthritis, again two out of five. Dental hygiene appears to be poor for an Iron Age population, with three of the five adults affected and one of the teenagers suffering from caries. The dental condition is probably related to diet. There are only three slight skeletal abnormalities.

Land Molluscs by C Mason

Columns were analysed from four of the occupation phases evident in the 1,000 years of habitation of the site. Phase 1 was the Neolithic ring-ditch, dealt with in a separate report (Fasham 1982). No samples were available from the Bronze Age. Phases 3, 4 and 6 were sampled as follows:

Features 8817/8818/8082	Samples	2641–2646	Phase 6	Enclosure ditch
F 1308/493	S	280–283	Phase 6	Enclosure ditch
F 8581	S	493/496	Phase 6	Pit
F 7372	S	308–323	Phase 4,6	Pit
F 6038	S	473–482	Phase 4	Pit
F 5GG	S	294–307	Phase 3,4,6	Enclosure ditch
F 5AA	S	225–236	Phase 3,4	Enclosure ditch
F 3935	S	71–75	Phase 3	Pit

Methods of extraction, identification and analysis can be found in Evans (1972). The results are available in table form in the archive. Most samples weighed 1.0kg. The exceptions were: 298, 150g; 295, 250g; 294, 400g; 225, 300, 299, 2641, 480, 500g; 306, 600g; 297, 296, 2643, 2642, 478, 474, 750g.

Interpretation

Feature 3935 Phase 3 was analysed and found to contain only six snails in all five samples. These were discarded. The samples contained more than 75% chalk rubble by weight, including a large quantity of fine chalk left as a residue after washing. This suggested deliberate backfilling of the feature allowing no molluscan colonisation.

Features 5AA and 5GG were different sections of the D-shaped enclosure ditch dated to the Early Iron Age. As in feature 3935, a lot of chalk residue remained after washing, particularly in the lower samples. The high rubble content in some of the layers effectively reduced the sample size being dealt with. For instance, samples 226 and 227 (5AA) weighed 1.0kg each before washing, but the residue weighed 950g and 970g respectively. This had the effect of reducing the potential snail-bearing material in these two samples to 50g and 30g respectively. This supports the case for increasing the sample size considerably, to 5kg, where excessively rubble-filled layers are being dealt with. Without exception, the Early Iron Age samples produced very few snails, probably due to the high rubble content as much as the unsuitability of the environment to support molluscs.

Only feature 5AA produced a reasonable Middle Iron Age ditch fauna. Samples 230 to 236 were dated to this phase and combination of the results produced 417 snails (Fig 83). The majority of these were open-country species with a predominance of *Vallonia costata*. A 12% occurrence of *Helicella itala* was suggestive of arable land use, as was the presence of fine silty soil in all samples. However, there was also a large proportion of chalk in these samples, though not as much as in the lower layers, mostly large rubble. The presence of almost 10% *Vitrea contracta* and 3% *Oxychilus cellarius* is worth noting since these species are capable of living in open ground normally considered hostile to them if there are shaded refuges available. The rubble-filled ditch, with its moisture-retentive properties and nooks and crannies between the lumps of chalk, would provide such refuges.

This could therefore be viewed as an embryonic rock-rubble fauna (Evans and Jones 1973), which was short-lived because agricultural activity aided the silting-up of the ditch. It also suggests that refuges for shade-loving species were to be found close to the settlement.

Two other ditch faunas were sampled, both Romano-British, from the rectangular enclosure ditches. Samples 2641 to 2646 were from a complex ditch of three features 8818, 8817 and 8082 (Fig 83). *Pupilla muscorum* dominated the fauna at 35%, with 22% *Vallonia costata* suggesting an open, dry environment with unstable ground bare of vegetation. The proportion of *Helicella itala* present increased towards the top of the section, suggesting the introduction of arable land use.

Ditch 493/1308 produced a similar fauna, high in *Pupilla* but with a much higher proportion of *H itala* (Fig 83) at 22%. This is typical of arable land use, except for the higher than usual occurrence of *Pupilla* which was probably accounted for by the local conditions pertaining to the ditch.

The rest of the analysis was carried out on pits which may not produce faunas representative of the surrounding area because of their tendency to produce microenvironments which may favour one or more species. They were also placed within the settlement, where the influence of man was at its greatest, with all its attendant effects on the wild-life. It should therefore be understood that each pit could have its own idiosyncratic fauna.

Pits 6038 and 7372 had Middle Iron Age faunas (7372 also included Romano-British levels) which were similar in species content but very different in proportional representation. 50% of the fauna of 6038 was *Vallonia costata* and 20% *V excentrica*, the remaining 30% being distributed fairly evenly between *P muscorum*, *H itala* and *Trichia hispida*. This was mostly from the top layers of the pit, the lower levels being impoverished, and therefore represented a time when the pit was largely filled and not much more than a shallow depression. The predominance of *V costata* suggests that there was a measure of instability in the ground surface, though this species can be regarded as synanthropic (certainly more than its congener), dwelling in close proximity to man where agricultural activity was not too intensive.

Pit 7372 had a proportionally more even distribution of species, *Trichia hispida*, *Vallonia costata*, *V excentrica* and *Pupilla muscorum* all falling between 18% and 26%, with *Helicella itala* at 10%. Once again the lower levels of the pit had few shells and the combination of all the Middle Iron Age samples (308 to 315) produced only 141 snails (Fig 83). The Romano-British layers of pit 7372 were more productive and the fauna was similar to that of the Iron Age with slightly more *V costata* and *P muscorum*. An open, dry environment with bare or unstable ground surface is suggested.

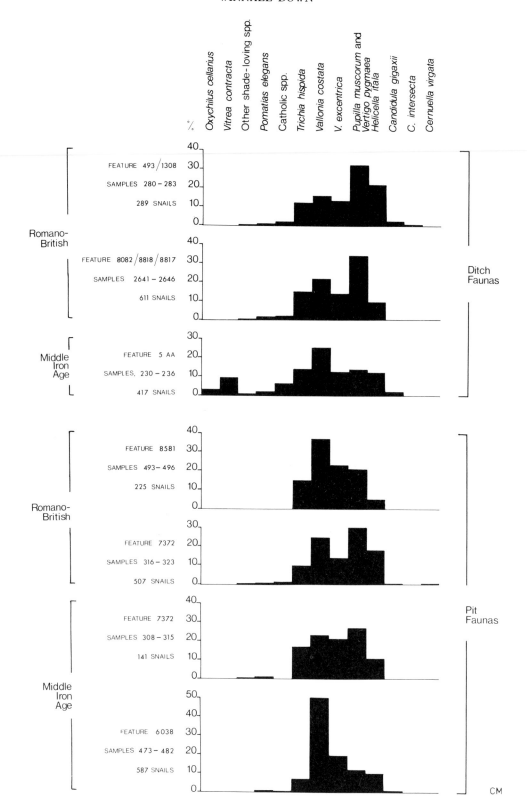

Fig 83. Winnall Down: summary histogram of snails from selected features.

Pit 8581 was exclusively Romano-British (Fig 83). *Vallonia costata* was the most abundant species and the fauna was similar to pit 6038, though not quite as extreme.

Winnall Down produced an impoverished fauna of a few species which were predominantly open-country inhabitants, representative of arable or bare, unstable ground. The faunal variations were probably caused by the proximity of man and his constant interference with the habitat. The necessity to combine samples into blocks, because of low numbers of shells, made the production of an environmental sequence of events an impossible speculation. It would appear, however, that open-country and possibly arable, land use was present throughout the occupation period of the site.

Chapter 5

Discussion and General Observations

Phase 2. The Bronze Age

The residual Deverel-Rimbury material indicates activity, possibly occupation, in the Middle Bronze Age. The Winnall Down pottery is broadly contemporary with the Type 1 Globular and the bucket urns discovered 500m to the west by Mrs Hawkes (1969) during the excavation of the Winnall II Anglo-Saxon cemetery. Recent work on the characterization of Deverel-Rimbury pottery from Cranborne Chase (Barrett *et al* 1978) raises the possibility that the material from both Winnall Down and Winnall II might be related to the suggested second cremation phase of burial at the Easton Down ring-ditch (Fasham 1982), or to the unexcavated ring-ditch 600m to the south, or to the Magdalen Hill barrow cemetery.

The later Bronze Age settlement was comprised of at least four houses and a fence. Houses A and C and fence 1 are dated by associated finds, and it seems reasonable to assume that houses B and E and structure A were broadly contemporary. The relationship of fence 1 with house C demands that there were at least two sub-phases of activity. The number of permutations of the structural sequence are so great that it is not worth speculating about them.

The settlement is in an area of 'Celtic' fields which would have been based on the probable double-lynchet trackway. Thus, if the fields are contemporary with the settlement, the landscape would have formed an integrated entity. However, the field system has been extensively damaged by ploughing and it is not possible to establish any relationships with other elements of the prehistoric landscape.

The four houses are the only Late Bronze Age examples from central Hampshire. They were 7–8m in diameter (floor areas of 38.5m² to 50.1m²) and were thus 1–2m larger in diameter than the Middle Bronze Age examples at Clanfield (Chalton Site 78 – Cunliffe 1970) and West Meon (Lewis and Walker 1976). Three of the Winnall Down houses had porches. House A had a simple rectangular porch created by two posts while houses B and C had complex arrangements with pairs of double or replaced posts, perhaps indicating doors in the porch. There were no finds in houses B and D although, in

the latter case, this may not be a real absence as the post-holes were, at the time of excavation, so small. Fragments of possible quern stones in post-holes 6482 and 6490 in house C suggest that food may have been prepared there. Although the structures are not contemporary, certain aspects of the settlement are reminiscent of Ellison's standard domestic unit (Ellison 1978, 36) of the Late Bronze Age, though with no larger hut and no evidence for grain storage facilities either above or below ground, unless post-hole 6482 is regarded as a small storage pit.

The available evidence does not permit much to be written about the social, economic or agricultural background except that a small mixed farming unit is suggested by the loomweights and the quernstones. The pottery was probably locally made, and the white quartzite (sarsen) fragments could have been obtained within a few kilometres of the site (Fasham 1980). The greensand quern is likely to have been imported from 20–30 km to the east from a source on the Hampshire/Surrey border. It must not be forgotten however that the settlement at Winnall Down would probably have played its part in a dynamic system of trade and exchange.

Phase 3. The Early Iron Age

A number of Early Iron Age occupation sites, apart from the hill-forts, have been excavated in Hampshire. There are enclosures at Old Down Farm (Davies 1980) and Portway (Champion pers com) and suggestions of early ditches at Owlesbury (Collis 1968 and 1970) and Ructstall's Hill (Oliver and Applin 1978). The early ditch at Meon Hill (Liddell 1933, 1935) has been interpreted as representing a 'palisaded enclosure' (Cunliffe 1978, 176). The open settlement at Wallington Military road was related to a linear ditch system (Hughes 1974). The diversity in the nature of Early Iron Age settlements is evident elsewhere in Wessex. At Gussage All Saints, the settlement was enclosed by a ditch and at Little Woodbury by a 'palisade' (Bersu 1940).

The Enclosure Ditch

The ditch itself was larger near the entrance, particularly to the south, than elsewhere. The cross-sectional area was up to twice as large near the entrance than on the east side. This may relate to a need for an impressive ditch by the entrance. The ditch at Bishopstone, amongst others, displayed some variation in dimension, but not so obviously related to the entrance (Bell 1977). The ditch at Winnall Down displayed no evidence of cleaning or recutting. It has been estimated that 85% of the ditch had silted up by Phase 4. It would appear that the significance of the ditch diminished once it had been dug.

Structures

House E, with the penannular gully, represents a well known form of Iron Age architecture.

It is a structural form more commonly found in the Middle Iron Age, although early examples are known from Overton Down (Fowler 1967), Sandown Park (Burchell and Frere 1947) and probably Aldwick (Cra'ster 1961). If it is assumed that the gully was structural and had posts set in it, rather than a drain, which would not have been topographically realistic, then the stakeholes in the upper fill of the gully must relate to a rebuilding phase.

The post-built circular houses may not look convincing, but several examples of irregularly-shaped but clearly isolated houses have been published, as for example at Tollard Royal (Wainwright 1968) or some of the houses at Maiden Castle (Wheeler 1943). The essential point with the Winnall Down examples is not that their post arrangements are irregular but that repeated analyses of all the post-holes on the site indicate circular structures of similar size to the published examples. The minor details may well not be right but the general impression is probably correct. Houses of both post-ring and penannular gully form are present in the Early Iron Age at Old Down Farm (Davies 1980). Of the three types of four-post structures represented in this phase, the large squarish ones, Group B, are similar in size to four-post structures found throughout the Iron Age and which are normally interpreted as granaries. This is a limited interpretation of a most utilitarian pattern of post-holes which could easily be used as a chicken coop, an animal pen, a small shed or a support for logs.

The small square structures of Group A probably do have a specialised function but it is too early for speculation.

It is the Group C set of four-post structures which is the most interesting. They form a long, thin rectangle and usually have two big posts paired with two smaller ones. It has been suggested that four-post structures are the sole remaining evidence of post or stake-built round houses (Jones 1975, 196). Alternative explanations should be sought for this distinctive and, as yet, unparalleled arrangement of posts.

Close to four-post structures *g* and *t* were pits 2630 and 2676 in which were found 41 fragments from about 11 loomweights and 25 fragments from 14 loomweights respectively. Loomweight classes A, D and E only were represented. The spatial correlation between these abandoned loomweights and structures *g* and *t* does suggest that this particular variety of four-post structure was related to weaving, and that the vertical loom may in fact have been A- or H-framed rather than represented by a single pair of posts. Despite Hoffman's belief that the upright loom was essentially portable, to be leant against a wall, there is no reason, apart from climate, why these four-post structures could not have been semi-permanent looms. This interpretation would not exclude the other, well-rehearsed, possible functions of four-post structures.

The other post-built structures worth noting are the small, circular or sub-circular arrangements of posts and stakes represented by structures *b* and *c*. The former is a particularly coherent example of what may have been a granary similar to the Scottish 'byre' (Dunbar 1932, Monk and Fasham 1980).

Activities outside the enclosure

The principal activity outside the enclosure revolved around the scoops to the northwest of the site. Stratigraphic relationships in the area strongly suggest that the digging of the scoops started in the Early Iron Age. Their purpose can only be guessed, but the completely amorphous form of these interconnecting features strongly suggests that they were quarries, rather than large working hollows (Bersu 1940) or occupation areas (Liddell 1935). The chalk might have been quarried for building purposes, for manufacturing loomweights and for marling the fields. It seems reasonable that the ditch was filled-in or bridged to allow easier access to the quarries. A few pits astride the south-east corner imply a similar bridging of the ditch.

Spatial relations and activity areas in the Early Iron Age

The use of a computer for basic manipulation of the data base made it possible to produce overlay plots of all classes of artifacts, structures and other features. Within the financial restraints of rescue archaeology it was not possible to statistically test any of the observed relationships of the plots. In the sections that relate to spatial analysis, the related distributions are accurate, though the deductive consequences which appear in this report will undoubtedly be modified by other scholars approaching the data with alternative models. The total, or almost

Winnall Down

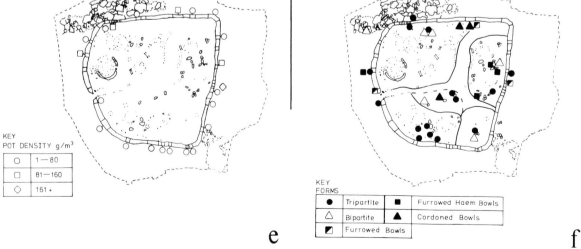

Fig 84. Winnall Down: distributions of selected elements in the Early Iron Age. a) Total density of animal bone fragments per m³; b) density of cattle bone fragments per m³; c) pits by volumetric range; d) distribution of triangular loomweights; e) pottery density per m³ in enclosure ditch 5; f) select pottery forms and outlines of the four activity areas.

total, excavation of an Iron Age site on the chalkland of central southern England is rare (Wainwright 1979 *viii–xi*), and consequently it is necessary to attempt to examine as many intra-site variables, albeit without statistical correlative analysis, as financial constraints allow. Simple distributions, and comments on those distributions, have been prepared for Phases 3, 4 and 6 of the settlement on Winnall Down.

There was a fairly even distribution of coarse and fine pottery except in one area (see below). Metalwork was limited to three iron nails (*eg* Fig 48.53 and 54), an iron goad (Fig 43.24), an iron object (Fig 47.48) and four iron fragments. The nails were from shallow scoops, and the remaining material from pits within the enclosure, except for one fragment from the enclosure ditch. Five objects of worked bone (*eg* Fig 74.12 and 14) and four of antler (Fig 73.1, 3, 4 and 5) were located thus: three bone objects in the quarry areas and one immediately to the south; an antler object from a post-hole near the entrance; and the remainder from the south-east corner of the enclosure.

The general plotting of artifacts, structures and features enabled four distinct areas within the enclosure to be determined (Fig 84).

Area 1 occupied the north-west corner of the site from the entrance as far east as fence 4 and contained the elaborate gully structure, house E, and the post-built circular huts F and L. It was characterized by a large proportion of four-post structures, particularly Group C, by a high depositional rate of triangular loomweights and fragments and by medium-sized pits. The densest concentration of animal bone, particularly cattle bones, occurred in Area 1.

Area 2 in the north-east corner extended from house H to a point 10m south of house K and west to fence 6. Area 2 contained, and was characterized by, a series of shallow pits/scoops.

Area 3 in the south-west corner contained very little. Worked bone objects were recovered from pits around the perimeter of the area; crucible fragments were found in the small pit 1053, which also contained a high density of pottery per m³, although this pit may relate to Area 4.

Area 4 occupied the south-west corner from four-post structure *n* in the east to *k* in the west and north to pit 3935. It contained two post-built circular structures, houses I and J, and was characterized by a small group of large pits and a considerable volume of daub and baked clay.

There was a fairly even distribution of fine and coarse wares between the Areas, except for a concentration of haematite-coated, furrowed and cordoned bowls in Area 2.

There are only limited repetitions of associations within each of the four Areas. The whole of the following discussion must be regarded as 'best-guess' interpretations of the observed relationships.

Area 1 contained the largest house attributed to this phase and two other huts, and would thus seem to represent the major family unit of occupation. This unit was provided with four-post structures (? granaries) and medium-sized pits. The predominance of Class C four-post structures and the high depositional rate of loomweights suggests that weaving was a specialised activity in this Area. The Area was bounded on the south and east by an open space which would have provided internal access around the site; it might have been fenced, though there is no evidence to support this. The relationship of house E and structure *b* shows that rebuilding took place, and that the function of the Area might have changed through time.

Area 2 contained the crude, circular house H, a possible circular structure in house K, and a series of shallow pits and scoops. There is no clear artifact distribution for this area and it seems that this was an area for activities of an unknown purpose. The Area is defined on its west side by a portion of double-fencing separating it from an open space.

Area 3 is ill-defined, relying for its separate identification on a central, blank area surrounded by peripheral pits. The absence of post-built structures attributed to this Area may be more illusory than real. The distinctive artifact associated with this area is worked bone.

Area 4 contained two post-built huts, houses I and J, some four-post structures (? granaries) and the largest pits, probably storage pits for seed corn. This Area appears to represent a second living-unit, perhaps where crop-processing took place.

The lack of vertical stratigraphy and the infrequency of horizontal relationships means that there are whole ranges of structures and activities not represented. Courtyards are not readily recognisable, although the areas to the east of houses E and F in Area 1 and to the north of houses I and J in Area 4 might be so construed. The functions of the different huts and their associated activities can only be crudely guessed; annexe huts and sties or byres are not identifiable, although they must have existed. Essential, but missing, activities include woodworking and metalworking, although the community might have relied on trade and exchange for finished metal objects.

The activities that have been identified include weaving, but not spinning, in Area 1, the working of animal bone in Area 3 and perhaps the butchery of animals and grain storage in Area 4. The distribution of quernstone fragments in the ditch around Area 4 suggests that flour-milling occurred in that Area.

Up to four houses may have been occupied simultaneously – houses E, F, I and J. House L was a little small, house H was crude and house K was incomplete; these three may have been workshops. If all four huts were occupied, the maximum roofed area would have been 240m²; if only house E and one other house were for living purposes, the available floor area would have been 182–199m². Following Cook and Heizer's (1968) model for occupancy related to the floor area of each house, the number of individuals living on Winnall Down in the Early Iron Age may have been about 41.

The distribution of pottery and animal bones shows generally similar trends, but with different details. Larger sherds and greater quantities of both artifacts (in terms of density per m³) were discarded in the pits, presumably as 'primary' rubbish, while 'secondary' rubbish was found in the enclosure ditch.

A number of separate elements may hint at the economic base of the Early Iron Age settlers on Winnall Down. There are the very specific Class C four-post structures (the possible semi-permanent looms), the relative high numbers of loomweights, and the small capacity for below ground storage. Mr Maltby's interpretation of the animal bones suggests that sheep formed an important component of the economy at Winnall Down. It is possible to suggest that, while Winnall Down was probably a mixed agricultural unit, some of the wealth that the occupants of Early Iron Age Winnall Down possessed may have been produced by the manufacture and exchange of wool or woollen products. This hypothesis could be proposed more strongly had more bone combs and beaters been recovered.

Phase 4. The Middle Iron Age

The characteristics of this phase are the clear separation of penannular hut gullies within the context of a settlement without prescribed limits.

The bank and ditch of the Phase 3 enclosure must still have been visible, since the Phase 6 enclosures are aligned on its east side. The immediate implication is that, on the west side, the earlier features had already been slighted or were deliberately flattened to allow houses M and N to be constructed. As many as six of these huts could have been standing at any one time.

The Structures

Penannular gullies have been interpreted as having a drainage function (Jones 1974), and/or used as stock enclosures (Lambrick and Robinson 1979), or as foundation trenches for timber-built round houses (Drury 1978), or as round-houses with mud walls (Smith 1979). Structures E, F and house V will be considered separately from the other seven gullies.

These seven features were all probably huts with the gullies containing posts separated by wattle panels (Drury 1978). The principal timbers in the huts may have been oak (Drury 1978, 116).

Structure F has the appearance of a hut gully, but there is no valid reason for only one-third of a complete circle surviving. There was no additional erosion east of feature 4607 which cut through it. That and the fact that it was isolated from the other gullies suggests that it was a length of fence/palisade rather than a fragment of a hut circle.

Structure E clearly was not a hut circle. It bore some resemblance to F1010 at Farmoor where such features were regarded as stock pens or yards for work or storage (Lambrick and Robinson 1979) and to the smaller ditch 346 at Ashville (Parrington 1978). At the entrance of structure E was a contemporary pit, 4006, which contained a high proportion of bones of larger mammals. This relationship might imply that E was used for a final form of stock-processing related to butchery.

Similarly house V, which represented about 50% of a complete circle, is not necessarily a house. Immediately south was pit 6595 which, apart from the almost complete skeletons of a sow and a dog and a chalk mould, contained a high proportion of larger animal bones. This structure may also have been related to stock processing.

If, therefore, three of the huts provided centres for activities other than purely living accommodtion, a total of eight structures, seven gullies and one post-ring, remain for occupation. A maximum of six houses may have been standing at any one time providing 645–658m² of covered floor area. Calculating the population for each house based on Cook and Heizer's figures (1968) indicates a population of 91 or 92 people.

The rectangular structure D with its open (perhaps gated) east side was probably associated with animal control and may have been a simple sheep fold. The partitioning of the north-west corner may indicate a more specific use of the enclosure, perhaps for gelding or branding. A radically different interpretation of this structure is that it was a shrine. Several rectangular Iron Age structures have been considered to be religious sites, but usually they are no more than about 10m by 10m (Drury 1980). There is nothing special or unusual about the artifacts associated with structure D, although its central position within the enclosure may indicate special significance.

The Pits

The contents of the pits are a reflection of activities rather than of areas of activities. Thus, for example, the animal bone data suggests specialised functions relating to animal butchery in the vicinity of pits 4006 and 6595. The greater volume of domestic refuse was found in the central pits around pit 7376 and may thus reflect that, at the height of prosperity during this phase, those pits were easiest of access, not necessarily the closest to the occupation and/or activity areas. There was clearly a greater grain storage capacity than in the Early Iron Age.

The pits of smaller volume fall into three groups, while the larger pits form one broad spread. Functional use of the pits may be the cause. Pits 2416 and 6038 may have been deliberately constructed within hut gullies 1821 and 200 respectively. Those pits that can be attributed to early in the Middle Iron Age tended to be small and occurred to the west of, or on the periphery of, the other pits. The later pits tended to be large and in the middle of the 'banana'-shaped wedge of pits.

Environmental

The charcoal indicates that there were similar sorts of wood and timber available as in the Early Iron Age, except that *Ulmus* sp (elm) was not discovered. The greater number of samples examined led to the additional identification of *Sambucus nigra* L (elder), *Rhamnus catharticas* L (buckthorn), *Taxus baccata* L (yew) and *Fagus sylvatica* L (beech). Oak and *cf* hawthorn were the most commonly burnt, followed by hazel and maple. Oak, hazel and hawthorn all provide good fuel, but oak is likely to have been used in buildings and hazel in wattles.

Six row hulled barley was the most important cereal grown, followed by wheat (probably spelt) and a few oats. Cultivated beans and peas survived in the archaeological record and give some indication of the variety of cereals and vegetables available. The weed seeds indicate that wheat (probably spelt) was sown in the autumn and the harvesting involved cutting the straw close to the ground, or even uprooting the stalk. In this way, the straw could have been dried and used for a range of domestic purposes, including bedding and kindling. Barley fragments were dominant in the east half of the site, particularly in the south-east corner and this may reflect winter storage whereas wheat, possibly residue from domestic milling, was the dominant species in the west half.

Pottery

Pottery was found mainly in the Phase 3 enclosure ditch 5 or in the pits. The sherds were larger in the latter context. The distribution of pottery around ditch 5 revealed the highest densities to be to the south and east. There were bigger sherds and denser concentrations in the central area of the pits, a distribution reflected in the density of animal bones. Higher densities of pottery in the north-east and south-east may indicate that the settlement extended in these directions.

Spatial Relationships in the Middle Iron Age (Figs 85 and 86)

There was a major division between the area containing the hut gullies and that containing the pits.

House V and structure *E* at the south differed in form to the others. Four-post structures were widely dispersed although they occurred only sporadically in the southern part of the site, structures *bb*, *ii* and *kk*. There was a small concentration of four-post structures on the east and four occurred either within or adjacent to the hut gullies in the north-west area.

Most of the pits were on the east half of the site with a marked clustering in the south-east corner of the disused Phase 3 enclosure. When the distribution of the pits was examined it was clear that pits of less than 1.6m³ volume (Groups 1 and 2) fell into three clusters in the north-east, the east central and the south central sectors of the site. The latter groups reflect, to a limited extent, the distribution of the larger pits. The north-east group contained relatively fewer finds. The more voluminous Group 3 and 4 pits formed a 'banana' shaped spine to the general scatter of pits extending from pit 1631 in the north to pit 8601 in the south. Pit 8601 may have been part of a sub-group of pits at the southern end which contained human remains. Pits 2022, 8095 and 8096 formed a small group of large pits at the north-east. There were no clusters of pits on the west side of the site where nine small and six large pits occurred. Of the larger pits, it can be postulated that 1491, 2416 and 6038 occurred within penannular hut gullies, and that the location of 2902 might be similarly interpreted, while 4006 and 6595 were associated with the southernmost of the gullies. A similar pattern does not emerge from the shallower pits.

It is possible, on ceramic grounds, to suggest that 14 of the pits were in use early in Phase 4; eight of these were of the smaller variety. All were fairly evenly distributed across the site apart from a gap in the central eastern area. It can similarly be suggested that thirteen pits were in use late in the phase. These all occurred amongst the general scatter of the pits on the east side and all but three were of the larger volumes. There were no late pits in the house area.

The artifact distribution is not so revealing as in Phase 3. For example, there is evidence for metal working, but the relevant artifacts are the bottom of a bowl hearth from pit 2002 in the north-east and a mould (Fig 65.12) from pit 6595 in the south-west. Most objects were disposed of in pits, and the pits in the central group around 7372 and 7376 appear to have the greatest concentration of finds.

The predominant recognisable pot form is the saucepan, and is the only form on the west part of the site, except in pit 6595 where jars and bowls were pre-

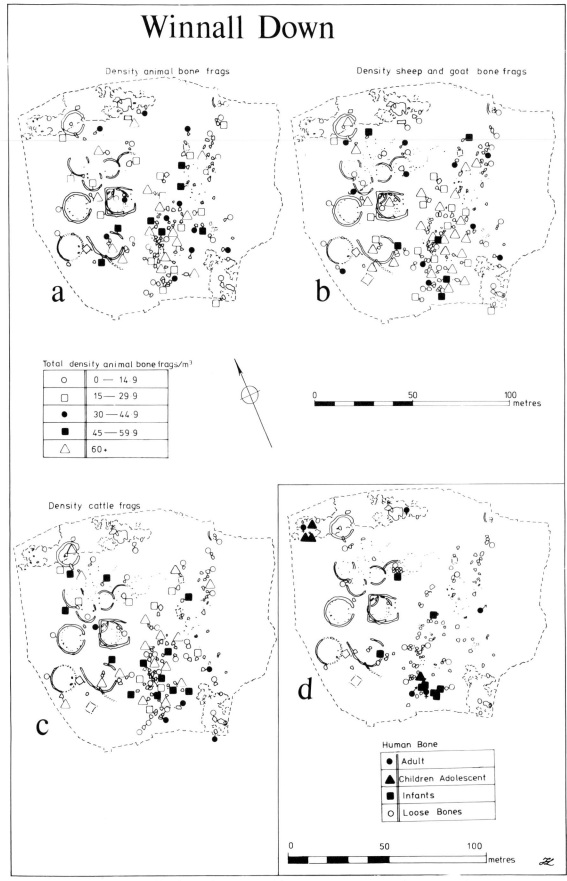

Fig 85.   Winnall Down: distributions of animal and human bones in the Middle Iron Age. a) Total density of animal bone fragments per m³; b) density of sheep/goat bone fragments per m³; c) density of cattle bone fragments per m³; d) human bone.

Winnall Down

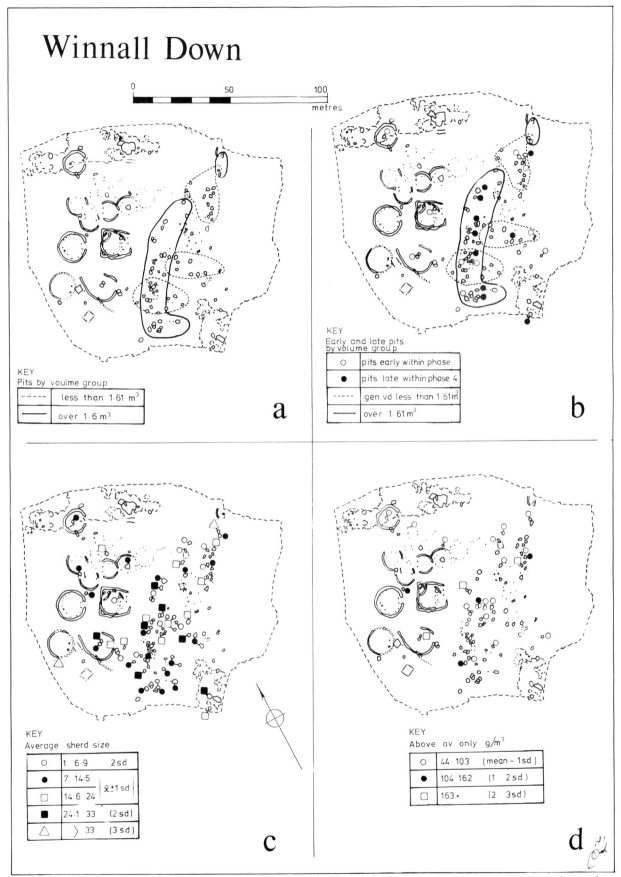

Fig 86.   Winnall Down: distributions of select elements in the Middle Iron Age. a) Pits by volumetric range; b) early and late Middle Iron Age pits within volumetric ranges; c) pottery sherd density in pits by grams per m³; d) average sherd size by weight.

sent. On the east part of the site, the saucepan form dominated but was associated with jars and bowls. Worked bone was restricted to the south-east apart from three isolated examples in pits 2553 and 1473 and the upper fill of segment FF of the Phase 3 enclosure ditch. Five of the ten nails came either from the fill of the gullies or from an adjacent feature and there were three pieces of slag in or near structure D.

Briquetage salt-making vessels, or vessels for transporting salt, or possible briquetage, was found in eight pits, usually in small quantities. Similarly, most of the baked/burnt clay, daub and tile was discovered in pits away from the settlement area. Although quern stones and fragments of quern stones were found across the whole site, they were a major component of the finds in the area around the houses. The gully of house N contained a greater amount of general building and domestic debris than any of the other gullies.

Trade probably included activity in the marketing of cereals and vegetables, of cattle and/or butchered meat. Imports included salt in briquetage from the south coast, and quernstones mainly from east Hampshire. Grain may have been produced in sufficient surplus for trade.

Phases 5 and 6. Late Iron Age – Early Roman

Only part of the Late Iron Age–Early Roman site was excavated. The full extent of the track and the enclosures was not recorded. At an early stage of the development of the enclosures (Phase 5 and Phase 6 period i) the evidence is fragmentary. Enclosures connected by tracks are not an uncommon feature of the early Roman landscape; they are known particularly in river valleys.

The enclosures were probably used for stock although the pits, scoops, quernstones, daub and concentrations of pottery and animal bones in and around enclosure C suggest that a considerable number of other activities took place there, including the processing of cereals. The six buildings are atypical of Roman dwellings and the likelihood must remain that a substantial part of the settlement area was not excavated. This may have been located in the partially excavated enclosure D, or further to the south.

The distribution of pottery is not only spatial but chronological, and reveals both a higher concentration and a greater average sherd size during Phase 6 period iii (Fig 87) than previously. This increase in the quantity of primary refuse may well derive from occupation activities.

Mr Mackreth's report on the brooches indicates that some of them were made by c 25 BC. The absence of any native forms of Roman pottery, however, suggests that this period of occupation probably did not start until around the time of the Conquest, in which case the brooches were quite old by the time they were lost.

Spatial Relations in the Late Iron Age – Early Roman Period (Figs 87 and 88)

Spatial analysis of artifacts revealed concentrations of pottery in the ditches of enclosures C and D, and of daub and clay in the pits and scoops within the former enclosure. Quernstones and fragments of quernstones were concentrated in the ditches on the east of enclosure D, and in the eastern parts of the ditches between enclosures C and D. In general terms there were higher densities of pottery and animal bones in the pits than the ditches, and daub was virtually absent from the trackway ditches. A concentration of nails and fragments of human bone in ditch 8088 of enclosure A perhaps indicate a disturbed coffin burial. The period i ditch 1300 produced a considerable amount of material including a ploughshare and an iron bar (Fig 44.26 and 27).

Although the structures do not seem typical of Romano-British houses, the quantity and concentrations of domestic refuse, particularly in and around enclosure C, suggest an occupation site within or close by the excavated area. Structure G did have associations with quern fragments and daub and clay, and also to some extent with the concentrations of pottery in ditch 1643 on the east of enclosure A, and in ditches 9805 and 9914 at the northern end of the west trackway ditches. Its influence on local artifact distributions and proximity to the disturbed burial might imply a domestic function for structure G. In ditch 660 of enclosure C there were high densities of animal bones, suggesting that the adjacent structure M could have been an ancillary building related to the processes of animal husbandry, possibly butchery. The concentrations of daub in the pits and scoops within enclosure C indicate some form of long-term activity. Little can be said of the other structures. Structure K was only partially excavated whilst structures H, J and L lay outside the enclosures and are seemingly unrelated to the recovered artifact distributions. Their functional and chronological relationships to the rest of the Phase 6 sequence are largely unknown.

General Considerations

The settlement excavated on Winnall Down is part of a complex of fields, enclosures and tracks which spread over the immediate area for 600ha. It is perhaps worth briefly summarising the basic sequence of the site. In the Neolithic an interrupted ring-ditch was constructed (Fasham 1982). The later

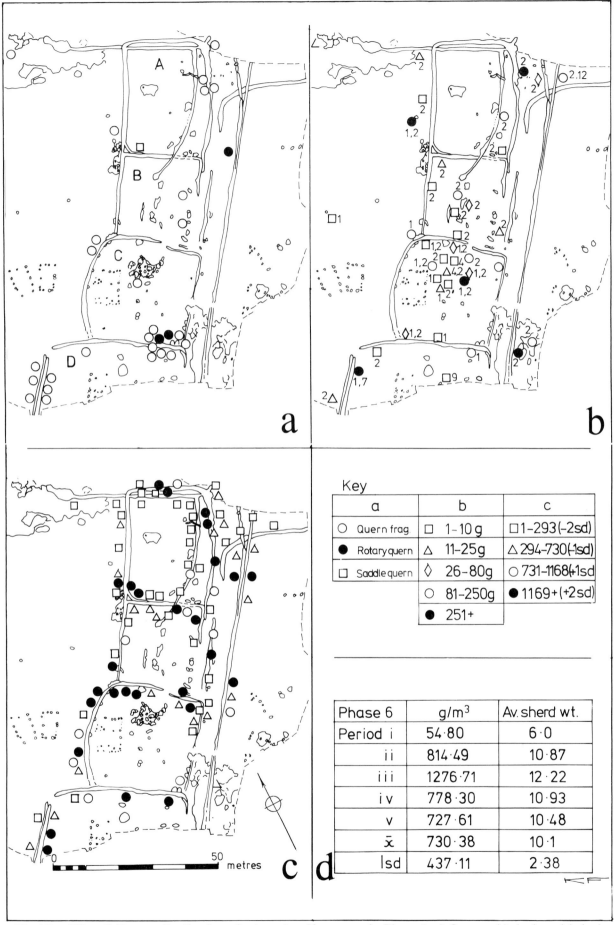

Key

a		b		c	
○	Quern frag.	□	1–10 g	□	1–293 (−2sd)
●	Rotary quern	△	11–25 g	△	294–730 (−1sd)
□	Saddle quern	◇	26–80 g	○	731–1168 (+1sd)
		○	81–250 g	●	1169+ (+2sd)
		●	251+		

Phase 6	g/m³	Av. sherd wt.
Period i	54·80	6·0
ii	814·49	10·87
iii	1276·71	12·22
iv	778·30	10·93
v	727·61	10·48
x̄	730·38	10·1
1sd	437·11	2·38

50 metres

Fig 87. Winnall Down: distribution of selected artifact types in Phase 6. a) Querns; b) daub and baked clay; c) density of pottery.

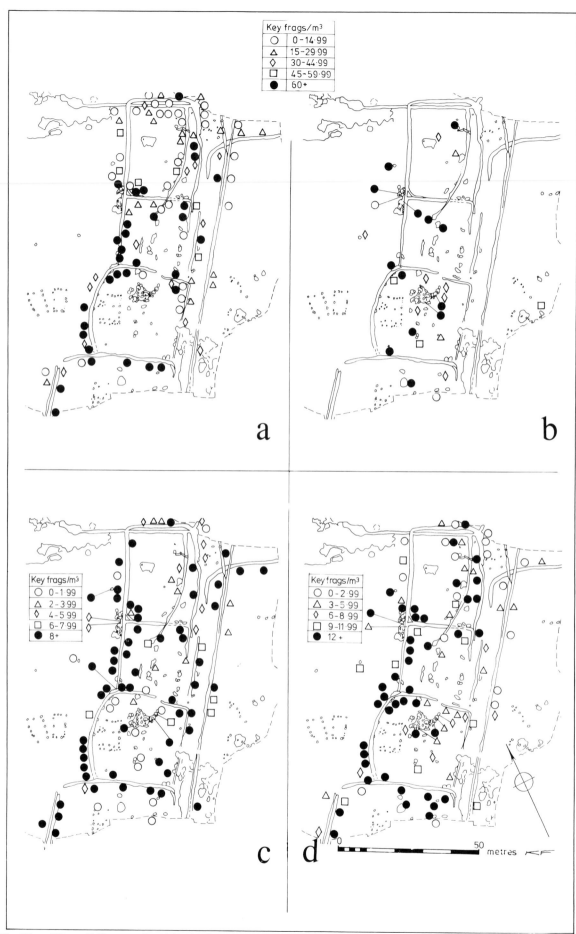

Fig 88.   Winnall Down: densities in fragments per m³ of animal bones in Phase 6. a) Total fragments in ditches; b) total fragments in pits and scoops; c) cattle fragments; d) sheep/goat fragments.

Bronze Age open settlement was abandoned and replaced in the Early Iron Age by a settlement located within a D-shaped enclosure. The enclosure ditch was partially filled by the Middle Iron Age and an open settlement established. By the Roman period the open settlement was superseded by an arrangement of enclosures linked by a track and seemingly laid out on the straight side of the Early Iron Age enclosure. This basic sequence was recovered from one element of the 600ha of soil and crop marks. It was impossible, from the aerial photographs, to detect the open (ditchless) settlements of the later Bronze Age and the Middle Iron Age and, indeed, very few individual features could be recognised from the aerial photographs. The aerial photograph in Fig 2 should be compared with that of Gussage All Saints (Wainwright 1979, Pl I) where many discrete features are visible. The irregular grey areas on Fig 2 – the so-called 'splodges' – proved to be quarries.

Although a long and interesting sequence of events was discovered by the excavation of the one enclosure at Winnall Down, this forms only part of the settlement history of the area. It must always be remembered that only part of the Roman element of the site was excavated – other enclosures existed to the south. A second large enclosure to the east, Winnall Down II, and the rectangular features within the pentagonal crop mark, were not excavated. A lot of questions can be asked of these two unexcavated remains. Was the latter site a form of Romano-British temple? If Winnall Down II dated to the Iron Age, was it contemporary with all, some or none of the occupation phases of the original Winnall Down? If there is any element of contemporaneity were the two sites related in terms of social or economic dependence? Did, for example, Winnall Down II provide the grain storage capacity during the Early Iron Age that was apparently lacking at Winnall Down I? These are some of the factors that need consideration, but which are not quantifiable in any discussion of the results of the excavation.

Animal Husbandry by J M Maltby

The analysis of the animal bones was carried out with two major objectives in mind. The first was to study in depth the nature of the faunal material, making use of the detailed method of recording. It was thus possible to examine the effects of differential preservation, butchery, carcase division and disposal strategies upon the faunal data. Secondly, the samples from Winnall Down form an important part of a longer term project of study of Iron Age material from settlements in Wessex, with the purpose of investigating the regional pastoral economy during that period.

Density Data

The study of animal bone densities in the pits, ditches and gullies proved to be a valuable exercise and one which should be applied to other sites. It was possible to determine general patterns in bone disposal in the three main phases and, in turn, suggest the areas of the settlement where most of the meat preparation and cooking may have been done. Pits consistently contained greater densities of bones than ditches and gullies, and comparisons of bone densities from different context types should be made with caution, since preservation conditions and other factors have to be taken into account.

Analysis of Bone Preservation

It was shown in all phases that differential preservation was a significant factor in the formation of the archaeological samples that were examined. It was also clear, however, that the bias towards certain categories was predictable and the standard of preservation could be measured by observations of the numbers of loose teeth, the proportion of the surviving articulations of the longbones, and the amount of weathering and gnawing on the bone fragments. On this site, it was found that the shallow features, such as the gullies and scoops, consistently contained less well-preserved bones than pits. Cattle and horse bones survived better than those of sheep/goat and pig because they were generally larger, denser and had fused epiphyses. The majority of the sheep and pigs represented were young animals, whose smaller, more fragile skeletons were more prone to destruction. Study of the bones in the Phase 4 pits showed that, although many of the bones survived in good condition, the evidence of canid gnawing on some of them suggested that some of the bones were accessible to dogs prior to disposal in the pits, and these bones may have been lying on the ground or in a midden before secondary disposal into the pits.

Butchery and Carcase Division

It was clear, particularly from the Phase 3 and 4 assemblages, that cattle and horse carcases were treated differently from those of sheep and pig. Concentrations of large mammal bones were found in some deposits in both phases. These had been disarticulated and stripped of meat. Similar concentrations of sheep and pig carcases were not found. The different treatment of large mammal carcases is not surprising since it is likely that more of the sheep and pig meat was cooked 'on the bone'. The occurrence of several dumps of large mammal butchered bones is interesting. Pit 3111 (Phase 3), for example, contained the major meat-bearing bones of at least three cattle and two horses dumped together at the same time. Pit 6595 (Phase 4) contained bones from a minimum of eleven cattle and three horses. Pit 4006 (Phase 4) contained the major meat bones from a minimum of five cattle and three horses. If these bones were processed at the same time, a substantial quantity of meat would have been made available. It is probable that some means of preserving meat (eg salting) was employed, unless this meat was to be distributed immediately to a relatively large number of people. Marrow production appears to have been of secondary importance, judging by the relatively large number of complete limb bones recovered.

The Exploitation of the Domestic Stock

The faunal material from Winnall Down, when seen in its wider regional and chronological context, provides an important body of data to further the understanding of animal exploitation in the Iron Age and early Romano-British periods. Striking similarities were found in the types of stock represented, the methods of butchery, the size of the animals and the mortality data of cattle and sheep with the assemblages examined at Balksbury (Maltby 1981a) and Old Down Farm (Maltby 1981b).

Similarities between Winnall Down and Old Down Farm are perhaps to be expected since the settlements have certain features in common. The similarity of the sheep mortality data from all three sites and some others of Middle Iron Age date is of particular interest. If these examples are typical of the regional exploitation pattern of sheep, it is possible to envisage sheep husbandry being basically at subsistence level with relatively little redistribution of stock or carcases. Certainly, if redistribution was taking place, it has not been reflected in the mortality data of sheep on the sites investigated to date.

Sheep farming was an important component of the inhabitants' economy at Winnall Down. The presence of neonatal mortalities implies that sheep were reared close to the settlement, and it seems probable that they were the stock species kept in the greatest numbers. Cattle were also important and it is possible that they provided the most meat. Ageing and sexing data from cattle bones were surprisingly limited, given the size of the sample. The majority of cattle represented in all phases were mature and this again is consistent with other Iron Age sites in Hampshire (Maltby 1981a, 1981b). Adult cattle could have provided meat, milk and traction power, although it is still unclear which, if any, of these functions was the most important in their exploitation. Some redistribution of cattle may have taken place, although there is no conclusive evidence for this. The Iron Age deposits at Winnall Down again showed that horses provided meat and that their carcases were treated in a similar way to those of cattle. Although preservation conditions may have been unfavourable to the survival of their bones, pigs seem not to have been a very important food resource. Wild species appear to have provided almost no supplement to the diet, although red deer antlers were utilised.

A full understanding of the Winnall Down faunal data will not be achieved without comparisons with assemblages from neighbouring settlements. The picture that emerges, however, from the Early and Middle Iron Age deposits is one of self-sufficiency. There is no evidence in these phases of large scale

organisation or redistribution of animal products. Even the evidence that, on occasions, several animals were killed and butchered at the same time is not beyond what we should expect from sensible culling strategies.

Pits, Houses and People by P J Fasham and J W Hawkes

The estimating of population for any settlement is fraught with uncertainties. It is possible to examine population figures by calculations based on floor areas of houses and on grain storage capacity represented by pit volumes. The problems of estimating population from pit volumes have been clearly stated by Bowen and Wood (1968) and Jefferies (1979). Not all pits would have been used for grain storage and shallow pits would probably not store grain satisfactorily, although experiments have shown that grain can be stored in pits 0.6m deep. Annual consumption of corn is not known nor indeed is the life of a pit. Ignoring all pits less than 0.75m deep and with a volume of less than 0.5m³ provides a total of 26m³ and 132m³ pit storage capacity for Phases 3 and 4 respectively. Assuming that these phases lasted 350 and 250 years respectively, the storage capacity was about 0.074m³ and 0.53m³ per year of pit life for each phase.

Jefferies assumed that pit storage equated with total grain storage, including seed corn. Reynolds' (1977) experiments have shown that, once the seal of a grain storage pit has been broken, the grain needs to be consumed quickly to avoid bacterial contamination. It can be argued that the necessity of ensuring successful storage by keeping the pit sealed implies that pit storage was for seed corn and not for domestic consumption, and that alternative forms of storage, in granaries or jars, was used for domestic grain (Monk and Fasham 1980).

Assuming that seed corn forms a minority (say one-third) of the annual yield and that it is stored in pits, with domestic grain stored elsewhere, and using, for comparative purposes, the same figures as Jefferies for annual consumption (6.5 – 13 bushels per person) – an estimate can be hazarded of 1.5 to 2.9 persons and 10–20 persons for Phases 3 and 4 respectively, also assuming a sowing rate of two bushels an acre, providing a yield of 16 bushels an acre (Reynolds 1977). Bersu and Jefferies allowed a pit life of ten years which produces a tentative population estimate for Phase 3 of 15–29 persons and for Phase 4 of 100–200 persons. It must be stressed that these calculations are an exercise based on a series of unprovable assumptions and should not be considered as anything other than tentative.

Another approach to estimating population is by calculations based on floor areas. Naroll (1962) estimated that each individual in a prehistoric population required ten square metres of floor space, based on a world-wide ethnographic sample. Cook and

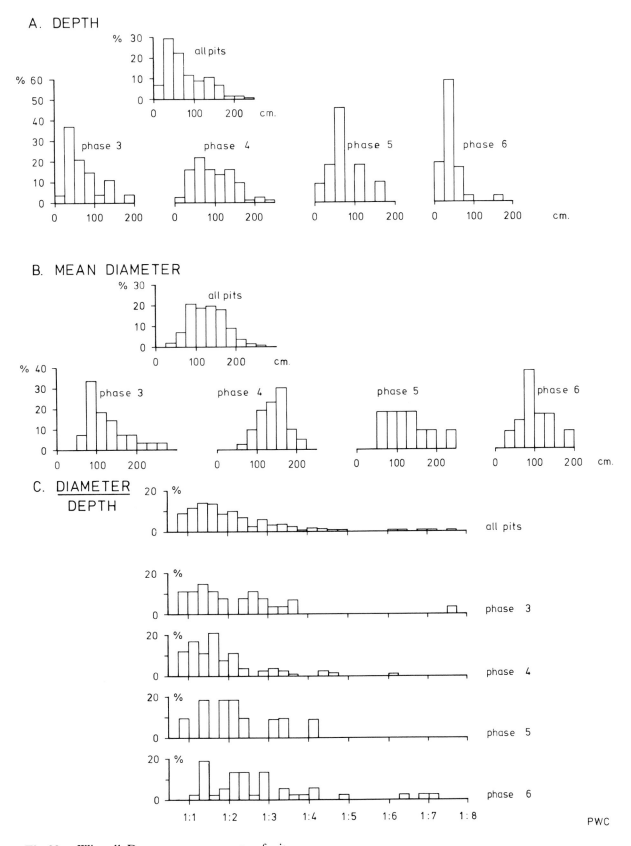

Fig 89. Winnall Down: measurements of pits.

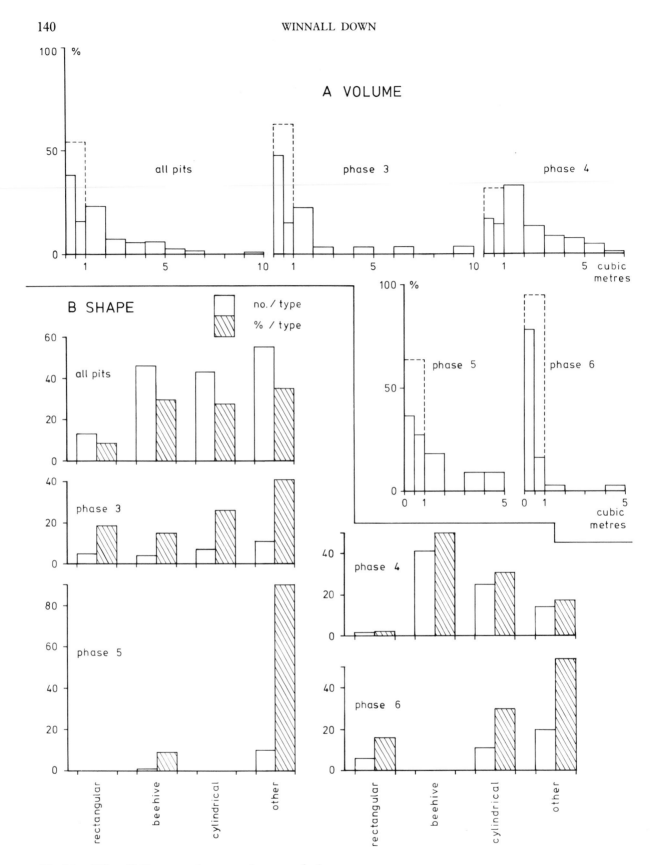

Fig 90.   Winnall Down: volumes and types of pits.

Heizer's (1968) study of Californian Indians indicated that a group of six persons would occupy twelve square metres of floor space, but that an extra individual would require an additional ten square metres. There are of course, many uncertainties relating to the life of a building, its function and how many buildings were contemporary.

Figure 91 shows the rank size order of houses in Phases 2, 3 and 4, indicating particularly large houses in Phases 2 and 3 and two larger houses in Phase 4. In Phase 3 between four and six houses may have been standing at any one time. This would provide for a population of between 24 – 34 (Naroll 1962) and 41–60 (Cook and Heizer 1968). Similarly, in Phase 4, up to seven houses may have been standing at any one time and could have supported a population of 75 (Naroll 1962) or 109 people (Cook and Heizer 1968). This range of values for the population during Phase 4 must, almost certainly, be

a maximum. If even the smallest house were not contemporary, then the population values for Phase 4 would be reduced by between six (Naroll) and eleven (Cook and Heizer). As with the estimates produced from pit storage capacity, these figures should be regarded as only tentative and treated, along with the underlying assumptions, with extreme caution.

In Phase 3, the possible population value derived from storage capacity was roughly comparable with the lower range based on floor area and considerably below the upper floor area range. However, in Phase 4, the capacity based on potential grain storage appears to outstrip the estimated population values derived from floor areas (Fig 92). If this is truly a reflection of circumstances in the Middle Iron Age, then one use for the apparent surplus of grain may have been trade. Indeed, it may even indicate a deliberate production of a grain surplus for trade.

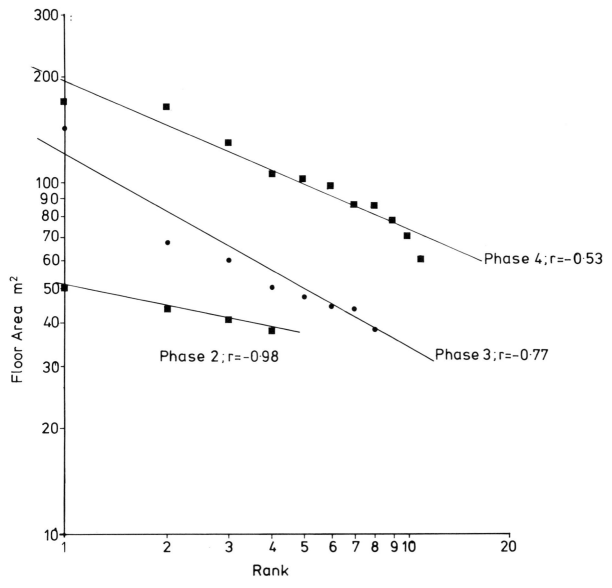

Fig 91. Winnall Down: Late Bronze Age–Middle Iron Age houses in order of rank size by floor area. Scales are logarithmic.

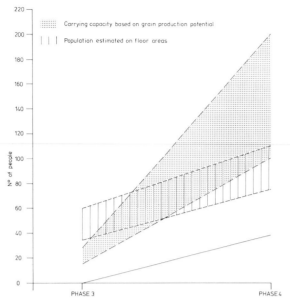

Fig 92. Winnall Down: figure demonstrating possible population sizes based on grain production and floor areas. The population estimates for Gussage All Saints are also shown (after Jeffries 1979). Trends are interpolated from Phase 3 and Phase 4 figures.

Social and Economic

The Late Bronze Age evidence consists primarily of the houses and a fence. There is no evidence of contemporaneity of one structure with another, but all four huts might have been in use simultaneously with the fence pre- or post-dating the huts, or any combination of the huts might have been contemporary. In any of the possible combinations it seems likely that there would have been at least one residential structure and one ancillary structure, a basic modular unit which Ellison (1981) has postulated for the Middle Bronze Age as being occupied by an extended familial unit. Such a kinship unit would probably have developed at least a level of self-sufficiency in terms of a mixed subsistence economy.

There was no continuity between the Late Bronze Age settlement and the Early Iron Age occupation. By the middle of the seventh century BC, when the enclosure on Winnall Down was probably constructed, it is possible that the development of iron technology had led, *inter alia*, to new exchange systems and to new economic structures.

Socially, the inhabitants of the Early Iron Age enclosure would appear still to have been related to an extended family-size unit predominantly occupying Area A, or with sub-groups of the unit living in Areas B and C as well. House E surely represented a major house both in terms of its complexity and its size. The grain-producing capacity of the inhabitants is likely to have been slightly more than was needed for a basic subsistence. It has been suggested above that some wealth may have been generated by the

production of woollen materials. The age at death of the sheep suggests that a balanced, viable flock was maintained.

By the Middle Iron Age a tribal society had developed. The population of Winnall Down was probably greater than in the Early Iron Age and the internal arrangement of the structures was quite different, as the marked separation of houses from the majority of the pits indicates. If a grain surplus was produced it could have been traded at the local hillfort (Cunliffe 1978, 328), either St Catherine's Hill (Hawkes *et al* 1930, Hawkes 1976), or in the later stages the developing site at Oram's Arbour, Winchester (*eg* Biddle 1970), or possibly with Danebury (Cunliffe 1972). The surplus might have been traded for goods produced elsewhere in the region, or outside the region (shale from the Isle of Purbeck), or even for continental goods entering the country via Hengistbury or even the Solent.

The Roman influence is clearly depicted in the layout of the site in Phase 5 and 6, and with a change in the agricultural practices on the site. The Roman occupation on the site was occurring when major public buildings in Winchester were being constructed (Biddle 1964), when the urban influences of Winchester would first have been felt, and when the land was being reorganised into new estates. The proximity of Winnall Down to Roman Winchester probably accounts for its apparent poverty, in structural terms at least.

In Conclusion

The excavation of Winnall Down was a rare exercise insofar as only a few Iron Age sites have been excavated to the extent that the whole of the recoverable plan was recorded and the greater part of the archaeological deposits excavated. Even so, earthworks, with their buried soils, and occupation levels had been flattened and ultimately ploughed away. The temptation to over-generalize from the site and its data must be resisted for, quite simply, there is at present insufficient information available for other sites in the area. Indeed, the date is not known of Winnall Down II.

It would certainly not be sensible to ascribe an especially high level of status to the settlement during the Iron Age. There are no elaborate entrances with antennae ditch and imposing timber structures; indeed during the Middle Iron Age there is not even an enclosure ditch. The increase in metal objects from the Early to Middle Iron Age can be seen in terms of a probable increase in population, and a greater availability of metal objects, as much as in an increase in wealth or status. The absence of personal ornaments in the Early Iron Age and the presence of brooches, rings, pins and the speculum object in the Middle Iron Age does indicate some increase in wealth. There were, however, similar numbers of personal objects found in the Roman phase and the Roman occupation, as excavated, was certainly not of a high level status.

There is evidence for metalworking in Phases 3, 4 and 6 in the form of crucibles, hearth slag and a single mould, but it is so sporadic as to make it unlikely that that particular craft was an important part of the life of the inhabitants of Winnall Down.

It has been suggested that cloth in the Early Iron Age, and grain in the Middle Iron Age were produced for trade. It is perhaps in the area of woollen goods, livestock and cereal production that any wealth should be measured and that the tangible forms of wealth are not so important as status indicators.

Even if it is not sensible to suggest a high level of status for Winnall Down during the Iron Age, one of the most interesting aspects of the site proved to be the internal dynamics of reorganisation between Phases 3 and 4. The occupation from the Early to the Middle Iron Age was apparently almost without a break. The change in layout from an enclosed settlement with seemingly discrete activity areas and a possible production of woollen garments, to an open settlement with clear separation of the houses from the pits, a change in the building style of the houses, an apparent increase in the population and a potential surplus production of grain represent the most interesting aspects of the Winnall Down settlement.

No matter what its status, the inhabitants of Winnall Down would have competed for their economic and social niche in the complex trading and agricultural society of the Iron Age with the many other farming sites in the Winchester area of the middle Itchen Valley.

This report is principally an archive and summary text report, and only for areas where new ground has been broken has much detail been published, as, for example, with the houses, of which so few have yet been published from Hampshire, or with the analysis of loomweights. The full story of the occupation on Winnall Down cannot be told while the second, similar enclosure remains unexcavated. However, it is hoped that some of the ideas presented will be considered in further detail and that the available data will allow not only the writer, but also other readers, to reconsider those ideas in the future, as Iron Age studies develop.

Chapter 6

The Archive

Structure Concordance

Throughout this report the terminology for the structures has been simplified to a basic, alphabetic system of reference for most structures, apart from the fences which have been numbered Fence 1–10. The following concordance is arranged by phase with the original context number given for the structures. It is the context number which is used throughout the site and other records.

Phase 2

Houses

House A	=	11184
House B	=	11185
House C	=	11186
House D	=	11187

Structures

Structure A	=	11188

Fences

Fence 1	=	11190

Phase 3

Houses

House E	=	224
House E1	=	11193
House E2	=	11194
House F	=	11191
House G	=	11256
House H	=	11225
House I	=	11214
House J	=	11205
House K	=	11219
House L	=	11202

Structures

2,3,4,5, and 6-post structures

a	=	11237
b	=	11195
c	=	11197
d	=	11216
e	=	11217
f	=	11226
g	=	11231
h	=	11233
i	=	11235
j	=	11198
k	=	11204
l	=	11234
m	=	11196
n	=	11215
p	=	11224
q	=	11228
r	=	11229

s	=	11230
t	=	11232
u	=	11192
v	=	11207
w	=	11206
x	=	11220
y	=	11221
z	=	11227
Structure B	=	11213
Structure C	=	11203

Fences

Fence 2	=	11208D
Fence 3	=	11208A
Fence 4	=	11242
Fence 5	=	11222
Fence 6	=	11223

Phase 4

Houses

House M	=	2
House M_1	=	11252
House N	=	200
House P	=	223
House R	=	444
House R_1	=	11264
House R_2	=	11265
House S	=	1820
House S_1	=	11262
House T	=	1821
House T_1	=	11257
House U	=	1847
House U_1	=	11263
House V	=	4022
House W	=	11258

Structures

Structure D	=	406
Structure E	=	1973/1989
Structure F	=	8795

2,3,4,5 and 6-post structures

aa	=	11251
bb	=	11218
cc	=	11266
dd	=	11276
ee	=	11241
ff	=	11243
gg	=	11247
hh	=	11249
ii	=	11250
jj	=	11238
kk	=	11209
ll	=	11239
mm	=	11240
nn	=	11244
pp	=	11245

qq	=	11246
rr	=	11253

Fences

Fence 7	=	11260
Fence 8	=	11261

Phase 6

Structures

2,3 or 4 post structures

ss	=	11276
Structure *G*	=	11267
Structure *H*	=	11277
Structure *J*	=	11278
Structure *K*	=	11272
Structure *L*	=	11271
Structure *M*	=	11275

Fences

Fence 9	=	11273
Fence 10	=	11270

Index to the archive

The finds, field records and the archive are housed at the Hampshire County Museum Service (Accession Number A 1978 20). A copy of the microfiche is with the National Monuments Record.

The archive consists of a computer record and manual, field records, field drawings, post-excavation drawings and ordered files on the different classes of artifacts and feature types. All these records, apart from the computer print-out, are on microfiche and are listed below.

Site plans	Aperture Cards 1–33
Site Sections	Aperture Cards 34–130
Post Excavation drawings	Aperture Cards 131–256
Site records	Fiche 1–191
Field sample records	Fiche 229–236
The Enclosure ditch 5	Fiche 201–202
Phase 4 pits	198–199
Unphased features	203
Postholes	204–206
Pits and scoops	213–214
Recorded find indices	224–225
Metalwork	195–196
Coins	210
Pottery – analysis	226–228
Pottery – drawings	218–223
Post-medieval pottery, worked bone, glass, shell and claypipe	192
Briquetage	209–210
Querns etc	217
Flint	193–194
Daub and burnt clay	211–212
Loomweights – analysis	215–216
Loomweights – drawings	237–238
Brick and tile	200
Slag etc	197
Animal bones	241–242
Carbonised seeds	208, 239
Charcoal	207–208
Human bones	207
Molluscs	240
Feature 1972	209
Technology (AM Lab)	210
Radio-carbon dates	210
Correspondence with specialists	207
General considerations	244

REFERENCES

The abbreviations used are generally those suggested in *Signposts for Archaeological Publication* (CBA 1979). *Proc* followed by a volume number always refers to *Proceedings of the Hampshire Field Club*. Bold numbers indicate volume of series numbers.

Addyman, P V 1972 Anglo-Saxon Houses at Chalton, Hampshire, *Med Archaeol* 17 13–31.

Addyman, P V and Leigh, D 1973 The Anglo-Saxon village at Chalton, Hampshire: second interim report, *Med Archaeol* 17 1–25.

Barrett, J C 1976 Deverel-Rimbury: Problems of Chronology and Interpretation, in Burgess and Miket (eds) *Settlement and Economy in the Third and Second Millenia BC*, BAR 33 207–389.

———— 1978 'The EPRIA Prehistoric Pottery' in Hedges and Buckley The Causewayed Enclosure, Orsett, Essex, *Proc Prehist Soc* 44 268–88.

———— 1980 The Pottery of the Later Bronze Age in Lowland England, *Proc Prehist Soc* 46 297–319.

Barrett, J and Bradley, R 1980 Later Bronze Age Settlement in South Wessex and Cranborne Chase, in Barrett and Bradley (eds) *The British Later Bronze Age*, BAR 83.

Barrett J C, Bradley R, Cleal R and Pike H 1978 Characterization of Deverel-Rimbury pottery from Cranborne Chase, *Proc Prehist Soc* 44 135–142.

Bell, M 1977 Excavations at Bishopstone Sussex, *Sussex Archaeol Coll* 115 1–299.

Bersu, G 1940 Excavations at Little Woodbury, Wiltshire, Part 1: The settlement revealed by excavation, *Proc Prehist Soc* 29 206–213.

Biddle, M 1964 Excavations at Winchester, 1962–3: Second Interim Report, *Antiq J* 44 188–219.

———— 1970 Excavations at Winchester, 1969: Eighth Interim Report, *Antiq J* 50 277–326.

Biddle, M and Emery, V W 1973 *The M3 Extension: An Archaeological Survey*, Winchester.

Boessneck, J and Driesch, A von den 1978 The significance of measuring animal bones from archaeological sites, in Meadow and Zeder (eds) *Approaches to Faunal Analysis in the Middle East*, Peabody Museums Bulletin 2.

Bökönyi, S 1974 *History of Domestic Mammals in Central and Eastern Europe*.

Bowen, H C 1979 'Gussage in its Setting' in Wainwright 1979.

Bowen, H C and Wood, P D 1968 Experimental storage of corn underground and its implications for Iron Age settlements, *Bull Inst Archaeol Univ London* 7 1–14.

Bradley, R 1975 Salt and Settlement in the Hampshire–Sussex Borderland, in Brisay (ed) *Salt, the Study of an Ancient Industry*, Colchester.

Brodribb A C C, Hands A R and Walker D R 1968 *Excavations at Shakenoak, Part I: Site A and D*.

Brothwell, D R 1972 *Digging up Bones*, London.

Burchell, J P T and Frere S S 1947 The Occupation at Sandown Park, Esher, during the Stone Age, the Early Iron Age and the Anglo-Saxon Period, *Antiq J* 27 24–46.

Clark J G D, Higgs E S and Longworth I H 1960 Excavations at the Neolithic Site at Hurst Fen, Mildenhall, Suffolk, *Proc Prehist Soc* 26 202–245.

Clay R C C 1924 An Early Iron Age Site on Fifield Bavant Down, *Wiltshire Archaeol Natur Mag* 140 457–490.

Collis, J R 1968 Excavations at Owslebury, Hants: a first interim report, *Antiq J* 48 18–31.

———— 1970 Excavations at Owslebury, Hants: a second interim report, *Antiq J* 50 246–261.

———— 1977a An Approach to the Iron Age, in Collis (ed) *the Iron Age in Britain – A Review* 1–7, Sheffield.

———— 1977b The Proper Study of Mankind is Pots, in Collis (ed) *The Iron Age in Britain – A Review* 29–31, Sheffield.

Collis, J R and Fasham, P J 1980 Excavations and Field Survey at Borough Farm, Micheldever, Hants, *Proc* 36 145–152.

Cook, S F and Heizer, R F 1968 Relationships among houses, settlement areas and population in aboriginal California, in Chang (ed) *Settlement Archaeology* 79–116, Palo Alto.

Cra'aster, M D 1961 The Aldwick Iron Age settlement, Barley, Hertfordshire, *Proc Camb Ant Soc* **54** 22–46.

Crowfoot, G M 1945 The bone gouges of Maiden Castle and other sites, *Antiquity* **19** 157–158.

Cunliffe, B W 1968 *Fifth report on the excavations of the Roman fort at Richborough, Kent.*

———— 1971 *Excavations at Fishbourne 1961–1969*, Res Rep Soc Antiq **27**.

———— 1972 Danebury, Hampshire: first interim report on the excavation 1969–70, *Antiq J* **52** 293–308.

———— 1974 *Iron Age Communities in Britain*, London.

———— 1975 *Excavations at Porchester Castle, Vol 1 Roman*, Res Rep Soc Antiq **32**, London.

———— 1978 *Iron Age Communities in Britain* (2nd edn).

Cunliffe, B and Phillipson, D W 1968 Excavations at Eldon's Seat, Encombe, Dorset, England, *Proc Prehist Soc* **34** 191–237.

Curwen, E C 1937 Querns, *Antiquity* **11** 133–51.

Davies, S M 1981 Excavations at Old Down Farm, Andover Part 2: Prehistoric and Roman, *Proc* **37**.

Déchelette, J 1904 *Vases ornés de la Gaule romaine* ii.

DoE 1975 *Principles of Publication in Rescue Archaeology*, London.

Dunbar, D 1932 Corn byres of Caithness, *Proc Soc Antiq Scot* **66** 136–7.

Drury, P J 1980 Non-classical religious buildings in Iron Age and Roman Britain: a review, in Rodwell (ed) *Temples, Churches and Religion in Roman Britain*, BAR **77**.

Ellison, A B 1978 The Bronze Age, in Drewett (ed) *Archaeology in Sussex to 1500 AD.*

———— 1981 Towards a socioeconomic model for the Middle Bronze Age in southern England, in Hodder, Isaac and Hammond (eds) *Pattern of the Past: Studies in honour of David Clarke.*

Ettlinger, E 1973 *Die römischen Fibeln in der Schweiz*, Berne.

Evans, J G 1972 *Land Snails in Archaeology.*

Evans, J G and Jones, H 1973 Subfossil and Modern Land-Snail Faunas from Rock-Rubble Habitats, *J Conch* **28** 103–129.

Fasham, P J 1980 Excavations on Bridget's and Burntwood Farms, Itchen Valley Parish, Hampshire 1974 (MARC3 Sites R5 and R6), *Proc* **36** 37–86.

———— 1982 The Excavation of Four Ring-Ditches in Central Hampshire (MARC3 Sites R17 Feature 1972, R7, R30 and R363), *Proc* **38**.

Fasham, P J and Hawkes, J W 1980 Computerised recording systems and analysis in an archaeological unit: some observations, in Stewart (ed) *Microcomputers in Archaeology*, MDA Occ paper **4**.

Fasham P J, Lloyd G D and Smith G 1976 Excavation Recording and Sampling in Fasham (ed) *M3 Archaeol 1975* 2–6, Winchester.

Fasham, P J and Ross, J M 1978 A Bronze Age Flint Industry from a Barrow site in Micheldever Wood, Hampshire, *Proc Prehist Soc* **44** 47–68.

Feugère, M 1977 Les fibules Gallo-Romaines du Musée Denon à Chalon-sur-Saône, *Memoirs de la Société d'Histoire et d'Archéologie de Chalon-sur-Saône* **47** 77–158.

Fingerlin, G 1972 Dangstetten, ein augusteiches Legionslager am Hochrhein (Vorbericht über die Grabungen 1967–1969), *Bericht des Römisch-Germanische Kommission* **51–2** 212–232.

Fisher, P F 1978 Soil Phosphorus Analysis at Winnall Down, in Fasham (ed) *M3 Archaeol 1976–77* 17.

Fowler, P J 1967 The Archaeology of Fyfield and Overton Downs, Wiltshire, *Wilts Archaeol Mag* **62** 16–33.

Fox, C F 1958 *Pattern and Purpose: a Survey of Early Celtic Art in Britain.*

Frere, S S 1954 Canterbury Excavations, Summer, 1946 'The Rose Lane Sites' *Archaeologia Cantiana* **68** 101–143.

———— 1972 *Verulamium Excavations II*, Res Rep Soc Antiq **28**.

Frere, S S and St Joseph, J K 1974 The Roman Fortress at Longthorpe, *Britannia* **5** 1–129.

Gavelle, R 1962 Notes sur les fibules gallo-romaines recuilles a Lugdunum Convenarum (Saint Bertrand-de-Comminges), *OGAM* **14** 201–236.

Grant, A 1975 Appendix B: the use of tooth wear as a guide to the age of domestic animals – a brief explanation, in Cunliffe *Excavations at Portchester Castle, 1: Roman*, Res Rep Soc Antiq **32**.

Griffiths, W E 1951 Decorated rotary querns from Wales and Ireland, *J Ulster Archaeol* **14** 49–61.

Haalebos, J K 1979 Primus, Celadus and Senicio, *Rei Cretariae Romanae Fautorum*, Acta 19–20, 121–135.

Harcourt, R A 1974 The dog in prehistoric and early historic Britain, *J Archaeol Sci* **1** 151–176.

———— 1979 'The animal bones' in Wainwright 1979.

Harding, D W 1974 *The Iron Age in Lowland Britain*, London.

Harding, J M 1964 Interim report on the excavation of a Late Bronze Age homestead in Weston Wood, Albury, Surrey, *Surrey Archaeol Coll* **61** 10–17.

Hawkes, C F C 1976 St Catherine's Hill Winchester: the report of 1930 re-assessed, in Harding (ed) *Hillforts: Later Prehistoric Earthworks in Britain and Ireland.*

Hawkes C F C, Myres J N L and Stevens C G 1930 St Catherine's Hill, Winchester, *Proc* **11**.

Hawkes, S C 1961 Longbridge Deverill, Cow Down, Wiltshire, *Proc Prehist Soc* **27** 346–7.

———— 1969 Finds from two Middle Bronze Age pits at Winnall, Winchester, Hampshire, *Proc* **26** 5–18.

Helbaek, H 1952 Early Crops in Southern England, *Proc Prehist Soc* **18** 194–233.

———— 1957 'Carbonised Cereals' in Burstow and Holleyman, Late Bronze Age settlement on Itford Hill, Sussex, *Proc Prehist Soc* **23** 167–212.

Hermet, F 1934 *La Graufesenque* ii.

Hodder, I and Hedges, J W 1977 Weaving Combs: Their typology and distribution with some introductory remarks on date and function, in Collis (ed) *The Iron Age in Britain – a Review*, Sheffield.

Hubbard, R N L B 1975 Assessing the botanical component of palaeo-economies, *Bull Inst Archaeol Univ London* **12** 197–205.

Hughes, M 1974 M27 (South Coast Motorway): Rescue Excavations of an Iron Age site at Wallington Military Road, Fareham 1972, *Rescue Archaeol in Hants* **2** 29–96.

Hunt, A forthcoming *Excavations at Friar Street, Droitwich 1975.*

Jeanin, Y and Lerat, L 1957 Catalogue des Collections Archéologique de Montbéliard, Historique (et) Les fibules Gallo-Romaines de Mandeure, *Annales Litéraire de l'Université de Besançon, 16, Archéologie* **4** 2–26.

Jecock, H M 1981 *The Production and distribution of prehistoric rotary querns in Wessex*, unpubl dissertation, Southampton Univ.

Jefferies, J S 1977 *Excavations: Record Techniques in use by the Central Excavation Unit*, DoE.

———— 1979 'The Pits' in Wainwright 1979.

Jones, R T 1977 *Computer based osteometric archaeozoology*, AM Lab Rep 2333.

Keepax, C A 1979 'The Human Bones' in Wainwright 1979.

———— forthcoming 'The Charcoal' in Fasham, *A 'Banjo' Enclosure in Micheldever Wood, Hampshire*, Hants Field Club Monograph.

Kiesewalter, L 1888 *Skelettmessingen an Pferden als Beitrag zur theoretischen Beurteilungslehre des Pferdes.*

Knorr, 1919 *Töpfer und Fabriken verzierter Terra Sigillata des ersten Jahrhunderts.*

Lambrick, G and Robinson, M 1979 *Iron Age and Roman riverside settlements at Farmoor, Oxfordshire*, Oxfordshire Archaeol Unit Rep **2**, CBA Res Rep **32**.

Lapinskas, P 1974 'The Flotation Machine' in Fasham (ed) *M3 Archaeol 1974*, Winchester.

Lerat, L 1956 Catalogue des Collections Archéologique de Besançon, II – Les Fibules Gallo-Romaines, *Annales Litéraires de l'Université de Besançon*, 2ˢ Tome III, fasc 1, *Archéologie* **3** iii–vi, 1–51.

Lewis, E R and Walker, G 1976 A Middle Bronze Age settlement site at Westbury, West Meon, Hampshire, *Proc* **33** 33–43.

Liddell, D M 1933 Excavations at Meon Hill, *Proc* **12** 127–62.

———— 1935 Report on the Hampshire Field Club's Excavation at Meon Hill, *Proc* **13** 7–54.

Limbrey, S 1975 *Soil Science and Archaeology*, London.

Lucas, A T 1958 An Fhóir: A Straw Rope Granary, *Gwerin* **1.1** 1–20.

Lyne, M A B and Jefferies, R S 1979 *The Alice Holt/Farnham Roman Pottery Industry*, CBA Res Rep **30**.

Maltby, J M 1981a Iron Age, Romano-British and Anglo-Saxon animal husbandry – a review of the faunal evidence, in Jones and Dimbleby (eds) *The Environment of Man: the Iron Age to the Anglo-Saxon Period*, BAR **87**.

———— 1981b 'The animal bones' in Davies 1981.

Manning, W H 1964 The Plough in Roman Britain, *J Rom Studies* **54** 54–65.

Mattingley, H and Sydenham, E A (eds) 1972 *The Roman Imperial Coinage*, London.

May, T 1930 *Catalogue of the Roman pottery in the Colchester and Essex Museum.*

Megaw, J V S 1971 A group of Late Iron Age Collars or Neck-rings from Western Britain, in Sieveking *Prehistoric and Roman Studies* 145–155, London.

Millet, M 1980 *Excavations at Cowdery's Down Basingstoke.*

Monk, M A forthcoming The Plant Economy of the Iron Age 'Banjo' enclosure in Micheldever Wood, in Fasham *A 'Banjo' Enclosure in Micheldever Wood, Hampshire*, Hants Field Club Monograph.

Monk, M A and Fasham, P J 1980 Carbonised Plant Remains from Two Iron Age Sites in Central Hampshire, *Proc Prehist Soc* **46** 321–344.

Morris, E L 1983 *Salt and Ceramic Exchange in Western Britain during the First Millenium BC*, unpubl PhD thesis, Southampton Univ.

Murphy, P 1977a *Early Agriculture and Environment in Hampshire 800 BC – 400 AD*, unpubl M Phil thesis, Southampton Univ.

———— 1977b *Carbonised fruits and seeds from R27, Micheldever Wood*, unpubl Level III archival typescript.

Naroll, R 1962 Floor Area and Settlement Population, *Amer Antiq* **27** 587–9.

Navarro, J M de 1972 *The Finds from the Site of La Tène*, London.

Oliver, M and Applin, B 1978 Excavation of an Iron Age and Romano-British Settlement at Ructstall's Hill, Basingstoke, Hampshire 1972–75, *Proc* **35** 41–92.

Parrington, M 1978 *The excavation of an Iron Age settlement, Bronze Age ring-ditches and Roman features at Ashville Trading Estate, Abingdon (Oxfordshire) 1974–76*, Oxfordshire Archaeol Unit Rep **1**, CBA Res Rep **28**.

Partridge, P 1974 *The Haematite Wares of Wessex: A Petrological Study of Some Aspects of their Production*, unpubl BA dissertation, Southampton Univ.

Peacock, D P S 1968 A Petrological Study of Certain Iron Age Pottery from Western England, *Proc Prehist Soc* **34** 414–27.

Perry, B T 1972 Excavations at Bramdean, Hampshire, 1965 and 1966, and a Discussion of Similar Sites in Southern England, *Proc* **29** 41–78.

Pitt-Rivers, A H L 1887 *Excavations in Cranborne Chase* **1**.

Philips, J T 1950 'A Survey of the distribution of querns of Holmbury allied types' Appendix 3 in Kenyon, Excavations at Breedon on the Hill, 1946, *Trans Leics Archaeol Soc* **26** 75–82.

Pliny 1961 edition *Naturalis Historiae* Books XVII–XIX, Rackham (trans).

Rees, S E 1979 *Agricultural Implements in Prehistoric and Roman Britain*, BAR **69**.

Renfrew, J M 1972 The Crops at Sitagroi, in Renfrew *The Emergence of Civilisation*, London.

Reynolds, P J 1974 Experimental Iron Age Storage Pits: An Interim Report, *Proc Prehist Soc* **40** 118–131.

———— 1977 Experimental Archaeology and the Butser Ancient Farm Research Project, in Collis (ed) *The Iron Age in Britain – a review.*

Riha, E 1979 *Die römischen Fibeln aus Augst und Kaiseraugst*, Forschungen in Augst, Band 3, Augst.

Roche, C D de 1978 'The Iron Age pottery' in Parrington *The excavation of an Iron Age settlement, Bronze Age ring-ditches and Roman features at Ashville Trading Estate, Abingdon (Oxfordshire) 1974–76*, Oxfordshire Archaeol Unit Rep **1**, CBA Res Rep **28**.

Rogers, G 1974 Poteries Sigillées de la Gaule Centrale: 1) Les Motifs non-figurés 28 (supplément à Gallia).

Saule, J forthcoming *Excavations at Droitwich – Bowling Green 1978–79.*

Silver, I A 1969 The ageing of domestic animals, in Brothwell and Higgs (eds) *Science in Archaeology.*

Smith, K 1977 The excavation of Winklebury Camp, Basingstoke, Hampshire, *Proc Prehist Soc* **43** 31–129.

Spratling, M G 1979 'The debris of metalworking', in Wainwright 1979.

Stanfield, J A and Simpson, G 1958 *Central Gaulish Potters.*

Stead, I 1976 The earliest burials of the Aylesford Culture, in Sieveking, Longworth and Wilson (eds) *Problems in Economic and Social Archaeology* 401–416, London.

Thompson, F H 1979 The Surrey hillforts: excavations at Artisbury, Holmbury, and Hascombe, 1972–1977, *Antiq Journ* **59** 245–318.

Trotter, M and Gleser, G C 1958 A Re-evaluation of estimation of stature based on measurements of stature taken during life and long bones after death, *Amer Journ Phys Anthrop* **16** 79–123.

Vanderhoeven, M 1978 Terra Sigillata aus Südgullien: Die relief verzierten Gefasse III, Funde aus Asciburgium, *Heft* 7.

Wainwright, G J 1967 *Coygan Camp.*

———— 1968 The excavation of a Durotrigian farmstead near Tollard Royal in Cranborne Chase, southern England, *Proc Prehist Soc* **34** 102–147.

———— 1972 The excavation of a Neolithic settlement on Broome Heath, Ditchingham, Norfolk, *Proc Prehist Soc* **38** 1–97.

———— 1979 *Gussage All Saints: An Iron Age Settlement in Dorset*, London.

Wainwright, G J and Longworth, I H 1971 *Durrington Walls: Excavations 1966–68*, Res Rep Soc Antiq **27**.

Ward, J 1911 *The Roman Era in Britain*, London.

Ward, G K and Wilson, S R 1978 Procedures for computing and combining radiocarbon age determinations: a critique, *Archaeometry* **20** (i) 19–31.

Werner, J 1955 Die Nauheimer Fibel, Joachim Werner, *Jahrbuch des Römisch-Germanischen Kommission, Zentralmuseums, Mainz* **2** 170–195.

Wheeler, R E M 1943 *Maiden Castle, Dorset*, Res Rep Soc Antiq **12**, London.

White, D A Reed, R 1970 The excavations of a Bowl Barrow at Oakley Down, Dorset, 1968, *Proc Dorset Natur Hist Archaeol Soc* **92** 159–67.